THE MEDIA ST

In this critical primer, Michael Z. Newman introduces newcomers to the key concepts, issues, and vocabulary of media studies.

Across ten chapters, Newman examines topics from text and audience to citizenship and consumerism, drawing on a myriad of examples of media old and new. Film and TV rub shoulders with mobile games and social media, and popular music and video sharing platforms with journalism and search engines. While the book takes a critical, cultural approach, it covers topics that apply across many kinds of media scholarship, bridging the humanities and the social sciences and looking at media as a global phenomenon. It considers media in relation to society and its unequal structures of power, and relates media representations to their conditions of production in media industries and consumption in the everyday lives of audiences and users. Spanning the historical periods of mass media and online participatory culture, it also probes assumptions about media that were formulated in a previous era and looks at how to update our thinking to address an ever-changing digital mediascape.

With its clear and accessible style, this book is tailor-made for undergraduate students of media, communication, and cultural studies, as well as anyone who would like to better understand media.

Michael Z. Newman is Professor in the Department of English at the University of Wisconsin-Milwaukee and in the programs in Film Studies and Media, Cinema, and Digital Studies. He is the author of Indie: An American Film Culture (2011), Video Revolutions: On the History of a Medium (2014), Atari Age: The Emergence of Video Games in America (2017), and co-author of Legitimating Television: Media Convergence and Cultural Status (2012).

THE MEDIA STUDIES TOOLKIT

Michael Z. Newman

Routledge
Taylor & Francis Group

NEW YORK AND LONDON

Cover image: Egor Suvorov / Getty Images

First published 2022
by Routledge
605 Third Avenue, New York, NY 10158

and by Routledge
2 Park Square, Milton Park, Abingdon, Oxon, OX14 4RN

Routledge is an imprint of the Taylor & Francis Group, an informa business

Library of Congress Cataloging-in-Publication Data
A catalog record for this title has been requested

ISBN: 978-0-367–44115-9 (hbk)
ISBN: 978-0-367–43252-2 (pbk)
ISBN: 978-1-003–00770-8 (ebk)

DOI: 10.4324/9781003007708

Typeset in Joanna
by codeMantra

For my students –
past, present, and future

CONTENTS

ACKNOWLEDGMENTS

Any book like this is the product of a whole network of cooperation, and I am grateful to many friends, colleagues, and family members for their support and input.

My former Routledge editor, Erica Wetter, encouraged me to pursue this project and gave me all kinds of essential advice. Rebecca Pearce was also helpful in the initial stages of proposing the book, and I am grateful for Martin Pettitt's copy editing. Emma Sheriff has been a patient and supportive editor throughout our time working together.

Many thanks to scholar-friends who read chapters of this book as work in progress and offered excellent advice and suggestions, including Kathleen Battles, Ron Becker, Katie Day Good, Elana Levine, Rick Popp, and Ira Wagman. The special expertise of David Allen, Kyle Barnett, Eric Harvey, and Michael Socolow helped me understand particular points. I am grateful to my broader social media networks, including many friends I also know offline, and even more I do not (yet). I also appreciate the feedback of anonymous reviewers. All of these friends and colleagues have made my work much better.

The Interlibrary Loan office at the University of Wisconsin-Milwaukee Libraries are heroes to me, as are the many ILL librarians, wherever they are, who work to facilitate the research and scholarship of people they will never meet. This resource was particularly essential during the months of the COVID-19 pandemic when my campus library was closed. I could not have produced this work without the support of our librarians.

I am blessed to have an amazing community of UWM media scholars (past and present) who are serious intellectuals, dedicated educators, and warm and supportive friends. I am so thankful for David Allen, Gilberto Blasini, Xiaoxia Cao, Christine Evans, Zach Finch, Lane Hall, Taisik Hwang, Richard Grusin, Elana Levine, Eric Lohman, Michael Mirer, Stuart Moulthrop, Rick Popp, Maureen Ryan, Jocelyn Szczepaniak-Gillece, Marc Tasman, Tami Williams, and Lia Wolock. Thanks as well to the students in the MA program in Media Studies who were the attentive audience for a presentation about this book project in its early stages of writing and asked sharp questions.

I was able to write this book in part thanks to a Fall 2020 faculty sabbatical. I am grateful to my colleagues and my institution, and to the University of Wisconsin System, for sustaining faculty sabbaticals and giving us time and space to do our work.

I am grateful to the many undergraduate students (a number in the thousands) whom I have been fortunate to teach over more than 20 years of offering courses on media, including those taking Introduction to Film Studies, Introduction to Mass Media, Principles of Media Studies, and New Media History. Some of these former pupils have become good friends and outstanding scholars in their own right, proving true the old saw that teachers learn more from their students than the students learn from us. The ideas in this book have been circling through my mind for as long as I have been teaching these courses. I could not have written this without my years of classroom engagement with introductory-level undergrads, some of the most rewarding teaching experiences I have ever had. This book is dedicated to them.

My family has given me so much, and made possible everything I do. My parents, Alvin and Ruby, were my first and best teachers, and their influence and example have shown me the way. My sons, Leo and Noah, have helped me more than they probably know. Just hearing them ask how the *Toolkit* is going, just knowing that they care, has been enough to push me along the road to finishing a chapter or even just work out an idea I was trying to express more clearly. I strive to be worthy of their admiration. Finally, Elana Levine has done way more for my writing than giving feedback on chapters or listening to me talk through ideas, both of which she does so well. She is my closest colleague, co-parent, and life partner, and I could not have written this book – or any book – without her editorial skills, but more importantly, her support, encouragement, and love.

1

INTRODUCTION

You already know a lot about media. Anyone who has come of age in the past century in most parts of the world has been exposed to a constant stream of reproduced images and sounds, storytelling, advertising, updates, and diversions — a torrent of information and entertainment. For modern folks like us, knowing about media is like knowing about driving automobiles or eating factory-made foods like canned soup and Doritos. It's just a normal, unremarkable part of life. But historically, these are all very recent experiences that would have been unfamiliar to our ancestors just a few generations back. We have known only a media-saturated world, though over time it feels like the saturation keeps getting more intense. In our own lifetimes, we have experienced so much media change.

Over the years, media has come to mean many diverse things as new forms of culture and technology have fallen under its umbrella. A hundred years ago, the media business was often called "the press" (after the printing press technology essential to newspaper publishing). Beginning in the 1940s in English-speaking places, cinema, radio, and television, along with print technologies like newspapers and magazines, were coming to be known as "the mass media." In later times, when dropping "mass" from "mass media," we lost the connotation of a one-to-many flow of culture from a small number of powerful sources like the broadcast networks and Hollywood studios. But we have retained the idea of many different kinds of published or transmitted culture belonging together in one category: books, shows, stories, songs, films, photos, videos, and games are all media.

DOI: 10.4324/9781003007708-1

Of course there is considerable heterogeneity among these different media, but we persist in thinking of them belonging together in one category.

So in the early decades of the 21st century, *media* covers journalism but also all kinds of popular culture, from movies to mobile apps. It refers to the channels and platforms that bring us content, like Netflix and Facebook, but also to the companies that make the media products we consume, or sell us access to them, like Disney and Comcast. Sometimes it seems as if practically everything is media, as we use our networked digital devices to shop, pay bills and exchange money, work and attend school, socialize, and express ourselves. As media historian Richard Popp (2021, 601) observes, "each generation of 'new media,' among other things, has generally meant more things count as media."

This book is about how we can make sense of this environment of media all around us and use what we already know to go deeper. At its heart is a set of concepts, of words and ideas. These concepts are tools for knowledge. Put together, they make up a toolkit to be employed in understanding media and their significance to our lives and in the world around us. Just as a screwdriver or a pair of pliers each has its purpose, each concept in this book allows you to accomplish a certain kind of task of understanding something better. This kind of understanding is the purpose of media studies, a loosely organized academic field made up of researchers and teachers whose focus is media of many kinds. Media scholars are experts, but not necessarily in making media, though many of us have some experience in media production. Our specialty as scholars is in understanding media, in creating new knowledge about specific media topics, and sharing that knowledge and understanding with others via our writing, speaking, and teaching.

The purpose of this book is to reveal the ways that experts think about media and help you think about media the way we do, using our vocabulary and background assumptions and our informed sense of media's past and present. In opening up the toolkit, I want to show you how each of the items inside works: how they help us to increase our knowledge about aspects of media by placing them in a meaningful context, and by making connections among ideas and examples. You might have encountered these concepts already, and some of them are similar to terms that come up in contexts other than media studies. But in this book they are explored as tools for use in particular kinds of analysis and interpretation within a field, a community of scholars who share common intellectual perspectives and investments, even as they may also disagree about some things.

Why should we want tools for making sense of media? For starters, media are among the most important ways that we are informed about the world beyond our immediate everyday experience. We live in large and diverse societies, where our fellow citizens number in the millions or the hundreds of millions. Our sense of our place in the world – and of the relationship between ourselves, our communities, and the broader social environment – comes largely via media. We need to know how we take in this information, what kind of information it is, and whose interests are served by its circulation. This helps us function effectively as citizens: as participants in our communities who feel a sense of belonging to them. Thinking critically about the relationship between media, ourselves, and our communities can ultimately make us better at participating in civic life.

Media are also the format and the conduit for much of our cultural life. While human societies once told stories, sang and danced, and participated in religious rituals in ways that we would regard as tech-free, our culture is largely mediated. Understanding media is understanding the whole symbolic universe of modern life. It means grappling with a media culture that plays a key role in shaping our social and political environments. Working toward a world characterized by equity and justice can be accomplished in many spaces. We should demand a media culture that addresses our problems rather than contributes to them, and media studies can help us appreciate these cultural dynamics, and maybe even work toward changing them.

For many people who find themselves in a media studies class, their ambitions also go beyond earning credits toward a diploma or degree – or learning for its own sake – to include working in a media industry, whether on the creative or business side or in some combination. If this describes you, understanding media can be instrumental in helping you become a well-informed and thoughtful, socially responsible producer. The critical and analytical perspectives informed by traditions of media studies research can serve you well by orienting you toward problems in media that should be on the minds of those with the power to do something about them.

Whether this book can help you become a more critical consumer of media or a more critical producer of media or both, the "so what" of it all really comes down to this: media are a crucial force in modern societies that have the power to shape our individual imaginations, our identities, and our sense of the world around us. The more we know and understand about these things, the better off we will all be.

Analytical, Critical, Cultural

Some key terms in this discussion so far have been *analytical*, *critical*, and *cultural*. The tools in this book's toolkit are meant to be all of these things. To be *analytical* is to break things down into their parts and appreciate how they fit together. Analyzing media means getting up close, and taking seriously even types of media that might seem trivial or ephemeral. It means wanting to know about how media products are made and how they are used and understood. These processes include the constraints on media production and consumption, the forces that give shape to media. And analyzing means exploring meanings and implications, and making connections between different examples of media and the ways they relate to the social world.

To be *critical* is not necessarily to be negative. In scholarly circles, a critical perspective typically includes questioning and probing, and digging beneath the surface to discover underlying assumptions. Just as critical thinking means testing the logic and evidence behind different perspectives, a critical approach to media studies casts a skeptical eye and asks, why is this the way it is, and how might it have been different? How can we imagine a media environment other than the one we have come to know?

In academic circles, *critical* also frequently has another shade of meaning suggesting a political investment. A critical media studies approach would not pretend to be objective in observing media. It would, rather, see the media of modern, Western nations as having important connections to an unequal and unjust social structure characterized by inequality of many kinds on a global scale. To be critical of media is to be critical of this status quo, to look at how media and larger structures are related, and to consider how current arrangements might be challenged.

Not all media scholars take a critical perspective, but no one book can represent every possible point of view. My orientation as a critical media scholar points me toward a perspective that takes media as one key institution within a capitalist, patriarchal, white supremacist society. The critical perspective in this book is concerned with media's role in either maintaining or resisting these forms of inequality and oppression. This isn't to say that every chapter and every section of every chapter addresses such matters directly. Some topics in media studies are closer to this critical discussion than others, and sometimes politics is an undercurrent rather than being at the surface. But the overall perspective takes media as having political functions within a given society, which only makes sense considering how pervasive and influential media tend to be.

Our third critical term, *cultural*, is always a challenge to define. The cultural theorist Raymond Williams (1983, 87) famously named it "one of the two or three most complicated words in the English language." To see media as culture is to recognize it as a part of our way of life and our everyday experience. It also means seeing culture as a system of symbolic objects and activities that have shared meaning and purpose within particular communities.

In its anthropological sense, culture is a vast area that includes language and food and religious practice and living arrangements. All media is culture, but not all culture is media. By this way of thinking, culture contrasts with nature and refers to all of the ways human societies construct meaning and organize our lives. It's our nature to speak a language, but it's our culture to speak North American English or any other particular language. In a different, more elitist sense, culture can refer to works of art, literature, and performance, practices valued for their beautiful or expressive qualities, and can also extend to "popular" forms like movies and TV, comics, and rock and hip-hop music, hence the term "pop culture." (What's elitist here is distinguishing culture proper, which is associated with class privilege, from popular culture, which is defined as being "of the people.") Thinking of media as culture draws upon both of these senses of the word. Media is deeply ingrained in our way of life, and media is also made up of many different kinds of cultural products that have their own qualities and meanings that we can approach critically and analytically, wherever they fall on a dubious cultural hierarchy.

Culture has one additional connotation in media studies. It relates to a particular school of thought called *cultural studies*, originally a British movement of the left that became influential in the 1970s and 1980s. For this tradition of media scholarship, separating the notion of culture from the elitist concept was a key move. Another was to recognize that culture is a site of struggle between groups in society, an arena in which the powerful assert their dominance and impose their ways of thinking, but in which less powerful groups can also exercise resistance.

One key contribution of cultural studies was to regard media (and other cultural objects) as part of a circuit that links production and consumption within a social world and its unequal structures. To do cultural studies of media can mean looking at all kinds of media products or experiences as worthy of our critical attention, as significant in playing a role in everyday life, and as potentially political. It can mean looking at media as the product of the social world and also as contributing to its systems of meaning and value.

To see media culture as a circuit, we have to cast aside the simplistic idea that producers create meanings that are transmitted via media to consumers who receive and understand them. This "communication model," in which a media text's purpose is to convey information from one party to another, is too simplistic according to a cultural approach to media studies. In place of this linear notion of transmission, the circuit of culture pictures a circle in which producers, texts (media content) and their representations, consumers or users, and the social world are all linked together by lines of influence, and the whole environment matters for creating meaning.

This requires taking into account many different things. As Richard Johnson (1986–1987, 46) describes his formulation of this circuit, "if we are placed at one point" on it, "we do not necessarily see what is happening at others." But to adequately study a cultural text, argues Paul Du Gay (2013, xxx–xxxi), drawing upon Johnson's theorizing, we must pass through all of the steps in its circuit. In reference to the example of the Sony Walkman, Du Gay argues that "to study the Walkman culturally one should at least explore how it is represented, what social identities are associated with it, how it is produced and consumed, and what mechanisms regulate its distribution and use" (xxx). Different versions of a circuit of culture might vary in their specifics, but they have in common a notion that conditions of production, consumption, and the social world all matter to the cultural study of media, and that we can better understand each one by thinking of it in relation to at least some of the others. The Media Studies Toolkit shares this basic orientation to the critical analysis of media, which comes from cultural studies.

Surveying the Terrain

Media studies is an unusual kind of field, and a relative newcomer to many colleges and universities. As media have grown and multiplied and become ever more enmeshed in our moment-by-moment existence, scholarly discourse about media has tried to keep pace. There was no field called media studies already established a few decades ago, and the study of media grew wherever hospitable conditions existed. The field as it exists today is the product of its origins in different kinds of fertile environments and its spread on the fringes of other academic disciplines. This can make media studies seem less cohesive than some academic areas of study, or more like a set of different clusters rather than one unified field. One introductory book cannot be representative of every approach to a sprawling topic like media, but I have tried in the *Toolkit* to present concepts that are widely shared and relevant to many kinds of topics.

One tradition of media studies, which is the one I come from, began in the humanities as an offshoot of English literature. (I was an English major as an undergraduate and earned a PhD in Communication Arts with a Film Studies concentration, and now I teach in an English department.) First film and later TV studies grew out of literature research, applying many of the concepts of textual interpretation and analysis to audiovisual media. Popular music and game studies have some things in common with this tradition as well, though these pursuits are also connected to other disciplines like musicology or anthropology. Humanities approaches to studying media often overlap with qualitative studies in the social sciences, and scholars from these different traditions can coexist within a department and draw on common theories and assumptions about media. But within the humanities tradition, it is more common to regard media as artistic forms of expression and to center authors, texts, genres, and representations in analysis, though this hardly accounts for all kinds of inquiry in this tradition.

Another strain of media studies, more distant from my own experience, began in the social sciences and has often been known as "mass communication" research. Journalism, public opinion, media effects, and other aspects of mass media have often been studied in settings that draw upon traditions in psychology, sociology, political science, and related areas. Whereas humanities research tends to be textual and interpretive, mass communication research follows a more objective approach in adherence with the scientific method. Whereas humanists might speak of doing readings of their objects of research, social scientists might speak of collecting and analyzing data about them. Actually both groups do both kinds of activities, but they surely differ in their worldviews and orientations toward their topics of study, and the way they formulate questions about them.

Both of these kinds of media studies grew as students wanted to take courses in media topics like journalism, advertising, public relations, and film and video production. They also grew as scholars in many disciplines wanted to understand more about media. As a new and hybrid field, media studies incorporated many ideas and approaches from other parts of the scholarly world. This book contains insights and concepts from an array of disciplines, including English/literary studies, communication, history, sociology, anthropology, political science, psychology, economics, and philosophy, as well as science and technology studies, gender and ethnic studies, and law. Media studies poaches concepts, blending them opportunistically. Different kinds of research borrow different kinds of ideas. It follows that media is not so much a discipline defined by the marriage of a subject and method as it is a broad topic to be approached by varied methods as they suit the agenda of the researcher. This book aims to be useful across these differing approaches by focusing on concepts that inform many kinds of media research. This book covers journalism and entertainment, old and new media, traditional one-to-many broadcasting and networked digital platforms. It aims to show that the tools in the toolkit can be useful across these distinctions.

Scholars, like any people organized into groups defined by their shared identities, sometimes draw boundaries around their areas of interest and police those boundaries by excluding some people from their circle based on a failure to conform to group expectations. In media studies, these boundaries can be based on topics of research (e.g., film scholars may avoid television) or on approach (e.g., humanists may avoid social science). I have written this Toolkit as a critical cultural scholar of popular media, especially film and TV. But I have tried to present the topics in this book in a way that would speak to the broadest possible media studies readership and avoid marking off stark boundaries. I have drawn for my examples on film and television, but also music, journalism, advertising, video games, and social and digital media. None of the chapters in this book are specific to any one medium or form of media, and all of them contain discussions of diverse kinds of culture. I propose that we see the field as a big tent rather than as scattered clusters of hostile factions.

The ten chapters that follow are all meant to be able to stand alone, which is often how books like this one are used. But they are all related to some of their neighboring chapters and are intended to be companions to one another. The chapters "Audience," "Text," and "Industry" are the ones most central to the circuit of culture, and this trinity is most essential for becoming oriented to the basics of media studies (at least in my opinion).

These three are also concerned more than the rest of the book with explaining how media research is conducted. "Representation" and "Ideology" are both connected to "Text" first of all, but also crucially to "Audience" and more tangentially to "Industry." "Citizenship" and "Consumerism" are both directly connected to "Audience," but also to the other two in the trinity. "Policy and Regulation" is most closely connected to "Industry." "Technology" is connected to all three, and also has some important links to "Ideology," in the discussion of the politics of technologies. "Global and Local" is connected to "Industry" and "Audiences," but also to "Ideology," in the discussion of the unequal global flows of media and the concept of cultural imperialism.

I have written this book from my own particular social position and perspective that I think should be acknowledged at the outset. I was born in 1972 and grew up in Toronto, Canada. I have lived in the Midwestern US since 1997, when I moved to Madison, Wisconsin, to go to graduate school. I am a straight, white, cisgender man, married, father of two sons. I am a tenured full professor at a public university, as is my spouse. I am Jewish, and aside from needing glasses and some hearing loss, I have no disabilities. Why are these things relevant? For one thing, I think we all bring our individual identities – our age, race and ethnicity, religion and nationality, gender and sexuality, class, ability or disability – to the experience of media and to the task of making sense of it. There is no disembodied brain that understands the true meaning of things and speaks in neutral, value-free facts. Every meaning is a situated interpretation. Your identity matters too, and shapes your understanding. For another thing, I find that I learn better from a teacher I feel some connection to, and I hope to appear in the pages of this book now and then as a person you can get to know a little bit, and not just as some authority who wrote a text you were assigned to read.

One more thing about me: I find the topics explored in the pages to come to be endlessly fascinating. I have assembled this *Toolkit* because I have sometimes struggled to introduce my own students to these concepts so that they could join with me in my particular kinds of deep interest in media. This book is meant as a guide along a journey not just into new knowledge but toward the satisfaction and even pleasure that come from working out new ideas and appreciating things you find to be fresh and revealing.

References

Du Gay, Paul. 2013. "Introduction to the First Edition." In *Doing Cultural Studies: The Story of the Sony Walkman*, edited by Paul Du Gay, Stuart Hall, Linda Janes, Andes Koed Madsen, Hugh Mackay, and Keith Negus, xxviii–xxxii. London: Sage.

Johnson, Richard. 1986–1987. "What Is Cultural Studies Anyway?" *Social Text* 16: 38–80.

Popp, Richard K. 2021. "Media." In *Information: A Historical Companion*, edited by Ann Blair, Paul Duguid, Anja-Silvia Goeing, and Anthony Grafton, 601–607. Princeton: Princeton University Press.

Williams, Raymond. 1983. *Keywords: A Vocabulary of Culture and Society*, rev. ed. New York: Oxford University Press.

2

INDUSTRY

Media has to come from somewhere, and most often commercial media comes from companies in an industry. An industry is an arena of production, so a media industry produces media. One industry, such as the newspaper industry, is made up of all of the companies that make the same kind of products, such as print papers and digital news sites. Media texts, often called content within the business of media, are the output of media industries. These include movies, TV shows, magazines, videos, records, and games. In the circuit of culture, industry is at one point along a circle that includes text and audience, and together these three concepts form a loop. You can't have one without the others. As a tool in our toolkit, industry tells us where media texts originate and what forces shape their creation. When media are produced by corporations in business to make money, their success or failure are measured in business terms.

The businesses making a particular form of media compete or cooperate to produce goods or services, and the term industry implies a certain size and complexity. It comes with a sense of scale, and brings to mind factories and warehouses, distribution channels, and established work routines and conventions. Industries of all kinds have their own trade papers tracking developments, and they have conventions where people who work in the industry and journalists who cover the industry come together to show what they have made and talk about what's new and what's on the horizon. Two of the oldest and most famous American media trade papers are Editor & Publisher and Variety, which have covered the news and popular entertainment

DOI: 10.4324/9781003007708-2

industries, respectively, since the early 20th century. An example of an industry convention is Cinecom, an annual gathering for film exhibitors.

If you set up shop making handmade jewelry to sell at art fairs, you probably wouldn't say you work in the jewelry industry as you would be missing that sense of scale. You would be a craftsperson or artisan, and perhaps an entrepreneur. But if you went to work for a company that mass produces jewelry to sell at Walmart or on Amazon, that would be an industry job. In an age of social media creators, it's increasingly hard to tell where amateur, artisanal production ends and professional, industrial production begins. This distinction can be pretty fuzzy. If you produce makeup tutorial videos for YouTube and get participation from brands that send you samples and help you earn advertising revenue, you might be part of the online creator industry, even if you can barely make a living at it. Your YouTube videos would be serving the commercial interests of the platform's parent company, Google, one of the biggest and most powerful forces in the media business of the digital age.

Industry is a singular term, but our topic here could as easily be plural – *industries* – as there are many. Each medium has its own, though they are interlocking and interdependent. Film, radio, television, recording (music), games, newspapers and magazines, publishing (books, comics), and social media are all media industries. There is also an advertising industry, which is integral to many of these other industries.

Industries are local, regional, national, and global. There are many film industries: the American film industry, often synonymous with Hollywood, also includes small-scale independent productions far from Hollywood, and other nations have their own industries. The British or Japanese or Brazilian film industries might have some points of contact with Hollywood, but they are also distinct. The American film industry is also in the television business as the same companies and the same workers might go back and forth between making feature films and television series, which are produced using many of the same tools and following many of the same conventions of production. Over time, the distinction between these media has become blurry as most content is viewed in the home or on mobile screens, and platforms like Netflix and Disney+ offer entertainment that can be hard to categorize as strictly either TV or cinema.

Netflix and Disney are global companies, but much of our media is produced locally for nearby audiences all over the world. Some media, like feature films, tend to be more national or global, but news is often local or regional in both its production and consumption. Where I live, in southeastern Wisconsin, in the Midwest region of the US, the newspapers, news websites, and the television and radio stations employ journalists who live in the community and report on matters of local concern. If they are advertising-supported, the local advertising industry and the local businesses that advertise (e.g., supermarkets, hardware stores, car dealers, health care providers, lawyers) are also part of this local news industry ecosystem. If you are aiming to work in media and don't plan to live in a major media capital like Los Angeles or Toronto, the most likely workplaces to employ you are probably local or regional news or advertising companies.

With some exceptions, these local media companies are for-profit businesses. Much if not most of the media you consume is made by media professionals working in a commercial industry. This would be true of the shows on Netflix, the songs on Spotify, the news stories watched or read on smartphone apps, and the games played on a mobile device or console. Commercial media means media run as a business, earning revenue to support the operations. A for-profit media company ultimately serves an agenda of keeping the business going and making more money than it spends. This may not be its only agenda – it also may aim to inform and entertain audiences – but we should never lose sight of it.

Some of the media that people consume in the US and other Western countries is professionally made but in the non-profit sector, such as public radio and television. The American media network NPR is funded differently from most other news organizations in the US. It gets a small amount of funding in grants from the government, and the lion's share of its budget – and of its member stations' budgets – is from contributions from charitable organizations, corporations, and individual members (people like me who support their local public radio station). Even though it is public and non-profit rather than private and for-profit, the workers at NPR and its member stations are part of the broader news industry.

Like the social media creator or the jewelry maker, there are many kinds of production that are smaller-scale than something you'd call industrial. In the case of YouTube, Instagram, TikTok, and Twitter, however, the users might be non-professional and unpaid, but the platforms are huge for-profit businesses, so we might consider this kind of media to be a hybrid of individual and industrial production that has some of the qualities of each. Workers in conventional industries labor under different conditions from social media content creators, with types of risk, reward, and compensation that vary from one kind of work to another.

These distinctions matter for the same reason that media industries more generally matter: we know more about how media work when we understand how they were made. Understanding how they were made needs to include understanding the goals and agendas of the individuals making media, and of the organizations they work in or work with. The agenda of public, non-profit media, or of individual online creators, might be different from conventional for-profit industries, but all types of media likely share the common agenda of needing to reach audiences and command their attention, driving their varied metrics of success and failure. The professional identities of the workers at public media companies often are defined in ways quite similar to for-profit media workers: they want to make an impact, to be recognized for their work, and to reach the public with meaningful messages.

The most basic, essential, fundamental truth of commercial media in a capitalist society, such as the media of the US and other rich free-market countries, is that it functions as any business functions, and is subject to the same incentives and constraints. When we ask, "why is this the way it is?" it always pays to remember that most media we experience are produced by an industry in business to make money.

Revenue Streams

For-profit media companies, whatever they produce, generally have two ways of generating revenue. (*Revenue* refers to all of the earnings coming into a company, while *profit* refers to revenue minus expenditures. It's possible to have large revenue and small profits, or none at all, if expenditures are high.) Some make money exclusively or almost exclusively from consumer spending, that is, from making a product that people are willing to pay for. When you go to the movies and spend your money to buy a ticket, some of it goes to the theater, and a lot of it goes to the film distributor, who divides it up among the many different people and companies that get paid a share of a film's revenue. It's true that some movie theaters show advertising before the feature, but revenue from those ads, which goes to the movie theaters, is a tiny amount compared to the money collected at the box office. Video games, books, recordings, cable television, and news are all businesses that sell something to the consumer. Anything that offers monthly or yearly subscriptions, like a magazine or a streaming service, is making money this way.

Some media forms make money exclusively or almost exclusively from advertising. Radio over the air, which you can listen to on the AM and FM dials, is free to you the listener. You probably receive many commercial stations over the air wherever you live, and these stations are mostly for-profit businesses that earn revenue from businesses that pay for the attention of audiences. Social media is another example of a for-profit media industry that is advertising-driven. No one yet pays to have a Twitter or Instagram account, except indirectly by being the target market for advertising on these platforms. If I buy a pair of shoes I saw advertised on social media (which I have done), you might think of the money I spent on them as an indirect cost that I paid to use a photo-sharing platform. As the old saying goes, "there's no such thing as a free lunch."

Some kinds of media rely on a combination of consumer and advertiser support. The news business is a good example, and so is cable television. A newspaper or website may charge readers for single copies of the paper or for unlimited digital access via a subscription. Cable providers offer dozens or hundreds of channels for the monthly fee they charge. But the news and the cable content you receive also carries ads, and with some rare exceptions, cable networks and newspapers absolutely need the revenue from both streams to sustain themselves. A network like CNN gets paid twice: once from the subscriber, whose monthly cable bill is sliced up into the many fractions that go to the various channels they receive, and once from sponsors like drug companies and insurance agencies, whose commercials run in between segments of the network's programs.

Traditionally, in the mass media industries, there have been clear demarcations of businesses by their revenue streams. Broadcasting was strictly advertising-supported. The recording industry earned its revenue from record sales for many decades, and as new formats emerged (LPs, CDs, MP3s), they adapted to selling their products for different kinds of devices and uses. Movies were made to be seen in the theater, by paying customers, and later adapted to being shown on television and released on home video for rental or purchase. Newspapers and magazines depended on a combination of both kinds of revenue for hundreds of years.

The digital age has upended many industry conventions and blurred many of the clear lines between the different industries. Television became a consumer-spending medium as cable TV grew in the 1980s. By the third decade of the 21st century, television is still broadcast for free over the air and supported with advertising, but it's also seen commercial-free via platforms like HBO Max and Netflix, and in both ad-free and ad-supported versions of platforms like Hulu and Peacock. Emerging media like podcasts and email newsletters have tried these different revenue streams with varying degrees of success. In some instances, new revenue streams have emerged that complicate the simple breakdown into two forms of income. For instance, some recording artists might earn as much revenue in the Spotify era licensing their work for use in television episodes or advertisements than in payments for streams. Catalogs of popular songs can have high value thanks to the revenue they earn this way (Hogan 2021). Podcasts might sell the rights to a story they told in an audio series to be made into a streaming series. In these examples, the customer for one kind of media is another kind of media. But these deals wouldn't exist if the products were not, in the first place, consumer-facing texts aiming for the attention and spending of a person listening to music or podcasts.

A key insight about advertising-supported media like commercial radio and television is that the audience is not the customer, and is only indirectly the source of the industry's revenue. The sponsor, not the viewer or listener or reader, is the one whose money the media producers are after. In this scenario, the audience functions as a commodity (Smythe 1981). Its attention is being packaged and sold by the media producer to the advertiser, who sees value in targeting commercial messages at desirable consumers. A movie producer benefits from the largest number of people buying tickets, and while studios market films at particular segments of the general public (for instance, addressing audiences of a particular age range and gender), they benefit from ticket sales being as high as possible.

For a strictly advertising-supported business, though, the measure of success is likely to be rather different. Since many or most goods and services are marketed to a particular segment of the population, advertisers are interested in engaging their potential customers more than they care about their appeals reaching the largest possible audience. Not all people who drive cars will ever seriously consider buying a new imported luxury vehicle, so Mercedes-Benz is wasting its advertising budget reaching the largest possible audience for its commercials. It makes more sense for them to spend their money to target people who might actually buy a Benz. So they advertise in places where they believe they are likely to capture the attention of these particular people.

In American ad-supported television, the key slice of the audience has long been viewers between 18 and 49 years of age, aka "the demo." These are the potential customers that many advertisers find most desirable, because people younger than 18 have less money and less power to direct consumer spending, and audiences 50 and older are believed to be set in their ways and harder to persuade. Many kinds of television are more narrowly pitched at male or female viewers 18–49, or at a smaller age range. If a sponsor is paying to advertise to men 18–49 (e.g., during a basketball game), then younger, older, and non-male audiences simply don't have value to the television network. They might watch, but they don't really count; the ads are simply not meant for them.

Being advertising-driven brings benefits to a media company, one of which is offering its products at a low price or even for free. Social media has become so enmeshed in our lives by being so easy to access at no direct cost. Broadcasting over the air continues to be free to the consumer, though most television is now accessed via some form of subscription service. Before the internet disrupted the news business, free papers were widely distributed in many cities from stands by the front doors of stores and restaurants. These "alt-weekly" tabloids contained local reporting and commentary, often from a sharply left-wing perspective, along with arts and culture criticism, events listings, classified ads, and display advertisements for local businesses. Some still exist as online news sites, or even as print publications. The revenue for these free papers would come entirely from the advertising, so the circulation of the papers could be as high as the number of people interested enough to pick up a free copy.

In many ways the functions of free papers and the revenues from publications like these have been taken over by digital versions of political, cultural, and personal discourse – social media. Platforms like Facebook and Twitter are likewise free to the user, generating their revenue from advertising. By being free, these platforms have extended their reach into the lives of enormous numbers of people. The power and reach of advertising-supported media can be staggeringly broad.

In advertising-supported media, the sponsor rather than the audience is the consumer, and the media producer might be mindful of the sponsor's interests. Many newspapers rely on advertising from car and truck dealers, and may be unlikely to cover the automotive industry in highly critical terms, given who their customers are. Advertisers are notoriously sensitive to controversy, and in some instances consumer activists have called for advertiser boycotts of broadcasting or cable programming that they find objectionable. Over the years, several personalities on Fox News have faced boycott calls targeting their advertisers after saying things many people found offensive, though the effectiveness of this strategy has been questionable (Adgate 2020). Producers of some kinds of radio or television programming might seek to avoid certain controversial topics out of a fear of offending advertisers. The product of these dynamics can be a logic of safety in mainstream media, and a tendency to repeat inoffensive but successful formulas (Croteau and Hoynes 2019, 93; Gitlin 2000). Of course, consumer spending industries also benefit from playing it safe in many instances, but the kinds of constraint and pressure they face is likely to be different without needing to account for the interests of advertisers.

By contrast to free ad-supported media, some media is expensive to the consumer, and being expensive also might bring advantages to the industry. Media industries that appeal to large audiences, such as Hollywood, can bank on significant revenues even from modestly priced offerings like movie tickets, which tend to be cheaper than many competing forms of entertainment, such as concerts, sporting events, and live theater. This allows them to make movies on a lavish scale, with budgets in the hundreds of millions of dollars. Media industries that base their business model on consumers' monthly subscriptions, including news outlets and streaming services, not only have the potential for large numbers of consumers, depending on their market and product, but also regular income month after month, avoiding some of the volatility of the industries that are constantly appealing to audiences. Regardless of the particular revenue sources of any particular company or industry, the money always matters. Thinking about industries in relation to their business models yields insights into how media are made to appeal in certain ways to particular people. This can shed much light on how they got to be the way they are.

(One bit of clarification may be useful here: advertisements are also commonly known as *commercials*, but any media company in business to make money is part of a *commercial media industry*, even if its revenue is entirely from consumer spending. *Commercial* means that the media industry functions within a market of exchange of goods and services for money. It means that value is judged in relation to earnings, to the bottom line.)

Political Economy and the Structures of Media Companies

The area of media studies that focuses on how media are produced within a capitalist system includes a number of different approaches, including prominently the *political economy of media* (McChesney 2013). Political economists look at connections between, on the one hand, media companies and their ways of making money, and on the other hand, the forms of media produced by these companies. It is highly critical of the for-profit nature of most media in Western, capitalist societies and sees the profit motive as a factor that generally trumps other values in media production, such as the need to inform citizens about the world they live in, the better to serve all of the citizens in a democracy. The terms *political* and *economy* here suggest the way that economic forces determine relations of power. Political economists argue that the capitalist foundation of media companies determines what kind of content they produce. The particular *kinds* of media companies in an industry (e.g., their size and scope, their ways of earning profits) are critical economic factors shaping media products.

An enduringly influential account of mass media as the product of a capitalist system or production is the 1947 essay "The Culture Industry: Enlightenment as Mass Deception" by Theodor W. Adorno and Max Horkheimer (2002), two German-Jewish critics from the Frankfurt School who escaped the Nazis and settled in the United States. By joining the terms "culture" and "industry," Adorno and Horkheimer meant to force a collision between incompatible ideas: culture had connotations of unique works of art, while industry by contrast suggested mass production of cheap amusements. To these critics, mass production of radio, music, movies, advertisements, and consumer goods was standardizing culture, imprinting a repetitious sameness on every product, and erasing the individualism of creators and audience members. This mass appeal, according to Adorno and Horkheimer, had the same kinds of effects on society as the fascist regime from which they fled: using media as propaganda to enforce conformity to one system, in this case the American capitalist system. It was being used, they argued, to keep audiences in a state of distraction or escape from critical thought, a mindset that would benefit the powerful within the economic system. This is a key point for a political economy of media: the products of the media industries ultimately serve the interests of those with the economic power.

Critical readers today might point out that the "Culture Industry" essay overstates some of its points for rhetorical effect, lacks an empirical basis, or fails to capture the authentic pleasures of popular culture and the potential of audiences to make their own meanings. But many of its points resonate so many years after its publication, and have given inspiration to critics of media industries from the left. Its argument about the standardized, formulaic qualities of mass culture, the conventionalized sameness of so much corporate media, makes a clear connection between political economy and the products of media industries that seems no less pertinent to 21st-century media than it was in the mid-20th century.

In the years since the publication of "The Culture Industry," the trendline in Western media industries has gone in the direction of increasing the power of the capitalist industries. In the last few decades of the 20th century in the US, there was a dominant pair of intertwined trends in media industries: a *concentration of media ownership* and a spread of *media conglomeration* (Croteau and Hoynes 2006). *Concentration* refers to the shrinking number of owners of media companies. When several big newspaper chains buy up many local papers, the total number of newspaper owners becomes smaller, and ownership of news companies becomes more *concentrated*. (Think of the quart and a half of orange juice being reduced to a 12-ounce concentrate in a frozen can for sale in the supermarket.) This is exactly what has happened as the American newspaper industry has gone from having thousands of locally owned papers to a small number of massive chains, basically the news equivalents of the CVS outlets that have taken the place of locally-owned drug stores. The urban region where I live, Milwaukee, once had two major daily papers, the *Journal* and the *Sentinel*, both with local owners. They merged in the 1980s to become the *Journal-Sentinel*, which meant that the city went from having two daily newspaper companies to having one. Ownership of newspapers in this town became more concentrated when the number of owners was cut in half.

But more recently, the *Journal-Sentinel* was acquired by a massive national chain, Gannett, which also owns *USA Today* and dozens of other daily newspapers, each of which was at one point independently and locally owned. Say 100 local papers with local owners eventually come to be acquired by one large chain like Gannett. In this case, media concentration will be much more drastic and intense than in the case of a single merger, as the number of owners will have shrunk down to 1 percent of its original value. A similar process has happened in many industries as the number of independently owned advertising agencies, record labels, and radio and television stations has shrunk considerably as major companies expand through mergers and acquisitions. You are probably familiar with this practice from the world of online media, such as Facebook's ownership of Instagram, WhatsApp, and Oculus.

Just looking at newspapers, the effects of media concentration on the content of media, i.e., the news, has been very clear. A single large chain standardizes the offerings in its outlets and reduces labor costs by eliminating positions in each city, substituting national chain content for what would previously have been local reporting. Local papers have fewer newsroom workers in the age of media concentration than they had when they were independent businesses. They have shed their television and book critics, their city desk reporters, and much of their coverage of local politics and local affairs more generally. These changes have many causes, but one of them is media concentration. The pursuit of profit by large national chains may be incompatible with producing news that serves local communities in every part of a country as large and spread out as the United States. In combination with the rise of digital media and other changes in media industries, these forces have led to a drastic reduction in the number of newsroom employees in the first decades of the 21st century (PEN America 2019; Walker 2021).

A related phenomenon is media *conglomeration*. A conglomerate is a big company made up of many other companies in different lines of business. Gannett is mainly a newspaper chain. It is not the best example of a media conglomerate because it focuses on just one form of media, the news. Disney, by contrast, is an excellent example of a media conglomerate as it is made up of many different kinds of media businesses that came together through mergers and acquisitions (Wasko 2020). Disney in the 2020s is a sprawling empire comprised of local television stations, a broadcast television network (ABC), cable channels (ESPN and Disney Channel, among others), a streaming platform to rival Netflix (Disney+), a massive film and television production operation that includes Marvel, Star Wars, Pixar, and 20th Century (acquired from 20th Century Fox), and Disney theme parks on three continents. The company began, under Walt Disney, as an animation studio that made cartoon films. In the 1950s, it expanded by creating a theme park, Disneyland, and a television show by the same name (Anderson 1994, 133–155), and this provided a model of transmedia synergy, with content from movies being turned into rides and television show segments, and with each product promoting the others (Wasko 2020). Many rides at Disney's parks have been based on Disney's feature films, and sometimes the process works in reverse, as rides like *Pirates of the Caribbean* and *Jungle Cruise* have been adapted into blockbuster films.

A media conglomerate has many tentacles in different areas of the business of media, and some of them will have little to do with one another.

But the bundling together of movies, television and streaming, and theme parks in the case of Disney lends itself to certain kinds of creative decision-making. Conglomerates often favor media franchises, such as Disney's Star Wars and Marvel properties. Franchises can milk intellectual property over a period of years or decades via multiple releases on various platforms, from feature films to comic books to video games to television or streaming series to theme park attractions (Johnson 2013). The structure of the conglomerate makes such convergences possible and profitable. It dictates that transmedia synergy will be one of the strategies for developing content. As a consequence, the development of movies that have little potential to become a media franchise, to be the basis for a theme park attraction or a streaming series spinoff, will be less central to the conglomerate's ways of doing business (Meehan 1991). A political economy approach to media industries prompts us to see these connections between media ownership and the products of media industries as deeply embedded in the logic of advanced capitalist media enterprises.

Horizontal and Vertical Integration

Looking at media industries and their structures of ownership, we can see two kinds of patterns of integration of their supply chain (Croteau and Hoynes 2006, 96–102). Integration here refers to the combination of two or more elements of a media business. If a business does nothing but sell products, you would not say that it is integrated at all, but if it produces products, moves them to market, and sells them to consumers, then you would say that it integrates production, distribution, and retail sales, controlling its supply chain. For example, if you make candles and open a candle shop to sell them, you integrate those two aspects of a candle business.

Some media companies are integrated in this way. The classic example was the Hollywood studios in their golden age, the 1920s to 1940s (Balio 2011). These studios, including Warner Bros., Paramount, MGM, and 20th Century Fox, were film producers as well as film distributors (they rented movies to theaters in exchange for a percentage of box office revenue) and film exhibitors (they owned cinema chains all over the US). As it happens, the major studios operated as a cartel that dealt only in their own and each other's products and required any theater renting their movies to take a whole block of pictures rather than rent them one by one, a practice called block booking. The Supreme Court of the United States found this whole setup to be an illegal business practice, and in 1948 ordered the studios to divorce from their theater chains, which meant they had to take an integrated business and dismantle it by selling off their movie houses to other owners.

The kind of integration that the Hollywood studios had in their golden age was *vertical integration*. They combined production, distribution, and exhibition of motion pictures into individual companies. But they were primarily in the movie business and had not moved into other kinds of media. In this period of American media history, each form of media was more or less in its own world. The recording industry, the broadcasting industry (radio and then TV), the newspaper industry, the magazine industry, the book publishing industry, and the motion picture industry were all much more separate from one another industrially than they would become later on. Other industries, like cable and satellite TV, video games, and online social or streaming media did not yet exist.

In the second half of the 20th century and into the first decades of the 21st, this separation between the different industries began to erode as many mergers and acquisitions brought together companies in different sectors of the media trade, ultimately forming massive conglomerates like Comcast and Disney (Balio 1990). By the beginning of the 21st century, all of the major Hollywood studios and national television broadcast networks were part of media conglomerates that included other media in addition to cinema and broadcasting. A conglomerate that combines news and entertainment, film and television, publishing and theme parks, is not necessarily vertically integrated like the movie studios were in the 1920s, 1930s, and 1940s. Rather, this kind of combination of different kinds of media within one large company is *horizontally integrated*.

It should help to visualize this spatially. Each industry is lined up side-by-side: movies, television, newspapers, magazines, video games, etc. Companies that combine production, distribution, and/or exhibition or sales are vertically integrated. A contemporary example of a vertically integrated media conglomerate would be Comcast, which is both the parent companies of movie and television producers (NBCUniversal) as well as internet and television service providers, effectively selling the means for consumers to connect to the content they produce. They are involved in making media but also in selling media products directly to consumers.

By contrast, companies that combine the production of two or more kinds of media are *horizontally* integrated. In its heyday from the 1980s to the 2010s, the Australian media mogul Rupert Murdoch's News Corp. combined many news and entertainment businesses, including major daily newspapers in several countries, 20th Century Fox studios in Hollywood, the Fox television network (he started it), cable channels including Fox News, and the book publishing giant HarperCollins. Before it was acquired by AT&T in 2018, Warner Bros. was part of a conglomerate, Time-Warner, that at various times included magazines, comics, video games, movies, cable television, music, an internet portal (AOL), and a broadcast network, the WB (one of the networks that merged to become The CW). When visualized spatially, each of these separate media is lined up one by one next to one another in a broad array, so integrating the different kinds of media is a horizontal combination. Time-Warner and Comcast are also examples of horizontal integration. The typical American media conglomerate since the 1990s has combined, at the very least, broadcast and cable television and movie companies with some other forms of media or entertainment, whether music, publishing, or theme parks.

The reason to pay attention to vertical and horizontal integration brings us back to the political economy of media. Vertically integrated businesses exercise control over every part of their product's lifespan. They can benefit from setting terms of their trade at all levels. A recent example would be the streaming media portals like Netflix and Disney+ (Lotz 2017). Netflix began as an online version of a video store, basically a retailer with a monthly subscription movie rental business. It was in need of large amounts of content to make the subscription worthwhile to the consumer, and it paid the Hollywood studios (among other producer-distributors) for this content, first by buying their DVDs, and then by licensing their shows and movies for online streaming. When it began to produce its own television series and movies during the 2010s, Netflix moved into vertical integration. Its original content is exclusive to Netflix, and is an attraction to non-subscribers to sign up, as well as a way of keeping consumers who already subscribe from dropping the service (which in the subscription business is called churn). It also benefits Netflix by saving it the expense of paying someone else for content, and may prove lucrative over the long run as the content produced now will likely continue to have value in the future, just as old movies and television series from before the streaming age (e.g., Friends, The Office, Harry Potter films) continue to make money in reruns and on the various streaming platforms. The point is that by moving into vertical integration, Netflix has strengthened its position in the media industries.

By contrast, Disney+, which launched in 2020, has given its parent company an opportunity to exploit both vertical and horizontal integration.

As a service (like Netflix) that directly charges users a monthly fee for its service, it is combining the sale of a media product with the production and exploitation of content. This includes its original series, as well as the library of movies and shows that Disney already owned at the time of launching the service. But as it develops new products – television shows like *The Mandalorian* and *WandaVision* – Disney is able to exploit the horizontal integration of a conglomerate that has many tentacles in different media: movies, games, theme parks, etc. Netflix might have a more impressively vast smorgasbord of video entertainment for now, but Disney has the advantage of its rich holdings of intellectual property. Its many television and movie series, under the various popular brands it has developed and acquired over time from Mickey Mouse to Marvel, contribute to its appeal as a streaming service. The logic of cross-platform integration will surely continue to inform Disney's choices about which products to develop and extend as the online audience becomes more and more dominant while motion pictures and theme parks continue to be strong attractions. It pursues these projects because they are profitable, and because they make economic sense when a media producer is part of a horizontally and vertically integrated conglomerate.

Legacy Media and the Tech Giants

As the contrast of Netflix and Disney makes clear, old and new media companies are often competitors to one another. Over the history of modern media, beginning in the early years of the 20th century, we have seen certain patterns repeat themselves. A new medium or technology emerges, and if it succeeds in capturing popular attention in a way that is commercially successful, an industry develops and grows, establishing its own conventions of doing business and trying to protect itself from rivals. This was true in the early 20th century with cinema, radio, and later television. At the same time, national advertising was growing along with the consumer economy, and advertising helped the magazine industry blossom and thrive. Later in the century, the music recording industry and the cable television industry were two strong players in shaping the direction of media and threatening established business practices, and at the very end of the century, the commercial internet emerged as a major force of change in communication and a cause of many disruptions. All of these are more than just names of a medium or a technology; they have all been industries in their own right. There is often a potential for conflict or cooperation among these businesses, and the clashes and negotiations among media industries have major consequences for the media landscapes we inhabit.

As in many established fields, in the media business, we can identify companies that have endured over a long period of time, such as newspapers, movie studios, and broadcast networks. Some of these are institutions, like the *New York Times* (est. 1851), Universal Pictures (est. 1912), and NBC (est. 1926), that seem so durable as to be almost like they are part of the natural environment. By contrast, some of the most profitable and powerful media companies are relative newcomers. Apple Inc. (previously Apple Computer, Inc.) and Microsoft are relatively elderly for technology companies, having been founded in the 1970s. Amazon and Google were founded in the 1990s. Facebook, Twitter, and YouTube all began in the 2000s. Netflix began with its DVD-by-mail service in the 1990s, but its online streaming platform did not debut until 2007 and its first original content debuted in 2012. So many of the dominant forces in the media today are barely older than teenagers.

For a time, there was considerable debate about whether big tech firms like Facebook could be considered "media companies." There is no magic formula for determining this kind of sorting, but it was revealing that Facebook would avoid being described as part of the media business, considering that its vast number of users were making and sharing media on the platform from the start, and were using Facebook to access many different kinds of media from mainstream journalism to viral videos and social media outrages making the rounds. Not to mention the fact that Facebook's revenue model, just like broadcasting and print media, is premised on selling audiences to advertisers. Of course, Facebook is a media company, but it's not the same kind of media company as a movie studio, television network, or news organization. It captures its users' attention in new ways and offers them experiences that previous media had not offered. Facebook, along with various other online media platforms, including Google, has been so successful at claiming the attention and engagement of people all over the globe that spending on advertising by companies looking to reach consumers has shifted to an extraordinary extent from print media, and to some extent from broadcasting and cable television, to Google and Facebook (Einstein 2017, 37–38). They have amassed unprecedented power by claiming so much attention from so many people, and in the media driven by advertising revenue, attention is currency.

In the media industries, the old, established firms from the pre-digital era are often called the *legacy media companies*. Here *legacy* references not just having roots in the past, but also durability, prestige, and honor. Companies like the *Washington Post* or CBS have stood the test of time. Any prominent digital media companies are likely to be regarded, in contrast to the legacy media companies, as newcomers shaking things up and threatening the established order. The legacy companies are *incumbents*, the competitors who come to the contest already having status and power. The online and digital and social media challengers are *insurgents*, upstart competitors aiming to diminish the power of the established companies. In reality, the two kinds of companies also typically work together and as part of a larger ecosystem. Facebook needs the legacy media companies to be content for its users to share and comment on. Netflix licenses content from Hollywood studios and other television and film producers around the world. And in pushing their content onto streaming platforms, companies like Disney and WarnerMedia are learning from the insurgents how a legacy media business can succeed in the online era by copying their strategies while also exploiting the assets a legacy company brings to the table.

The tendency in advanced capitalist economies such as the US in the early 21st century has been toward a small number of large firms dominating a particular business. When one company controls all of the sales of a particular product, that's called a *monopoly*, and we generally dislike monopolies because they have excessive power and exploit consumers for the enrichment of their owners. Many nations have laws against monopoly business practices that encourage competitive business environments. In the US, the key statute in this area is the Sherman Antitrust Act of 1890, which can be used to force companies to be broken up into different smaller companies under separate ownership to create competition.

In some areas of media business, such as cable and internet service providers, we do observe monopoly or duopoly situations (a duopoly is an environment in which two companies dominate). A more common arrangement is an *oligopoly*, which is the domination of a trade by a small number of companies that work in cooperation with one another. The Hollywood studios were an oligopoly when the Supreme Court ordered that their theater chains be sold off in 1948. The major media conglomerates of the early 21st century, including Disney, Comcast, and Viacom, operate as an oligopoly as well. The biggest problem with an oligopoly has to do with its scale. When media is such a big business, with so much capital involved, it inhibits participation by newcomers. The only options are the major corporate mass media.

In the digital age, however, we have seen that the status of the media conglomerates has been threatened by the tech giants, the insurgents like Netflix and Facebook, which threaten to become new iterations of media monopolies. Innovation in the media industries often comes from outside of the established firms, from technological change and entrepreneurial newcomers (Wu 2011). It remains to be seen if the old and new giants of media will continue to compete with one another, or if one of them will attempt to absorb the other. In either event, the power of big companies or conglomerates is likely to remain undiminished within the advanced capitalist marketplaces of Western economies. The legacy media giants are facing competition from the new media giants, but the massive scale of media industry corporate structures continues despite the many changes observed over the first decades of the 21st century.

Studying the Media Industries

When we want to know more about the media industries, where can we go to learn about them? Some things about the inner workings of a business can be hard to find out, as private companies may prefer to keep their affairs private. But media businesses, like many companies, also like to publicize their successes. Many aspects of the workings of media industries are fairly well known because they have become part of the publicity that circulates around the media as an industry whose fortunes depend on capturing and holding the attention of the public. For decades, the movie studios have hyped their weekly box office revenues, and the television ratings are also widely reported as a form of entertainment news. Books are marketed as "bestsellers" and music recordings have traditionally been honored by sales milestones such as "gold" and "platinum" records. All of these quantifications of success appear regularly in the popular press, in news reports and marketing discourse.

Much more information can be gathered from tracking a more specialized form of journalism: the industry trade press. Most industries have at least one trade paper dedicated to covering the business for readers who work in that business. Media industry trade papers like *Broadcasting & Cable* (for the television industry) and *Billboard* (for the recording industry) are rich sources of information about how media industries work. If you are studying media industries in a class, an assignment might ask you to locate articles on a particular topic in an industry trade publication, and these are often accessible through periodical databases accessible via a school or public library website. Sometimes these publications are also available for free online. A great deal of knowledge of media industries can be gathered from these sources, both the popular and trade publications.

Many studies of media industries want to get closer than just reading articles about how a business works. There are drawbacks to the trade press, which often presents an optimistic side of the business that powerful people within an industry want to see circulating in coverage of their work. It can be hard to be critical of a business when your sources and subscribers all work in that business. But there are some alternatives or compliments to using trade press sources when doing research on the media industries. One method would be to talk to people who work in the media business and hear from them directly about how their industry works, and about their "cultures of production" (Caldwell 2009). Some researchers attend trade conventions where they might have a chance to interact with media professionals. Some conduct interviews via phone or email, or in person. An advantage of interviews over reading about an industry in the press is that the researcher can ask the questions they want answered, rather than be content to get the answers to someone else's (a reporter's) questions.

A deeper level of engagement with the people who work in media industries can be achieved by spending time among the workers at their places of business, on site in media production spaces. This method is called *ethnography*, a term from the discipline of anthropology (Stokes 2013, 104–112). An *ethnographer* is a participant-observer whose object of study is a group of people. Ethnographic research is a form of fieldwork, where the researcher spends time in a location and among participants, getting to know their values, their forms of knowledge, and their ways of living and working. One kind of media ethnography that has been fairly widely practiced involves the study of journalism as a profession. Journalism researchers have spent months or longer in the offices of online newsrooms, producing richly detailed accounts of the professional practices, the norms and conventions, of news workers during the digital transition (e.g., Boczkowski 2004; Paterson and Domingo 2008; Robinson 2010). Their insights have yielded knowledge about media that no amount of trade press coverage could reveal.

Many media industry researchers are just as interested in the past as the present, and while trade papers and interviews can be ways of accessing the history of media industries, another rich source of knowledge about the past is located in archives, such as collections of the papers of media professionals. As private entities, many companies do not make their archives public, but some have donated papers such as memos and correspondence to libraries and archives, in addition to media like film prints and videotapes. Archives of several American movie studios are held at the University of Southern California and the University of Wisconsin-Madison. These materials are open to researchers and many articles and books have drawn on their contents. Archives can shed light on the internal workings of companies, conflicts within business among workers who had different roles and interests, and strategies pursued or avoided.

These forms of research can offer new ways of understanding the industries as businesses, but many of the insights that researchers find most useful that come from interviews, ethnographies, and archival study pertain to media texts. Knowing how the text was made within its industrial production setting can help us understand why it came out the way it did, why it contains certain kinds of form or style, or certain meanings. Newsroom ethnographies can help explain why and how journalists follow particular routines of reporting and writing, and what pressures or constraints they work under. This can help us understand the news as a business, but also the news as a product. The archives of the Hollywood Production Code Administration reveal the negotiations between film producers and the industry's internal censors, who applied a set of rules to Hollywood film that allowed for certain kinds of representation but not others during the period when the studios all adhered to the same code. Research on media production can yield many kinds of knowledge.

For students doing research projects for a class assignment, ethnographic and archival research may be beyond the realm of possibility. But there are so many ways of accessing information about how the business of media works in our digital age, so many publications widely available, and so many media industry workers who are easy to find online and possibly willing to answer your questions. Media industry research can be particularly rewarding to students who have the goal of working in the media business, as the knowledge produced via research in this area can be applied directly in future work, or can serve as a kind of orientation or background set of assumptions that guide students as they enter the field.

Following the Money

The incredible variety of media that we encounter on a daily basis makes it hard to generalize about their origins in industries that produce these many different kinds of texts, from news stories to video games and from social media environments to advertising campaigns. But there are some things that media in an advanced capitalist society will have in common, and the vast majority of the media in our everyday lives continues to be the product of major commercial industries of enormous power. Even the small-scale performances we see on YouTube or Twitch or TikTok, or whatever the currently popular platform is, come to us via devices and networks that are enmeshed in the same big media and tech world as the legacy media conglomerates. When it comes to digital and electronic media, there really is no going "off the grid" of the corporate, commercial system. Even media branded as "independent" or "alternative" is likely to be enmeshed in systems of distribution and publicity that are part of the larger network of commercial mass media.

Whether or not there is advertising paying the bills, commercial media functions as a business and a business has interests other than the public good. A truly public media system, a system funded by tax revenue rather than subject to the vagaries of the market, might offer a worthwhile alternative that would better serve democratic goals of sharing information widely and engaging citizens in community affairs. But the power of for-profit commercial media in modern Western societies has been much greater than that of public media. This has profound consequences on the culture that makes up the landscape of our everyday lives. Media as the product of a commercial industry may be made to appeal to consumers, but ultimately the agenda of any commercial business is profits. When you wonder how the media you love or hate, or merely find familiar day in and day out, got to be the way it is, you can usually learn something informative if you simply follow the money.

Discussion Questions

1. What is the difference between these revenue models: consumer spending, advertising, and a mix of the two? Why do they matter?
2. What are vertical and horizontal integration? Why might it give a company an advantage to be either vertically or horizontally integrated?
3. Choose any example of media that you find interesting and find out which company produced it. What does knowing about the origins of the text in an industry help you understand about it?
4. What are some similarities and differences between legacy media and new media? Do you think one or the other has a better chance of continued success over the next few decades?

References

Adorno, Theodor W. and Max Horkheimer. 2002. "The Culture Industry: Enlightenment as Mass Deception." In *Dialectic of Enlightenment: Philosophical Fragments*, translated by Edmund Jephcott, 94–136. Stanford: Stanford University Press.

Adgate, Brad. 2020. "Do Advertiser Boycotts Work? It Depends." *Forbes*, June 17, 2020. https://www.forbes.com/sites/bradadgate/2020/06/17/do-advertiser-boycotts-work-it-depends/?sh=1fb10cb04ed8

Anderson, Christopher. 1994. *Hollywood TV: The Studio System in the Fifties.* Austin: University of Texas Press.

Balio, Tino. 1990. *Hollywood in the Age of Television.* Boston: Unwin Hyman.

Balio, Tino. 2011. *The American Film Industry*, rev. ed. Madison: University of Wisconsin Press.

Boczkowski, Pablo. 2004. *Digitizing the News: Innovation in Online Newspapers.* Cambridge, MA: MIT Press.

Caldwell, John Thornton. 2009. "Cultures of Production: Studying Industry's Deep Texts, Reflexive Rituals, and Managed Self-Disclosures." In *Media Industries: History, Theory, and Method*, edited by Jennifer Holt and Alisa Perren, 199–212. Malden: Wiley-Blackwell.

Croteau, David and William Hoynes. 2006. *The Business of Media: Corporate Media and the Public Interest*, 2nd ed. Thousand Oaks: Pine Forge Press.

Croteau, David and William Hoynes. 2019. *Media/Society*, 6th ed. Thousand Oaks: SAGE.

Einstein, Mara. 2017. *Advertising: What Everyone Needs to Know.* New York: Oxford University Press.

Gitlin, Todd. 2000. *Inside Prime Time.* Berkeley: University of California Press.

Hogan, Marc. 2021. "What to Know About Music's Copyright Gold Rush." *Pitchfork*, January 25, 2021. https://pitchfork.com/thepitch/what-to-know-about-musics-copyright-gold-rush/

Johnson, Derek. 2013. *Media Franchising: Creative License and Collaboration in the Culture Industries.* New York: New York University Press.

Lotz, Amanda D. 2017. *Portals: A Treatise on Internet-Distributed Television.* Ann Arbor: Michigan Publishing, University of Michigan Library. http://www.amandalotz.com/portals-a-treatise-on-internetdistributed-television

McChesney, Robert. 2013. "The Political Economy of Communication: An Idiosyncratic Presentation of an Emerging Subfield." In *The International Encyclopedia of Media Studies*, 1st ed., edited by Angrahad N. Valdivia. Malden: Blackwell, 2013.

Meehan, Eileen R. 1991. "Holy Commodity Fetish, Batman! The Political Economy of the Commercial Intertext." In *The Many Lives of the Batman: Critical Approaches to a Superhero and His Media*, edited by Roberta Pearson and William Uriicchio, 47–65. New York: Routledge.

Paterson, Chris and David Domingo, eds. 2008. *Making On-Line News: The Ethnography of New Media Production*. New York: Peter Lang.

PEN America. 2019. "Losing the News: The Decimation of Local Journalism and the Search for Solutions." PEN America, November 20, 2019. https://pen.org/wp-content/uploads/2019/12/Losing-the-News-The-Decimation-of-Local-Journalism-and-the-Search-for-Solutions-Report.pdf

Robinson, Sue. 2010. "Traditionalists vs. Convergers: Textual Privilege, Boundary Work, and the Journalist-Audience Relationship in the Commenting Policies of Online News Sites." *Convergence* 16.1: 125–143.

Smythe, Dallas W. 1981. "On the Audience Commodity and Its Work." In *Media and Cultural studies: Keyworks*, edited by Meenakshi Gigi Durham and Douglas M. Kellner, 253–279. Malden: Blackwell.

Stokes, Jane. 2013. *How to Do Media and Cultural Studies*, 2nd ed. London: SAGE.

Walker, Mason. 2021. "U.S. newsroom employment has fallen 26% since 2008." Pew Research Center (July 13, 2021). https://www.pewresearch.org/fact-tank/2021/07/13/u-s-newsroom-employment-has-fallen-26-since-2008/

Wasko, Janet. 2020. *Understanding Disney: The Manufacture of Fantasy* 2nd ed. Cambridge: Polity Press.

Wu, Tim. 2011. *The Master Switch: The Rise and Fall of Information Empires*. New York: Vintage.

3

TEXT

What are media? One way of answering such a crucial question is by giving examples we all probably agree on. Print publications like newspapers, magazines, and books are kinds of media, as are their digital and online versions. So are television and streaming video, movies, photos, recorded music, digital games, and apps and websites. All of these are formats of what the media industries produce, which they usually call *content*.

Media content refers to things that have value for both industries and audiences: they can be exchanged (for money or attention) and experienced. Media of communication and expression come in-between producers and consumers, and they take material forms: words printed in ink on a page, pictures recorded on film, sound recorded on disk, or any kind of content encoded in a digital format and delivered to our devices over the internet. A media *text* is an individual instance of media, something made by a producer and received by a consumer, an object like a magazine for sale by the cashier at the supermarket, or something we can regard as an object, like a social media interface or a show streaming on Netflix.

The text goes by other names, and it might be weird at first to start calling things texts that all along you have been calling something else. *Text* and *content* are close siblings, and in ordinary conversations, we may have little need for a term that does what *text* does: reference the object, the commodity or product, distinguishing it from its production or consumption. Or else we use a more specific word such as movie, game, meme, or ad. The category of *texts* gathers together all of these various forms of media that

DOI: 10.4324/9781003007708-3

might appear not to have that much in common, but still share one central fact of their existence, which is that they are media texts.

One important thing about a text, and the most important for media studies in distinction to the media industries, is that you can analyze it. The usual reason to analyze a text is to talk about the meanings in the text, and scholars call this *textual analysis* (or *critical analysis* or simply *criticism*), to distinguish this work from other forms of analysis, such as audience or industry analysis. Whether we're doing media studies or not, we all probably do textual analysis all the time, almost never calling it that. Written textual analysis is often called criticism, and the person doing it can thus be called a critic, whether or not they're saying something critical or fault-finding.

We also use the same word, *text*, in other ways. It refers to letters and other characters: text as opposed to images, videos, or sound files. We call our school readings texts, including perhaps this thing you are reading right now. We refer to the text of a speech to distinguish the words, the language, from the speaker's delivery. In these instances, texts are things to read.

Now it's true that you don't read a film or song or game in the same way as something in the medium of text, like a news story or a tweet. But in analyzing a text in any medium, we do read it in another sense of reading: interpreting, like reading a situation or a facial expression. When media scholars or students in a media studies class do textual analysis, they are in some ways reading, or interpreting, a text.

Interpretation might sound like something subjective or arcane, the stuff of intriguing theories based on exhaustive study or deep dives into fandom. Sometimes it works this way, but not necessarily. Interpretation means making sense, doing the work of saying what something means, eventually making another text that speaks about the first one. This kind of work is central to the academic fields of the humanities. Philosophers, historians, art historians, literary scholars, legal scholars, and media scholars among other humanists do interpretation of various kinds, on many kinds of objects. One of the jobs that media scholars do is the interpretation of media texts.

Interpretation is not usually idiosyncratic and personal. It's also a different activity from judging the quality or value of the text. Interpretation tends to be limited and shaped in particular ways. In order to be a persuasive interpretation, an analysis of media will have to make an argument based on sound reasoning and clear evidence from the text and other informative sources (such as sources that shed light on how the text was made), and will likely function to illuminate the text under discussion, to help a community of readers understand it better, to show us the text in a way we would not otherwise have seen it. The point of research, after all, is to contribute to a field of knowledge, not to produce novel but unpersuasive interpretations.

Many students are drawn to media courses because they are interested in or excited about texts, and they might even assume that texts will be the main objects of study. Often, they are. Film studies emerged out of English and literary studies, where the analysis of texts (of literature) is the discipline's most basic business, and television and popular music studies sometimes follow this tradition. Other areas within media studies, however, have often been as interested in understanding audiences/users or in media industries and their economic and political workings. And text-centered study often places a text in context, which means seeing it in relation to its production or consumption, or to the broader society that it reflects and speaks to. (The Latin prefix con means with, so context is that which is with the text.) It is rare, and probably ill-advised, to be interested in texts all by themselves without also being interested in who made them, and for whom. But however much we might base our understanding of texts on their relation to contexts – to their makers and users – analyzing them means doing some of the most basic work of media studies, producing an understanding of individual examples of media, and making sense of media as objects and experiences.

The texts that have come up so far, like movies and newspapers, are clear examples of media. But are there limits on what you might consider as a media text? It really depends on you as the person doing the analysis. If you are interested in analyzing the meanings of parks, chairs, smartphones, yoga pants, Jell-O, Wikipedia, or soda cans, go make them your texts. No inherent property gives something a quality of being a text, and it would be impossible to distinguish all of the texts of the world from everything else that is not a text. Perhaps a thing becomes a text when you think of it that way, as something meaningful that you can analyze. But since the academic field of media studies tends to treat certain kinds of things as texts, typically the products of the media industries, these will be the main examples here.

Breaking It Down

Any text in any medium can be broken down into its component parts, which is to say that it can be subjected to an analysis. The word comes from ancient Greek and literally translated it means "loosening up." A better definition of the modern sense of analysis would be "taking apart." Analyze, take apart, break down, look at the pieces, and see them as they work together to form a whole (or not). This breaking down is a critical process at the heart of many kinds of scholarship, leading to greater understanding and new knowledge. Thinking analytically means wondering how things work and why, which leads us into a process of intellectual discovery. This doesn't merely help us understand media because we find it interesting. It also sharpens our critical thinking skills, helps us understand the world around us so that we can engage as informed citizens and consumers, and has the potential to shape the work of the next generation of media creators who benefit from understanding how such things work (perhaps that means you).

What are the parts to be broken down? It depends on the text and its medium. An advertisement in a magazine combines image and text. A typical pop song has music and lyrics, rhythm and melody, vocals on top of an arrangement of other instruments. A movie has music, dialogue, acting, camerawork, costumes, editing, and numerous other parts. A news story has a headline, a lede, a nut graf, quotations, a kicker.

While texts of different media may have much in common, analyzing texts in a particular medium often calls on some medium-specific knowledge. Film scholars know that to do a good analysis of a film, it's important to observe the techniques specific to movie-making, such as conventions of editing often used in narrative feature films to help them tell stories effectively. These include specific devices like a "POV shot" (from a character's perspective) and "shot/reverse-shot" (alternating between two characters). Being able to recognize and describe these and many others can be essential to doing some kinds of film analysis effectively (Bordwell, Thompson and Smith 2020).

Consider these two images from classic Hollywood films made several decades apart, Casablanca (1942) and Jaws (1975):

In order to discuss these films effectively, not just as stories but as visual texts, it helps to have some critical vocabulary that is specific to photographic representation. In addition to differences in color and aspect ratio, i.e., the ratio of width to height of a picture – Casablanca is in black and white while Jaws is in color, and Casablanca is in the Academy ratio (approximately 1.375:1) while Jaws is in a widescreen format (2.39:1) – there are many other differences worth noting in these two frames. The Casablanca shot of Humphrey Bogart as Rick is an interior in shallow focus: the man is in focus and the rest is not. Shadowy, low-key lighting is used to contrast highlights

Figures 3.1 *and* 3.2 Analyzing film images from *Casablanca* (1942) and *Jaws* (1975) benefits from close attention to specific details such as lighting and depth of field.

on one side of the human figure against a dark background. It was shot on a soundstage on the Warner Bros. lot in Hollywood with highly controlled artificial lighting. In contrast, the *Jaws* shot of Roy Scheider as Brody is an exterior with considerably greater depth of field (the face in the foreground and the beachgoers on the left of the frame are all in focus). It was shot on a beach during the daytime with plenty of natural light.

The meanings of these texts are in the images as visual representations, not just in the stories they tell. These details of the image help in conveying the meanings of the stories: Rick's brooding appearance and drinking establishes character, as does Brody's concern over the possibility that a shark attack could spoil the fun of the people all around him.

It's also generally a benefit when doing textual analysis to have some knowledge of the history and context of the specific type of text under consideration. An analysis of a Hollywood movie from the 1940s like *Casablanca* or from the 1970s like *Jaws* will undoubtedly benefit from familiarity with American cinema of that period, its production norms, prevailing styles, popular genres, and audience practices. What is true of film criticism is no less true than criticism of advertising, video games, web design, and really any medium or genre of text. Texts make more sense in context.

Texts like these films tell stories, though certainly not always. A still photograph or a Subaru ad might not really tell a story, though your imagination might fill one in. In many texts, these stories, the narrative content of the text, came from someplace else. Artworks in a museum are often subjects from scripture, history, and mythology. *Casablanca* had an original screenplay based on an unproduced stage play, but *Jaws* was a bestselling novel before it was a movie. A video game might be the latest in a long series of similar video games with familiar situations. Some television shows are spun off of other television shows, with characters migrating from one setting to another. Many stories continue from one text to another, like *The Lord of the Rings*, or overlap and extend across media from comics to cartoons to Hollywood blockbusters to theme park rides.

These translations, adaptations, serials and sequels, spinoffs and extensions suggest that we can split the *content* of a text from its form or its medium. Harry Potter can exist as words on a page in J.K. Rowling's fiction, or as images on a screen in the films made from her books, or as an actor playing a role on the stage in *Harry Potter and the Cursed Child*, a pair of plays she co-authored. The content – the character and his story – may be brought to life in different forms. In analyzing a text, then, it can be possible to isolate form from content, or content from form. It would make sense to discuss the editing and camerawork in the film version of a story, and to discuss the sentences and paragraphs in the literary version. In principle, perhaps the two can be cleanly divided, form over here and content over there. In practice, however, they tend to blend together inseparably, and the meanings of the text can be hard to grasp without understanding form and content as one.

One way to test this is by considering the translation of literary texts. Is an English version of the Hebrew Bible the same text as the original, or is it another version of the same stories? Biblical scholars believe that the interpretation of the Hebrew Bible demands an understanding of the original ancient Hebrew, and they would regard any translation as a unique text in its own right. If form and content were truly separable and independent of one another, then a translation of a Hebrew text into English should potentially contain *all* of the same content, *all* of the same meanings, as the original, but of course it does not. Every text's meaning is shaped – at once constrained and made possible – by its form.

Assuming that any media text has parts combining to form a whole (thought experiment: try to imagine a text that cannot be broken into parts), an essential thing to know before subjecting any text to an analysis will be: what kind of parts are you looking for? To determine what you're looking for, you might apply previous knowledge of what a certain kind of text looks like and how it functions. This knowledge will be specific to the type of text, its form, its medium, and especially its *genre*. Genre is really just another word for kind, type, category, but it's a category that is widely shared and easily recognized by media producers and consumers. So before you can look for the parts, you will need to assess what kind of text it is, to size it up. There may be some kinds of extraordinary texts that are hard to fit into any category, but these are rare if they even exist. The usual object of textual analysis will be so easy to identify as a particular kind of text that it will probably just seem obvious and unremarkable.

The parts of the text might have names you already know, or they may have names you need to discover or perhaps invent. And the parts might appear clearly marked as separate from one another, or you might need to do some work to identify them. For instance, in a movie or television show, the opening and closing credit sequences are usually clearly separate from the rest of the text, and mark a beginning and end, respectively (though the opening credits sometimes appear after one or more scenes, or sometimes not at all; and though the closing credits sometimes include additional scenes that interrupt them or come at their conclusion). The term "credits" is fairly widely known – another word for them is "titles" – and you might not need to discover those terms.

Another way movies and television shows are often analyzed is by identifying their "acts," which is a theater term that screenwriters and others in the film and television industries borrow, and which some critics and scholars have also adopted (Newman 2006). In a television series with commercial breaks, the acts are typically identified as the segments in-between the ads, and the cut to commercial is often called an "act out." But in a movie or a television show without interruptions, nothing clearly marks an act out, and the person analyzing the text has to do their own segmentation, likely based on how the plot develops (Thompson 1999). In *The Wizard of Oz*, for example, you might identify the first act's end with the arrival of Dorothy in the land of Oz, which appears in the text as a clear moment of passage as it is also when the film switches from black-and-white to color photography. The segmentation of the whole film into a series of acts would be a way of understanding how it tells its story, which is itself a part of the film to be identified during an analysis. Books that have chapters do some of that work for us, and music and video games often segment themselves into verse, chorus, and bridge, and levels and worlds, respectively, but movies usually lack such neat divisions.

There are also more fine-grained divisions into parts in a movie or television show: scenes, sequences, and shots. When the text unfolds in time, the parts may be segments that appear in a particular order. For texts that are single images or words on the page, their parts might be organized differently, such as the photography and text in an advertisement, which means the analysis will proceed according to the specific characteristics of that text and its form. In any event, the medium, genre, and format of text you are working with will indicate what kind of parts you are looking for and what kind of expectations you have about them.

Levels of Analysis

In approaching any text, you can organize your task by thinking of the work occurring in discrete levels of engagement. Or rather than levels, you may prefer to think of them as moments of analysis, or stages in a process, or perhaps as the layers of analysis similar to the layers in a Photoshop image, with the possibility of overlap or transparency. What's important is that they name types of activity, whatever we call them. It's not essential to think about the task so systematically, but it might help clarify your thinking to sort your work into these categories.

While these steps can function as an order of operations, they do not necessarily need to all follow one another in a linear fashion, and some of the levels are inessential or maybe even undesirable, depending on the analysis.

Levels of Textual Analysis:

- ☐ Anticipation
- ☐ Experience
- ☐ Description
- ☐ Analysis
- ☐ Interpretation
- ☐ Evaluation
- ☐ Appropriation

Anticipation: information we learn about a text before we encounter it will shape our experience of it, so acknowledging this can help us see how we experience texts through our anticipatory frameworks. Peter Rabinowitz's (1987) book *Before Reading* discusses many ways that prior knowledge shapes the experience of literature, the way readers apply implicit, unwritten rules to the process of reading, such as paying special attention to titles and beginnings and endings. In his book *Show Sold Separately*, Jonathan Gray (2010) examines *paratexts*, the things like trailers, promos, posters, book covers, and bonus features that run alongside and shape the meaning of texts. Those like the trailers and posters that we encounter before a movie are part of a category he calls "entryway paratexts," and they can powerfully shape our experiences. Audiences often choose what media to consume on the basis of expectations formed in this way, such as expectations about a genre or media franchise, or personnel involved in making the text (e.g., an author or another creative artist). Sometimes these expectations are formed as we seek out information about the text, as when looking up reviews or going to Wikipedia. Spelling out the expectations we bring can help us see how we found or didn't find what we were looking for in our experience of the text.

Experience: here is the consumption of media, the watching, listening, playing, reading, interacting. I suppose one could analyze a media text that one has not experienced, but that would probably involve some degree of dishonesty. We take for granted that a critic has read the book or watched the show or played the game. When experiencing media knowing that an analysis will be coming next, it can be useful to do so with one's critical attention focused on the experience, thinking about points of discussion and breaking it down while watching. Some critics watch movies or TV with pen and paper or a computer on their lap. But this can also be challenging or distracting. Anyway, you might not know you are going to do an analysis when experiencing a text. Many analyses are done after repeated encounters with the text, and subsequent experiences can be more focused on the task to come.

Description: when doing an analysis, it's usually necessary to describe the text before breaking it down or ascribing meaning to it. As an exercise, look at a newspaper or magazine review of a movie, book, play, or any example of culture, even a restaurant or hotel. Note how the critic mixes description with other kinds of discussion. In reading textual analysis, we often encounter examples of texts we have not ourselves experienced, and reviews are written for just this kind of reader. Description helps us grasp what is being analyzed, and done well it evokes images and feelings that fill in for us not being able to experience the text under discussion at the same time as reading the analysis of it. Here is a television critic, Emily Nussbaum (2019), describing one of the characters in the Hulu series PEN15:

> Maya is a true-blue alienated weirdo, seething with contradictions. She 's a horny tomboy with a bowl cut, both worshipful and contemptuous of the popular girls. She's a showoff desperate to disappear, a bullied kid who calls other kids sluts. She galumphs past the school lockers, punching people in the shoulder to be friendly. At one point, she's so tense that her hands turn into claws.

This writing doesn't tell you what this television show means so much as it gives you an impression of what it's like to watch it, using vivid language to portray a character from this story world.

Analysis: while it's confusing to call one stage of an analysis *the analysis*, I want to preserve here the essential quality of this task, which is breaking a text down into parts. Description is often mixed together with analysis, as the individual parts (e.g., a character like Maya) themselves will need to be identified and described. Analysis can be sensitive to form and style, picking apart the techniques of the text, and can look at compositional elements of an image or narrative unfolding of a story. Analysis often looks for patterns such as repetition and alternation, recurring themes, tropes and conventions. A standard tool of analysis is comparison of one text to another, and identification of traditions and precedents for the text under discussion.

Interpretation: to interpret is to assign meaning, to offer explanations, to pose arguments about the text. Facts don't speak for themselves. We interpret them when we put them into a context and speak for them, drawing out their significance. Textual interpretation takes the representation in a text, the images, sounds, stories, experiences, whatever the text is made up of, and speaks for it. To interpret effectively, it's usually necessary to have done some work to describe and analyze, and to use these passages of description and analysis in defense of your interpretive criticism. The evidence in support of an interpretation might just be in the text, but it might also come from other texts or from contexts, depending on your analysis and its goals.

Evaluation: while it's entirely possible to do a textual analysis without making a claim about its value or quality, the choice of a text to analyze often implies a judgment that it is worthwhile of critical attention. Beyond that, some analyses of texts are concerned not just with establishing what the meanings of the text are, but with glorifying and celebrating the text, or perhaps condemning it. I consider this type of overt evaluation to be entirely optional and unnecessary when doing textual analysis of media, but some kinds of criticism are rather invested in it. Reviews are the most typical form of analysis to engage in evaluation (and often include scores or grades, which can be aggregated as in sites like Metacritic and Rotten Tomatoes), but much academic media studies is more engaged with thinking of texts in relation to media production and consumption, or in relation to representation and ideology, than with the evaluation of texts as aesthetic works, or works of art. In the humanities, the tradition of looking at texts such as literary works has tended to imply a positive judgment of evaluation, but cultural studies of popular media like television, cinema, music, video games, and digital culture might tend more toward looking at media in their sociological significance rather than, or in addition to, their aesthetic dimensions.

Appropriation: this last stage is the most different from the others. A media text sometimes offers a critical response to another media text in a way that makes use of the original. Authors appropriate media for purposes of appreciation or parody, and many forms of art explicitly and self-consciously build on existing works of art, as in found footage works edited together from existing video and film. When the purpose of appropriation is critical, as in a feminist found footage film made out of clips of pornographic movies (e.g., Peggy Ahwesh's 1994 film *The Color of Love*), there can be both an aesthetic and an analytic purpose.

Memes and fan art are good examples of appropriation of media texts that repurpose original creative works for new agendas and audiences. Some of these pluck a moment out of a text for a novel purpose, but many memes and GIFs that appropriate popular media do so in a way that sheds light on the original. A GIF of Judge Judy rolling her eyes can be a way for someone to express their own eye-roll, but it also works as an affectionate tribute to Judge Judy's facial expressions. The fan practice of *vidding*, editing clips into a video set to music that identifies patterns or finds meaning in new juxtapositions, is an excellent case of appropriating media texts for the clear purpose of introducing new ideas about the original texts (Coppa 2008). But often the analysis in an appropriation of a text will be more implicit or subtextual. However overt the analytical purpose, one way that texts circulate and become part of the texture of our everyday lives is through repeated appropriations of many different kinds.

Textual Analysis in Practice

To put these levels into practice, and to go deeper into the identification of the parts of a text and see what happens when you take them apart, I am going to look at one text in its entirety. Sometimes the technique I'm about to practice is called "close reading," though there are degrees of closeness and some readings go much closer than I'm going. Texts of different scope and size require different kinds of analysis, with varying degrees of depth and detail. I'm using an example of a text of modest size suitable to a succinct analysis of the whole thing: Elton John's "Rocket Man." A text of a different shape and size might not be so easily analyzed in a few pages, and some texts, like television serials and other long-unfolding formats that continue for many years, may be impossible to analyze comprehensively, and especially difficult if one wants to practice close reading of more than a sliver.

As you listen to the original studio recording of "Rocket Man," think about what its parts are. If it's a song you already know, try to imagine listening for the first time and discovering it with fresh ears. At this moment you are either in anticipation or experience. Reflect on what this is like: what are your expectations? What are you noticing as the song plays?

Now come description, analysis, and interpretation. Most basically, we can describe "Rocket Man" as a pop song (this is its *genre*). Yes, it is obvious – it's not a cartoon or a first-person shooter, it's not a billboard by the side of the road, etc., etc. – and yet it's worth stating the obvious here because we are spelling out our assumptions. They matter. A pop song is typically of a certain length and style, with lyrics and music, rhythm and melody, verse and chorus, hooks and riffs.

"Rocket Man" is a particular kind of pop song: a soft rock ballad (this is a *subgenre*). If you are not familiar with this category, it might not be obvious to you what kind of song it is, but if you recognize the combination of tempo, vocal style, and instrumentation, it fits into a category. You might also say it's an Elton John song or a 1970s song. All of these are correct descriptions. Even the briefest research will turn up some more information, and maybe looking this stuff up was part of your anticipation of the text: "Rocket Man (And I Think It's Going to Be a Long Long Time)" was composed by Elton John (music) and Bernie Taupin (lyrics). It was released in 1972 on the album *Honky Château*, runs 4:41, was a hit in several countries, was inspired by a sci-fi short story and by the song "Space Oddity" by David Bowie. It is a unique text, but it also behaves a lot like a soft rock song by Elton John from the 1970s. The first step in a textual analysis will be sizing up the text, sorting it into categories, looking for the parts to break down based on what we expect of a text of its type.

A key set of parts in practically any kind of song will be the music and lyrics. They typically go together in making the meanings of the song. These parts often include repetitions, such as the repetition of a phrase of music or of words. An example in "Rocket Man" is the phrase "And I think it's going to be a long long time," over two different phrases of music in the chorus. Songs also have patterns, similar to stories, of beginnings, middles, and ends. "Rocket Man" has this in the soft opening of the song, the fuller sound of the chorus and second verse, and the repeated "long long time" phrase as it builds toward a conclusion. This is analysis, by the way, but it's also description.

How can we put into words what the parts of a text are? We begin by observing (listening, watching, taking it in) and describing what we see or hear. In these next few paragraphs, I am describing and analyzing, but soon enough this will also shade into interpreting.

"Rocket Man" has the musical form of a rock ballad, in a medium-slow tempo of 4/4 time, with a pattern of verse-chorus-verse-chorus. Verses and choruses typically have different melodies, which are repeated – each verse and each chorus sound mostly the same – but the lyrics of the verses are different, while the lyrics of the choruses are repeated. This song has a hint of a country sound, which was typical of rock ballads in the 1970s, from a combination of strummed acoustic and slide guitars, adding a note of melancholy. The verses begin with a moody G minor chord on the piano ("She packed my bags last night …"), while the choruses launch with guitars pleasantly strumming a B-flat major chord ("And I think it's going to be a long, long time …"). (My contrast there of moody and pleasant could be description, but it's also my interpretation of their emotional quality, which goes along with the earlier reference to a melancholy sound.) In addition to the guitars, the instruments include piano, bass, drums, and synthesizer, as well as Elton John's vocal and several background singers.

The song builds as it goes along, following a trajectory. How does it do that? The verses push toward the choruses. The choruses emphasize the central theme of the song: the rocket man's loneliness and isolation out in space. "Rocket Man" begins with a sparse arrangement of piano and vocal, and more instruments are added as the song moves toward the first chorus, with a swell of volume as the whole band plays. The first instrument added to the piano is an electric bass, then cymbals, drums, acoustic guitar, and slide guitar come in, and then additional vocals, and the chorus has a much fuller sound than the song had when it began.

These points of description are useful because they identify the parts of the whole that have the potential to contribute to its meanings and pleasures. You may not have a clear idea of what every little thing a text is doing actually means, but every little thing has the potential to be meaningful, and the more we pay attention, the more likely we are to notice meaningful elements of the text.

While describing and analyzing, we often mix in some interpretation of meaning. Here is an example: after the line that gives the song its title, "I'm a rocket man," with its vocal emphasis on rocket, a slide guitar glissando ascends as if to follow the trajectory of a spaceship launching into orbit, possibly away forever, and it later descends as well as if falling into oblivion. In the second verse, a synthesizer riff added around the line "and all this science I don't understand," suggests a high-tech, computerized world of space exploration with the potential to malfunction and lead to catastrophic results.

The lyrics of the verses, written in the first person, paint the picture of a lonely astronaut on his way to Mars and missing his family. The chorus introduces a critical detail about the astronaut: "I'm not the man they think I am at home." This establishes a contrast between an appearance − a hero, a celebrity, a "rocket man" − and the disappointing reality beneath the surface. (That last sentence is interpretation, by the way.) This meaning is reinforced in the second verse, when he sings, "It's just my job five days a week," as if space exploration is work not much different from staffing an office or factory. The choruses end with an ambiguous statement: "Rocket man, burning out his fuse up here alone," followed by the line that repeats several times as the song ends, "And I think it's going to be a long, long time," meaning he will not return home soon to reunite with the people who love him or misunderstand him, or perhaps he will not ever return depending on how we read "burning out his fuse" and "long long time."

The song has a structure, so typical of pop songs as to be a kind of formula, of verses alternating with choruses. The song also has a pattern of other repetitions, including the phrase repeated as the song draws to a close. These repetitions and alternations organize the text and give emphasis to certain feelings and ideas, which are those most central to its themes. (This paragraph so far is analysis.) This sense of organization around repeated phrases and running themes is what gives a text a sense of coherence and unity. Not all texts work this way, but it's quite common for popular media texts to be structured to give just this sense, which is appealing as it feels harmonious and complete.

The themes in "Rocket Man" emphasized via this structure are typical of science-fiction, such as disillusionment with advanced technology and its effects on humanity. The feeling expressed by the astronaut is not the optimistic rhetoric of the typical narratives of the American space program of the 1960s and 1970s, filled with hope and promise for the future, but does have something in common with Bowie's "Space Oddity," with its chorus of "Planet Earth is blue and there's nothing I can do," its astronaut, Major Tom, stranded in space in his "tin can." These examples also echo Stanley Kubrick's film 2001: A Space Odyssey, from which the Bowie song borrows its title, which represents a space mission gone horribly wrong and technology being a threat to humanity.

Bernie Taupin took the title and situation of "Rocket Man" from a science-fiction short story called "The Rocket Man" by Ray Bradbury (1951; Rosenthal 2001, 48). In the literary version set decades in the future like Kubrick's film, the narrator is an astronaut's son, who misses his absent father for long periods he spends away on his rocket, and in the end the father perishes in outer space. However much it borrows from these sources, the "long, long time" in this song expresses a sense of modern alienation, of technology having left us alone in a vast universe, while longing for home and human connection. (This paragraph has mixed together description, analysis, and interpretation. You might also have noticed how the description and analysis stick to the text, but some of the evidence for my interpretation comes from outside of the text.)

There is a name for the ways that one text like "Rocket Man" is fashioned out of bits and pieces of other texts, of references and allusions, of familiar tropes, and of sometimes unacknowledged quotations, homages, or plagiarisms. This quality of one text owing debts to other texts is known as *intertextuality* (Allen 2011). This term varies in usage, so that sometimes intertextuality might mean explicit reference of one text by another, like an actual quotation in quotation marks or a bit of one film inserted into another, while other times it refers much more generally to the basic condition of texts building on other texts, as in any instance of a familiar textual structure or convention. Intertextuality is opposed to the logic of absolute originality. It is the antidote to seeing culture as highly individualized, unique works of genius. If all texts build on other texts, none are ever totally original.

In the case of "Rocket Man," intertextuality works on multiple levels. It explains how the song follows conventions of a 1970s soft rock ballad and how it fits into the body of work of its songwriters John/Taupin and the recording career of John. It also explains how the song works with its particular influences and sources. Paying attention to the qualities that any text draws from other texts helps us to see how all texts are enmeshed in a dense network of intertextuality, which enriches our sense of their meanings. The more we know about texts of any particular kind, the more we understand of new texts we encounter that belong in the same intertextual network. Seen this way, textual analysis necessarily involves putting one text into conversation with other texts. The more we know, the harder it is to see any text as a truly unique object. We can do our best to examine "Rocket Man" strictly on its own terms, but our knowledge of other texts will almost certainly shape our effort to make sense of it.

Now let's go back over the points I have offered about "Rocket Man" and observe them as elements that together make up the whole. I split the lyrics from the music, and I identified parts of both: verses, chorus, repetitions. The music can be broken down by instruments that appear at particular times, and by changes such as minor to major and back again, and softer for the verses and louder for the choruses. I also isolated certain elements of the text: moments of music like a glissando and phrases of the lyrics like "I think it's going to be a long, long time." I took care to identify meanings for these isolated elements. I also explored some of the story as a narrative, analyzing the character and his situation, the way the story is told (in the first person, from the Rocket Man's perspective), and the themes of the song. I placed this kind of story into contexts: the genre of science-fiction, the work of another rock artist who might have influenced Bernie Taupin and Elton John (Bowie), and the source material for the lyrics.

Some of the meanings of this song, as I pointed out, are ambiguous. It might not be clear from the lyrics whether the rocket man will return ("touchdown brings me round again") or not ("burning out his fuse"); I'm not concerned with interpreting it decisively one way or another, but rather am content to point out alternative possible meanings. I might also have pointed out some non-obvious meanings, or points about how the song works that might not have occurred to you. My interpretations of the slide guitar phrases and of the computerish synth notes both conveying meanings to do with the song's space travel theme are intended this way.

Ultimately, my reading of this song is that it presents an astronaut as an alienated, unhappy, surprisingly unheroic figure disillusioned by space travel and endangered by the advancing technology of modern life. At the same time, the mellow soft rock ballad form of the music is at odds with the more negative mood of the words, and there is a tension in the song between the laid-back feel of the melody and rhythm and the alarming meaning of the lyrics, a tension that cannot be fully resolved in the repetition, as the song is ending, of "and I think it's going to be a long, long time," with its ambiguous meaning. The song leaves us hanging, like the character out in space.

To support a reading of a text, one might look deeper into its background and production or into its reception, which is to say one might go beyond the text for evidence of its meanings. While I have referred to some information outside of the text, such as the intertexts identified – the Bradbury story and the Bowie song – note what I have left out of my analysis: the biographies of Elton John and Bernie Taupin and how they came to write this song or what they have said it meant, to them; where the song was produced and recorded; which musicians performed in the studio; how it became a hit record; its history of concert performances, cover versions, and uses in movies and television; or its significance to particular audiences or to me in my own life. I left out the fact that the President of the United States used the name "Rocket Man" as an epithet taunting the North Korean dictator Kim Jong-Un in 2017, and that a hit movie based on Elton John's life called *Rocketman* was released in 2019. (These would be appropriations).

All of these things might help shed light on "Rocket Man," but they are all outside of the text. They are matters of production or distribution or reception, or of other texts that build on the text we are analyzing.

And yet it's hard to make sense of a text without any ideas that come from outside of it. The title of the song is not part of the text itself, and it helps us understand what it's about. Knowledge about the form of songs and particular styles of music, about the genre of science-fiction, about the history of space exploration will inform our understanding. The feeling of the song to its listeners might also be rather different from what these meanings suggest. Not everyone listens carefully to song lyrics, and to some listeners "Rocket Man" might just be a laid-back ballad that gives them an easy, relaxed feeling, similar to other Elton John soft rock ballads of the same period in the same style, like "Your Song," "Daniel," "Candle in the Wind," and "Goodbye Yellow Brick Road."

(By the way, I think "Rocket Man" is a great soft rock piano ballad by one of the outstanding artists of the style, a genius of pop music, and I probably would not have chosen a text that I dislike to serve as an extended example here. But my analysis has pretty much avoided evaluation until this aside, and I doubt that it would have benefited from more of it.)

Meaning can reside in different places for different people, and not everyone experiences a text the same way. Some listeners, perhaps many or most, pay little attention to song lyrics and their sense of the song might come more from its rhythm, tempo, melody, and overall vibe than those themes and narrative meanings I have identified. I personally have found myself surprised to learn what the actual words of a song are after long periods of not paying close attention. I had heard "Rocket Man" casually for years playing on the radio or in public places before discovering that the hard-to-discern words Elton John sings in the chorus are "burning out his fuse up here alone." The meaning of the song was enriched and transformed for me when I made that discovery, and all it took was paying closer attention.

Meanings and Intentions

You might hear something different in "Rocket Man," something missing from my analysis, or understand its message differently from the way I do, and that's fine. This variability of textual meaning from one listener to another, from one audience to another, is one way that textual analysis can be dynamic and unpredictable. The quality of media texts that admits this diversity or instability of meaning is called *polysemy*, and it is an inherent property of many texts that makes them potentially endlessly fascinating. The roots of this word are Greek: *poly* (many), and *semeion* (sign) and it refers to a quality of multiplicity. A typical case would be a text that has two or more clearly different possible meanings or values.

The television series *All in the Family*, a situation comedy created by Norman Lear and Bud Yorkin that aired on the CBS television network from 1971–1979, is a classic case. The characters in *All in the Family* are Archie and Edith Bunker, a middle-aged, working-class married couple in Queens, New York, and their adult daughter, Gloria, and son-in-law, Mike, who live with them in their modest single-family house. The show appeared at a moment when American society was riven by conflict between generations and social upheaval over the changes marked by the 1960s: the civil rights and women's rights movements, the Vietnam War, the youth counterculture, and soon enough the Watergate scandal. Archie is a bigoted family patriarch hostile to many of the changes of those years. He is given to humorous, ignorant outbursts revealing the limitations of his own old-fashioned worldview. Mike and Gloria are idealistic, earnest, intelligent young adults on the side of progress, often sparring verbally with the man of the house. While the humor is often at Archie's expense, making fun of his verbal blunders and his blustery style, Archie is also the moral and comical center of the drama, and the conflicts of the show's episodes often resolve with Archie learning his lesson or getting his comeuppance.

When *All in the Family* first appeared, some liberals feared that the representation of Archie Bunker, complete with bigoted epithets used in reference to racial and ethnic minorities and obsolete opinions about conventional gender roles, would be viewed as sympathetic or even heroic to the intolerant "silent majority" that had elected Richard Nixon as president. But to these same liberal viewers, the representation would have clearly been mocking Archie. The show was a huge success and was regularly viewed by millions of television viewers, presumably across the political spectrum. To some audiences, Archie was a familiar figure and an everyday hero, while to others, he was a clown. You could admire Archie, but you could also feel superior to him. This is how polysemy works, admitting varying or even opposed meanings. Comedy is often polysemic in the way it bends to accommodate the audience's agenda. *Laughing at* and *laughing with* can be diametrically opposed reactions to the very same text.

The instability of meaning in an example like this is hardly unusual. Meaning might reside in the text, and texts are limited in the range of meanings they admit. But meaning also resides in the audience as products of a social world, and texts only convey meanings when an audience makes meaning of them.

Alternatively, you may be wondering, If there are meanings in texts, isn't it their authors who put them there? Can we settle matters of ambiguity or polysemy by asking the author what they meant, or looking for evidence of it? If we want to know what really happens to the Rocket Man burning out his fuse, can we just ask Bernie Taupin, who wrote that line?

Stepping back, we might also wonder whether one purpose of textual analysis ought to be the discovery of what an author intended in making a text. In the case of All in the Family, we know from many published accounts that the character of Archie Bunker was based in part on Norman Lear's own father, who was blustery and bigoted (though Lear's family is Jewish rather than Protestant). Does the author's account of how he created the character matter for our interpretation? Does Archie seem more sympathetic, knowing that he was based on Norman Lear's dad? Maybe he does. For better or worse, I think knowing this detail makes me look at Archie with more reluctant affection than I would otherwise. All in the Family was inspired by the BBC television comedy Till Death Us Do Part (1965–1975), and Archie has also been seen as a version of the main character in that series, Alf Garnett, so perhaps we might also wonder about the intentions of this program's authors.

Some textual critics might object to this way of thinking. There is an influential concept that media studies inherited from literary criticism called the intentional fallacy, which opposes looking to authorial intention as the justification for an interpretation. To W.K. Wimsatt, Jr. and M.C. Beardsley (1946), who coined the term in an essay published in 1946, any meaning to be found in a text ought to be there in the text. As they say: "If the poet succeeded in doing it, then the poem itself shows what he was trying to do" (469). The novelist and literary critic D.H. Lawrence (1923, ch. 1) also captured this way of thinking when he wrote: "Never trust the artist. Trust the tale."

Wimsatt and Beardsley were talking about the critical analysis of poetry, and a poem, unlike many forms of media, is typically the product of one individual. The same goes for many forms of "high" art; symphonies and oil paintings, like literary works, tend to have a single author. By contrast, most texts you will analyze in a media studies class are products of collaborative workplaces in which many people, from dozens to hundreds or thousands, contribute to the creation of a text. Even if you think it's a good idea, identifying authorial intentions might be challenging in analyzing a poem or painting centuries old, but thinking about the intentions of the many workers who contribute to a news broadcast, an advertising campaign, a Hollywood blockbuster, a music video, or a AAA video game can involve so many different kinds of authors in various different roles that the complexity level can overwhelm the task of attributing authorship. Media produced in such an industrial setting might better be considered as the product not of an individual author but of a corporation or institution. The collaborators who produce a text might not all have the same agenda, and the purpose of many forms of media may be rather different from the expressive and personal nature of much literature.

And yet information about production – about authorship in its many forms – can be very informative and can undoubtedly benefit the enterprise of textual analysis even of highly collaborative media. Knowing what kind of considerations went into making a media text can guide us as we break it down. This might not be about intentions when it comes to interpreting specific meanings so much as intentions in using certain tools of production to create certain effects in the text. Authors might not always tell the whole truth about the process, but the more we know, the more we can weigh the evidence of their statements against other sources.

So, for instance, Joey Soloway (2018), a writer, director, and producer of films and television shows, is an outspoken genderqueer feminist who advertises their intention in texts like the Amazon series *Transparent* and *I Love Dick* as "toppling the patriarchy." I take Soloway's stated intention to be sincere and true, and the kinds of stories and representations they create are clearly the products of this intention. When I read interviews with creators like Soloway, it often deepens my appreciation for their work and adds to my understanding.

As these examples of Lear and Soloway illustrate, with some kinds of media that are highly collaborative, such as television and cinema, a discourse of authorship can seize on one individual as an author whose vision leads the production, making all of their collaborators in some sense subservient to a strong leader. In film history, this has usually been a director, and when the film director is identified as the author, they are regarded as an *auteur*. *Auteur* is just the French word for author, but within this discourse it means something more. An *auteur* is an artist whose signature is visible across a body of work (an *oeuvre*) and whose authorship can be used as an organizing principle for promotion and marketing, for critical discussion, even for thinking about the history of the art of cinema.

Other popular arts also have *auteurs*; in TV, it is often the *showrunner* like Soloway or Lear, a hybrid of writer and producer, who attains this status. Since so much cinema and television comes to us without such a strong sense of being the work of one individual (think about some movies and TV shows you have watched lately, including news and sports, and see if you can name all of their authors), those instances that do have a single name attached to them may be instances of *conspicuous authorship*. This mode of authorship is as much a social circulation of knowledge about texts as it is a characteristic of texts themselves. And yet it surely organizes our experience of media if we are attuned to it. Some kinds of media are more or less likely than others to be conspicuously authored.

Where does that leave us? It's tempting to endorse the *intentional fallacy* and the assertion that meanings in a text should be discoverable from the text, and yet we have seen that prior knowledge about texts almost inevitably shapes our encounters with them. Sometimes that knowledge includes ideas about their authorship, about how they were made and by whom. How much you care about that information will probably depend on the kind of text you are analyzing and the kind of things you want to say about the text. Sometimes knowledge about authorship, or about production more broadly, can be incredibly informative in establishing the meanings of a text. Sometimes it might matter little, or be hard to access, and even if we can ask an author about the text and its production, it's not always best to believe everything they say. They could have an agenda other than simply telling us the truth, or they could be forgetful or inarticulate. Textual analysis is ultimately an interaction between an instance of media and a critic engaged with making meaning out of it. The author is an optional and sometimes undesirable ingredient in this recipe.

Denotation and Connotation

Whether the author appears in our analysis or not, one way of thinking of the meanings in any given text is by contrasting the more basic and literal ones with higher-level meanings that tap into an audience's associations and values. This shows the audience (or reader) to be a crucial factor in producing meaning regardless of how much author we put into our criticism.

The French cultural critic Roland Barthes (1977) distinguishes between two types of meaning called *denotation* and *connotation*. Denotation refers to the meanings that are obvious and surface-level, which he calls the "literal message" of a text. Connotations are by contrast "symbolic" and require the audience reading the text to have some prior knowledge. In a classic essay called "The Rhetoric of the Image," Barthes illustrates this distinction using the example of a magazine advertisement for Panzani, a brand of packaged foods (and a good example of the kind of text that we typically do not identify with an author). The image in the advertisement represents Panzani dried spaghetti noodles in their packaging, Panzani parmesan cheese and a can of Panzani sauce, as well fresh onions, tomatoes, mushrooms, and green pepper, all spilling out of a white net shopping bag as if just brought home from the market and set down on a table. The text at the bottom of the image reads (in French) "pasta – sauce – parmesan/Italian luxury."

Beyond showing products for sale, for Barthes this image conveys *Italianicity* and draws upon the French reader's familiarity with this national stereotype, which is also reinforced by the Italian brand name and the text reading "Italian luxury." Its color scheme emphasizes the tricolor of the Italian flag. The subjects of the image, the foodstuffs, are placed against a red background. A tomato in the foreground is red, the pepper is green, and several items in the image are white, including the cheese, the mushroom, and the bag. Barthes also notes the similarity of the composition to still life artworks and the association between this kind of scene and the activities of preparing food at home. He identifies "plenty" as a symbolic meaning of this scene, a connotation of enjoying a nourishing meal and being well fed. Barthes continues to argue that Italianicity suggests a panoply of meanings to do with one particular nationality, but also assumes ideas about nationality such as distinctions between Italian and other identities such as French, German, and Spanish. One is defined in relation to the others.

The meanings of this advertisement are both literally there in word and image, but also reside in the shared knowledge and experience of the people looking at the image and bringing their prior understandings to the work of making sense of it. To the French reader of this advertisement many decades ago, *Italianicity* might have meant something more specific, drawing on a deeper set of associations, than it does for you. The connotations of the text come from the social circulation of knowledge within a particular culture. At the same time, they also are built on the denotative, literal meanings of the text. One of Barthes' key insights is also that denotation and connotation cannot be easily separated as discrete elements of a text, but rather work together and through one another.

Bundling variability of textual meaning together with these ideas about denotation and connotation, literal and symbolic meanings, we see that texts are not singular, timeless, unified objects with straightforward or unequivocal values. The text itself as a physical object might not change significantly over time, and it might not vary from reader to reader (though some texts, like a game or a "choose your own adventure" story, are designed to do so). Audiences, in their infinite diversity, make meanings from texts based on a combination of what they find in them and what they bring to them.

Texts and Readers

Texts are objects whose meanings we discover through a process of analysis. There are two ways of looking at these meanings: first, as already contained in the text, perhaps put there intentionally by the text's authors, awaiting your attention; and second, as produced or constructed by you, the reader, during your encounter with the text and your analysis after the fact. Texts have meanings, but readers also make meanings from texts.

Both of these statements can be correct, and at the same time, neither one can work without the other. Because the audience doesn't invent the text out of whole cloth, and because texts typically are more or less the same object for all of the audiences that encounter them, we should recognize the integrity of the object. At the same time, the text has no effective meaning until it has been experienced by a reader, by an audience, and each person's experience will be shaped by their background and culture, by their prior knowledge, and by their agenda in looking at media. You and I might interpret the same text in ways that both agree and disagree. We might base our interpretations on some overlapping evidence – the same text and context – and some that are unique to our own perspectives. Each instance of textual analysis will draw on some resources that we all share, including the text, but any interpretation will also draw on some resources – knowledge, evidence, a point of view – that the person doing the analysis has come to on their own. When we share our analysis with others, they get an opportunity to see the text in a new way. The variability of textual meaning is one of the things that makes media studies endlessly fascinating. In every reading, every encounter with media, we can find an opportunity for discovery and insight.

Discussion Questions

1. How is the term *text* related to the similar term *content* – what are their similarities and differences?
2. What does it mean to analyze a text and what is the point of textual analysis?
3. What are *intertextuality* and *polysemy*, and how do these terms help us understand texts?
4. Choose another song to analyze along the same lines as the discussion in this chapter of "Rocket Man," breaking it down and offering an interpretation. How does the genre of the song shape your analysis of it?
5. Choose any example of a media text and describe its meanings as denotation and connotation. Are these meanings easily separable or overlapping?

References

Allen, Graham. 2011. *Intertextuality*, 2nd ed. New York: Routledge.

Barthes, Roland. 1977. "The Rhetoric of the Image." In Roland Barthes, *Image-Music-Text*, translated by Stephen Heath, 32–51. New York: Hill and Wang.

Bordwell, David, Kristin Thompson and Jeff Smith. 2020. *Film Art: An Introduction*, 12th ed. New York: McGraw Hill.

Bradbury, Ray. 1951. "The Rocket Man," In Ray Bradbury, *The Illustrated Man*, 97–111. New York: Doubleday.

Coppa, Francesca. 2008. "Women, Star Trek, and the early development of fannish vidding." *Transformative Works and Cultures* 1.1. https://journal.transformativeworks.org/index.php/twc/article/download/44/64

Gray, Jonathan. 2010. *Show Sold Separately: Promos, Spoilers, and Other Media Paratexts*. New York: New York University Press.

Lawrence, D.H. 1923. *Studies in Classic American Literature*. https://en.wikisource.org/wiki/Studies_in_Classic_American_Literature

Newman, Michael Z. 2006. "From Beats to Arcs: Toward a Poetics of Television Narrative." *The Velvet Light Trap* 58 (Fall): 16–28.

Nussbaum, Emily. 2019. "Middle School Mortification on 'PEN15,' " *The New Yorker*, February 25, 2019. https://www.newyorker.com/magazine/2019/03/04/middle-school-mortification-on-pen15

Rabinowitz, Peter. 1987. *Before Reading: Narrative Conventions and the Politics of Interpretation*. Columbus: Ohio State University Press.

Rosenthal, Elizabeth J. 2001. *His Song: The Musical Journey of Elton John*. New York: Billboard Books.

Soloway, Jill. 2018. *She Wants It: Desire, Power, and Toppling the Patriarchy*. New York: Crown/Archetype.

Thompson, Kristin. 1999. *Storytelling in the New Hollywood*. Cambridge, MA: Harvard University Press.

W.K. Wimsatt, Jr. and M.C. Beardsley. 1946. "The Intentional Fallacy," *The Sewanee Review* 54.3, 468–488.

4

AUDIENCE

I wake up to an alarm that plays music. Over breakfast, I read the newspaper (on an iPad). Riding the bus, I listen to a podcast or read a book. Over lunch, I watch YouTube videos and read social media posts that I missed while teaching or attending meetings. A friend shares a link to a story and I read it on my phone standing in line for coffee. While making dinner, I listen to the news on the radio. Later in the evening, I turn on the television and watch a basketball game or a TV drama. Before falling asleep, I scroll through Twitter and Facebook, liking and commenting, following links and saving stories to read later. On the weekend, I play video games with my kids and go out to the movies. I post photos to Instagram and look at other people's pics, double-tapping to "like" them. In all of these moments, I am experiencing and consuming media. I am reading, watching, listening, and interacting. In every instance, I am part of a media *audience*.

The people in attendance at a concert or a play are most literally an audience. *Audience* and *auditorium* both come from the same Latin word, *audentia*, which means hearing or listening. The same Latin root also gives us *audio* and *audible*. An audience is a group of people who come together to pay attention to the same thing, and this could mean listening but also watching. A radio or television or social media audience also comes together, though not face-to-face in the same room, to look or listen.

Audiences are people, the people who receive media as viewers, listeners, readers, or users. One person might be a reader or a spectator, but an audience is a group. There's a special feeling of being part of an audience

DOI: 10.4324/9781003007708-4

who feel suspense, who laugh, who applaud as one. When I watch a comical movie in a theater along with other moviegoers, their laughter enriches my experience (or annoys me if I don't like the jokes). When we all laugh at once, we are part of something greater than ourselves.

Movie screenings are one kind of media experience, but most media aren't consumed in public, in a crowded theater. The readers of a book or newspaper are its audience. Particular genres are often associated with an audience that can be characterized in demographic terms. Think of the audience for YA novels, typically girls and younger women, or the audience for 24-hour cable news, mostly older adults. The broadcast media of radio and television often have more varied audiences of listeners or viewers driving in cars or working in offices or drinking in bars or relaxing at home. They might be listening or watching alone or in small groups, maybe as many as dozens in a crowded pub for a big game. But if you add up all of these people watching the same show, this combination of perhaps millions of people make up its audience. These viewers might not have that much in common demographically or otherwise, and they are probably spread out all around the country or the globe, but we still call them an audience.

Naming and Counting the Audience

Audiences are called by many different names. Each has its own meanings, but they're all ways of capturing the experience of media for the people who pay attention to it, who learn from it and take pleasure in it. Radio and music have audiences but also listeners. We talk about TV audiences but also viewers. Movies are seen by audiences, but also spectators or moviegoers. Books, magazines and newspapers have readers. Games have players and maybe gamers, if they see themselves that way. Each of these is its own kind of activity and its own identity. But all have in common that the people who experience media take it in through their senses, and make sense of media by understanding and appreciating the content of the media experience in whatever medium: a show, a song, a film, a story, a game. If the making of media (usually in the setting of a media industry) is production, the experience of media by audiences is reception, and we the audience are its recipients. Or it is consumption, and we are its consumers.

When it comes to digital and online media, the word user often takes the place of audience. These words are more different than the ones above like reader, listener, and viewer. User is more similar to the player of video games who watches and listens but also inputs data via the controller and interface, moving the avatar this way or that, jumping, firing. We speak of Facebook or Reddit or TikTok users, and the way we interact on these platforms may be different from watching TV or reading a magazine as it often involves giving input as well as receiving output. Some scholars use the term *prosumer* to capture the dynamic of users (e.g., YouTubers, Instagrammers) at once producing and consuming media on the same platform (Ritzer and Jurgenson 2010). It's true that some people go on social media just to look, listen and read, sometimes called *lurking*. But there is always the potential for this experience to involve both reading and writing (comments, replies, posts of your own) and clicking like or fave, upvote or downvote, or using emoji, gifs or stickers. This difference between audiences and users is sometimes portrayed as one between passive viewing and active or interactive navigation of the digital, online environment. I think we should reject such a contrast between audiences and users, but for now, I want to acknowledge that a user is an active, engaged participant in media. If audience means listening, user means doing. *To use* is a verb, but *to audience* is not. (*To listen* is, though.)

Despite some differences, audiences and users (or prosumers) have a whole lot in common, more than any contrast implied by their names. From the standpoint of media industry workers, audiences and users are their consumers and it matters little what you call them as long as they buy magazines, subscribe to Netflix, go to the movies, and check in on their social media feeds. They're the people who see the advertisements that pay the bills for the TV networks, websites, and news organizations. Industries are constantly trying to figure out who their audience is and what they want, and calling these people users does nothing to change this basic fact. Whether the audience is literally the customer who buys the media product, like an issue of *USA Today* or a new version of *Madden NFL*, or the target of commercial messages from sponsors, like the ones on TV or online, the audience is the holy grail of all work in the media industries and for many social media prosumers: capture their attention, and you've succeeded. The users who are actively engaged in media consumption might be even more desirable than the audiences who merely pay attention, because users are involved and dedicated.

But much depends on who this audience is and how numerous its members are. A critical mass of affluent adults often matters more to the media business as an audience, unfortunately, than audiences of greater numbers who are older, younger, or poorer. Media industries often have particular audiences in mind for different kinds of content: men for sports, women for lifestyle content on food or family, children for cartoons, and so on. There may be impressive numbers of women who like football and men who like interior decorating shows, but these viewers are irrelevant to the industries producing this content if their underlying purpose is to deliver one gender or other to the sponsors, the brands eager to reach their target market.

When it comes to the effects of media on its audiences or users, individually or more broadly, it matters little what we call them. What's interesting about audiences to people engaged in media studies is how they use media, take pleasure from it, make meaning of it, let it into their lives to shape their imaginations and form common points of reference for their social worlds. All of these things happen whether media are experienced using eyes, ears, fingers, or some combination of senses, whether media are printed on paper or projected on screens or carried around in our pockets. So we will refer to these people as audiences, understanding that their activities are really too varied for one word to capture fully.

Some media, like movies, are made for audiences in the old sense of persons assembled for a performance. When we go to the movies, we often find ourselves in an auditorium filled with strangers, our fellow moviegoers. Many theater auditoriums contain only a few dozen seats in the 2020s, but a century earlier, there were many theaters built with more than 1000 seats in a single auditorium, and a movie audience in a big city could be larger than the populations of many small towns.

Yet even that audience would be practically nothing compared to the *mass audience*, the audience of all of the spectators in all of the theaters all across the country and the world watching that same movie at the same time. A popular film could be seen by millions of people. Radio and television made this kind of mass audience experience routine in modern life, and truly simultaneous. In the early days of television, events like the coronation of Queen Elizabeth II in 1953 and a live performance of the Rodgers and Hammerstein musical *Cinderella* in 1957 were seen by tens of millions of people all watching at once, a world-changing novelty. The idea of an audience as one group experiencing a show together, laughing or cheering or applauding as one gathering of individuals becoming one whole, may be hard to extend to millions of people watching or listening in their own private spaces, in many different regions of the country or the globe.

Thus the old idea of the audience implies a commonality that is probably lacking from typical experiences of mass media. This is one reason why the audience is a metaphor or figure of speech as much as it is a factual description. It's only figurative that a million people all watching the same show are an audience. Actors in a play or musicians performing a concert sometimes characterize an audience as one whole: a lively or raucous audience, or a dead crowd. Individuals coming together as one might be possible in a room the size of a theater, but a million or 50 million people are an audience only in the sense that they're all looking at the same thing. Even so, the ideal of an audience as a group sharing a common experience can be useful for the media industries. If they can imagine their consumers as fundamentally the same, it helps them figure out how to make and sell their products.

Why Care About Audiences?

Why should we care about media audiences? One reason is that the people who make and sell media care about them. Decision-makers in the media industries choose what kinds of media to invest in based on what they imagine their audiences will like, sometimes based on their audience research and sometimes relying on their own beliefs, opinions, and experiences. There is always some degree of fit between media production and media audiences. This could be about who the audience is. You can tell from watching Pixar films that they are made to be seen by kids (though not exclusively), and you can tell from R-rated comedies like Bridesmaids that they are made to be seen by adults. Knowing about audiences helps us to know about media more broadly, explaining how media got to be the way they are.

Media industries care about who their audience is, but also how their audiences use media, and under what conditions. People often listen to the radio while doing other things like working, driving, or cooking. This explains why radio of many different formats – sports, talk, music, public radio – tends to be repetitious, with frequent breaks and brief segments, and redundant updates with news headlines and weather and traffic conditions that suit listeners who don't always pay sustained, focused attention. Radio formats are tailored to patterns and conditions of use among radio audiences. One reason movies and television have been different from one another is that their audiences experience media differently, typically in public for movies and in private for TV, though these conditions have changed over time and the distinction between movies and TV has become blurry as a result.

A more important reason to care about media audiences is that we generally believe that media can have powerful, far-reaching effects, and shape our lives in a great many ways. Media have impacts on individual people, but also on society more broadly. By studying media audiences, we can improve our understanding and appreciation of these forces that media exert on us, which is one vital part of understanding how our world works.

Students new to media studies often arrive with strong opinions on the subject of how media influences audiences. You might believe that images of women in magazines or Instagram feeds cause girls to have a negative body image, or that excessive time spent with media can lead to obesity, or that playing violent video games inspires real-world violence, or that false news stories can deceive readers and affect their voting behavior. You likely would agree that racial or ethnic stereotypes in media can contribute to racism in society, and maybe also that positive representations can have an opposite effect of teaching tolerance. If media is an important topic of study, it must be because it contributes to shaping the world we live in. That shaping can happen on a societal level only if it happens at the individual level, with the people who make up the audience.

You may be right or wrong about these particular *media effects*. It's up to researchers to prove them convincingly. We should be skeptical of claims of strong, direct effects of media on individuals without seeing clear and persuasive evidence of it from academic research, but there is no question that media has given form to our world in many, many ways.

Audiences Making Meaning

Even in one theater auditorium, it's a mistake to assume that everyone in an audience is affected by a show in the same way. In some audiences, you might see everyone laughing at the same gag or crying at the same sentimental moment. But sometimes you hear just one voice laughing, and we know from having post-movie conversations and Monday morning discussions of the previous day's games and shows that opinions differ about practically any instance of media. Much of what's interesting about audiences is what they don't all have in common. We know that children respond differently to many kinds of media than adults do, and kids of different ages are different from one another. Urban and rural, male and female, straight and gay audiences are often assumed to be distinct from one another. Cultural background plays a big role in shaping media experiences and audiences who share a frame of reference, a set of common experiences and assumptions, will likely have a much different time with any particular media product than a more varied group. So even if the term *audience* suggests commonality, the reality is often that members of an audience are all seeing and hearing something a bit different from one another, and responding in their own ways.

Differences among audiences have been studied systematically by media researchers, showing us how varied our responses can be and how factors like culture and nationality shape our perceptions. One of the most popular television series worldwide in the 1980s was *Dallas*, an evening soap opera about a rich extended family in the oil business in Texas. Media researchers Tamar Liebes and Elihu Katz (1990) showed episodes of the show to viewers of six different cultural backgrounds, and followed the screenings with a discussion led by a trained interviewer who asked the participants to summarize the episode, discuss the characters. and comment on the situations in the narrative and their meanings. They asked questions like "Is there a moral, a lesson, a message in *Dallas?*"

The researchers found that each group understood the show in its own distinct way. Four of the groups were in Israel, where *Dallas* was very popular: a group of Arab Israeli citizens; a group of Moroccan Jews; a group of kibbutz (collective settlement) members, mostly born in Israel; and a group of recent Russian immigrants. Two other groups were American viewers in Los Angeles, whom the researchers regarded as sharing the same culture as the show's producers, and viewers in Japan, a country where *Dallas* failed to become popular and was removed from the broadcast schedule shortly after its debut.

The viewers described as "Western" in this study, which includes the Americans, Russians, and kibbutz members, were more likely to regard the show critically as an aesthetic object. The viewers categorized as more culturally "traditional," the Moroccan and Arab viewers, were more likely to read the show literally and focus on the narrative and characters rather than the producers' storytelling choices. Arab viewers were more likely than others to interpret the messages of the show to include "Americans are immoral." Kibbutz members were most likely to say one message of the show is that "the rich are unhappy." Japanese viewers, who disliked the show most of all, felt that *Dallas* did not fit with their cultural values, and they found it hard to comprehend situations like rich people setting their own tables and carrying their own luggage. In many ways, the show did not conform to Japanese expectations of a "home drama," a familiar genre in Japanese culture. Some viewers (Arabs) focused more on the morality of the characters as a way of distancing themselves from the show's message, while others (Russians) showed more concern with the program's aesthetics as a way of showing that they were not falling for the producers' ideological manipulation. Each of these perspectives fit to some extent with the cultural background of the viewing groups. *Dallas* didn't impress American values on the rest of the world, but rather gave viewers around the world an opportunity to respond to American culture in their own local ways.

Evidence like this of different audiences' meaning-making shows us something critical about media reception: we are not passive and gullible consumers. Passivity of media audiences is a widespread assumption. People can be quite invested in it, so it can be hard to give it up, but the *active audience* is one of the most fundamental assumptions of media studies (Ang 1985; Fiske 1987, 62–83).

Why do people often assume that media is consumed passively, uncritically, with naïve acceptance? It's undoubtedly true that our bodies are not usually in motion while reading, watching movies or TV, or listening to the radio, though you might be watching a video on a treadmill at the gym or listening to music when out for a walk. The stereotypical image of a "couch potato" in front of a TV set is a body at rest, a vegetable with eyes unable to move on its own. The implication might be that watching television has immobilized us, taken away our power to get up and turn it off. A potato is about as passive as it gets.

But the concept of the passive audience really has to do with our minds. According to passivity logic, audiences of mass media are easily programmed. Newspapers, movies, radio and television, and social media function effectively as propaganda – as media made to persuade a mass audience to subscribe to some powerful group's agenda – if audiences are not actively, critically thinking about their messages. This propaganda could be used for catastrophically harmful political purposes, as in Nazi Germany under Hitler and the Soviet Union under Stalin, but also for the purpose of spreading the gospel of consumerism in an advanced capitalist society like the United States. The idea of media audiences as passive receptacles for state or corporate propaganda was popularized in particular in the middle of the 20th century and in some ways is still with us in the assumption that mass media has such powerful effects over mass audiences.

A famous example of this supposed ease of manipulation at a time when radio's popularity was still new and the power of mass media was increasing was the broadcast of *The War of the Worlds* (Pooley and Socolow 2013; Schwartz 2015). *The War of the Worlds* was a radio drama adapted from the science-fiction novel by H.G. Wells broadcast on CBS in October 1938. The story depicted an alien invasion of the New York City area, and the drama was presented in the format of a news bulletin reported from New Jersey. Although audiences were told at the start that it was a fictional play, some listeners misunderstood and took the drama to be a real news story about breaking local developments, reacting with alarm, calling newsrooms and broadcasters for confirmation of the Martian attack and alerting the neighbors. In the days that followed, newspapers spread an exaggerated account of mass hysteria, of large audiences easily duped into the belief that America was being invaded, and reacting in a frenzy of panic, including mobs filling the streets and attempts of suicide. People seemed eager to believe such a story of the influence of radio over its listeners.

Whatever the extent of the chaos that unfolded that night, the legend of *The War of the Worlds*, which has circulated ever since, was one of mass communication having a fearsome power to be used for the deception and manipulation of an easily influenced, uncritical audience. Thinking of audiences as passive subjects of media, as helpless victims, is a key element of this idea. A passive audience is a pliable audience that those in power can control in any way that suits their interests.

This way of thinking might sound like a relic of the past. It's been many decades since a radio play had the potential to wreak such havoc. But the same kind of thinking about audiences also informs more recent concerns about media influence. For instance, consider the notion that "fake news" circulating on Facebook could help elect a candidate for public office, such as an American President, or that terrorist groups or white supremacists could radicalize impressionable young people using YouTube videos and online forums. These examples assume that some social media users are vulnerable and might believe practically anything they read, especially if it conforms to some existing opinions and beliefs. This is not so different from the audience of *The War of the Worlds*, likewise imagined to be ripe for deception.

Passivity logic often seems particularly appealing when thinking about others who see the world differently from yourself. People like to think of themselves as being savvy and safe from deception, while regarding others as susceptible to influence. This can be especially true politically, as liberals might imagine conservatives willing to believe anything right-wing media tell them, and vice versa, as if audiences unlike yourself are eagerly ingesting any barely plausible message uncritically. The name for this coined by the public opinion scholar W. Phillips Davison (1983) is the "third-person effect." It's the idea that we tend to believe mass media has stronger effects on others than on ourselves. To take a less political example, many people have believed that some advertising contains subliminal messages, such as sexual language spelled in the ice cubes of a whiskey ad, which is almost certainly false. It's a seductive myth. The attractiveness of this phony idea probably comes from people being willing, even eager, to believe that when it comes to media influence, others are less critical and more vulnerable than they are (Acland 2012).

In contrast to the idea of the audience being passive, there are several ways we can regard them as active. All of these are going to be forms of mental or cognitive activity. It's certainly true that some kinds of media, like digital games and social media, are creative and interactive in a way that's different from reading, watching a movie, or listening to music. But there are forms of activity common to all of these media that are different from creative activity like taking a photo and posting it on Instagram or playing *Mario Kart*.

The active media audience is busy making meaning. This involves our senses first of all. We read or watch with our eyes, hear and listen with our ears. Some media are haptic, which means they appeal to the sense of touch, as in a 4D movie or a video game controller with force feedback. But our eyes, ears and hands are never independent of our brains. Anything we take in through the senses has to be processed, interpreted, fit into our expectations of what the world looks, sounds, and feels like.

Even if much of that process is practically automatic, consuming media also requires higher-level processes of understanding, judging, and responding with feelings like amusement, anger, or excitement. We take pleasure from media, which is a big reason why we seek out stories and shows. In one famous study of romance novel readers, Janice Radway (1991) found that women who were regular readers thought of the time they spent reading as a pleasurable escape from housework, as time of their own. Sometimes we also experience displeasure, and even seek it out ("hate-watching" and "hate-reading" were coined to capture this dynamic). We evaluate media and decide if we like it or not. Much of our conversations about media are focused on evaluation, like when you tell someone your opinion of a particular show or piece of music, a podcast you listened to or a movie you saw. If you tell me you saw a new movie last weekend, my first question might be: Did you like it? Liking it or disliking it and having reasons why or why not is a kind of activity.

Our reception of media involves applications of moral judgment when we approve or disapprove of a character's behavior, or of the creators' choices in telling a story. Reality television offers great examples of media made to be judged in particular ways by its audience. So-called docusoaps like the *Real Housewives* series on Bravo are all about offering the audience a mixture of admiration for characters who are richer than they probably are (admiration of their lavish lifestyles if not their actual lives), and feelings of superiority over these same people's ridiculous, outrageous behavior (Lee and Moscowitz 2013). *Real Housewives* characters act in ways that invite viewer scorn, such as spending their money frivolously, gossiping about one another and stabbing their friends in the back, and failing to care adequately for their children. The shows wink at the audience as if to say: look at what self-absorbed liars or hypocrites these women are! The audience might love some of the characters and hate others, but regardless of whether they feel positively or negatively, their responses about characters being good or bad is a kind of activity, and often leads to another kind: talking to other people who watch the same shows you do about the stories and characters.

Much of our cognitive activity in media reception falls under the category of *interpretation*: we make meaning out of media texts. Often our process of making sense of a text is called a reading, and reading is a term with multiple layers. Literally, it means looking at words and understanding their meaning. This is what we usually mean by "reading a book" or "reading the syllabus." But a reading is also a person's take on things, their own distinctive understanding. You might read *The Office* as a comedy about quirky characters in familiar situations, but I might read it as a biting satire of the modern corporate workplace. We can both be right, but either way our readings are signs of our cognitive processing. When we are reading, which we can define as the activity of media reception, we are active in understanding, assigning meaning, drawing conclusions, and identifying themes.

Dominant, Oppositional, Negotiated

Often when taking pleasure from a particular media text, we are reading it as its authors or creators might have intended. When listening to Marvin Gaye singing "Let's Get It On," you might feel the sexual charge expressed by the voice in the lyrics inviting his lover to bed. When watching a news report about a violent crime, you might respond with sympathy and concern for the victim and outrage at the perpetrator. These seem like the sanctioned readings, the intended effects. The song was made to excite that feeling, and the news segment was made to spark that concern. Stuart Hall (1992, 134–136), a key figure in cultural studies of media, called this a *preferred reading* or *dominant reading*. It would be the reading that adheres to common-sense ideas about how the world works, and likely serves the interests of those with the most power in society.[1]

But other readings are always possible. You might read "Let's Get It On" as a song that endorses problematic conventional gender norms, and find yourself irritated by the expectations that men should pressure women into sex and that women should submit to male seduction. Maybe you dislike that song for that reason. A viewer of the crime story might object to how it sensationalizes violence, appealing to the audience's fascination with lurid subject matter, giving a false sense that the city is a violent and dangerous place. You might avoid local TV news because you've come to expect this kind of treatment of urban life. These readings against the grain push back against the more typical, expected responses, and the resistant reader is fully capable of thinking critically about media. Any time you reject the preferred meanings, the underlying assumptions or taken-for-granted ideas in a media text, any time you feel outraged or offended by something in the media, you are what Hall terms an *oppositional reader* (137–138).

We can accept or reject the meanings offered to us, but there is also a third way, a position in the middle. You might have mixed feelings about some of the media you experience, appreciating some things and finding fault with others. The TV comedy *Modern Family* has been praised for its inclusive representation of a diverse cast of characters, including a gay male couple raising an adopted daughter and a white man married to a Latina woman with a son from a previous marriage. The show is often charming and funny in a way that many viewers might find relevant to their own lives, feeling familiar and ringing true. It sometimes pushes boundaries in a progressive direction while still maintaining its popularity with conservative audiences. (During the 2012 presidential election in the US, the more conservative candidate's wife named the show as her favorite.) *Modern Family* certainly advances a liberal message of tolerance, of recognition of our shared humanity, but its appeal is quite broad. There is much to admire in it for viewers of many backgrounds and political orientations.

Still, one might lament some of *Modern Family's* tired sitcom elements and its reliance on some old-fashioned conventions. In all three of the marriages in the show, in its first several seasons, there was one male breadwinner, with a woman at home caring for children in two of the three (and a same-sex caregiver in the third). Some characters are stereotypes: the sexualized bombshell Latina with a humorous accent, the affluent, high-strung gay men with urbane good taste. In the early years of the show, fans agitated to have the show overcome its chaste approach to the gay pair, who were never shown exchanging any type of physical affection. The public campaign to get Cam and Mitchell to kiss onscreen eventually succeeded, but this was itself a sign that the creators of *Modern Family* were avoiding representing some kinds of sexuality, treating gay and straight relationships differently (Martin 2014). More generally, *Modern Family* reinforces the old-fashioned ideal that a family consists of a pair of parents in a committed relationship, leaving little room for alternative conceptions. So even while it challenges some norms, it reinforces others.

This discussion has been what Hall would call a *negotiated reading* (137) of *Modern Family*, following Hall's scheme of audience responses, at once accepting and critical of its message. It goes along with its intended meanings of inclusion and diversity to a point, but also goes against the grain, wishing for a different kind of image of modern families. Whether you read with or against the grain or whether your reading is somewhere in between, i.e., negotiated, your interpretive meaning-making is evidence that you are active rather than passive in your media reception.

Communication as Transmission and Ritual

The activity of reading media, of interpreting texts and making meaning of them, is not the only thing we do with media, and some kinds of texts might lend themselves more or less to reading than others. Do you read a sporting event in the same way as an advertisement or pop song? Is everyone who engages with media always thinking about meanings and values, seeking the moral of the story or its ideological agenda? It surely varies, depending on the person and their situation, and on the type of media.

One way of thinking of meaning is to see it as the reception of a message via the channel of the media text. Decoding a meaning is part of a communication between the creators of media and their audience. But the transmission of meanings between media creators and consumers is not the only way of thinking about the experience of media for audiences. The communications scholar James Carey (2009, 11–28) distinguished between a *transmission* view of communication and a *ritual* view of communication. The ritual view, according to Carey, is not about sending and receiving information but rather sharing and participating, taking part in a community. (*Communication* and *community* both derive from the Latin *communicare*, "to share.")

To see the audience for media as engaged in ritual is to appreciate a different kind of audience activity than receiving meanings from media, though transmission and ritual are not necessarily opposed or mutually exclusive. Viewed as participants in ritual, the media audience engages in a drama in which its shared values are performed. This is a secular rather than religious drama, but it has some of the qualities of sacred ceremonies. These include habitual engagement in a communal act, and a familiar routine or script that participants follow. Often these ceremonies mark special occasions like annual holidays or life passages like baptisms and weddings, but rituals can also be more frequently occurring in everyday life.

Many kinds of media can be seen in ritual terms: reading the newspaper over breakfast (or news on an app), going to the movies, posting updates on social media, watching live television events. Major media events like a royal wedding or a political convention in particular lend themselves to being seen this way. The ritual functions of such occasions include a shared simultaneous experience in which, in Carey's words, "a particular view of the world is portrayed and confirmed" (6).

When watching the Olympics, we do so at the same time as millions or billions of others. The games confirm some taken-for-granted ideas about competition and nationalism. We come to expect the peaceful parade of nations in symbolic attire, the spectacle of opening ceremonies with the lighting of the Olympic flame, the stories of the athletes and their struggles against adversity, the races and matches, the awarding of medals and interviews with medalists. Often the new games awaken memories of old games, and past heroes resurface as commentators showing their age.

Watching is ritualized, but so is the social dimension of media consumption. For audiences of the Olympics, as for many kinds of media, our casual conversations about the games might be just as meaningful as the television event itself, and the competition gives us something in common to discuss. Seen this way, along with the athletes and broadcasters, we the viewers are also participants in the ritual drama of the Olympic games, and the experience binds us into the community of viewers who share these same values and interests, and who take part with us at the same time via representation across multiple media platforms. The same can be said for many kinds of media that give us fodder for gossip and small talk, for trading opinions and informing one another about what we have seen and heard. Media as ritual gathers us together in a shared practice of media experience.

Fans in the Audience

There is another name for a certain type of audience member or media user that hasn't come up yet in this discussion, which you might have thought about while reading so far: the fan. Not all audiences are fans, but fans stand out as exemplary active audiences. I often watch TV or read books in a dispassionate way, with interest but maybe not fascination or commitment. I've seen a few James Bond movies and been entertained, but I don't love them or carry around a strong opinion about which actor played the character best. If another Bond movie comes out, I'll be unlikely to see it.

I feel differently about *Star Wars*. I have seen the movies multiple times and would never skip seeing a new film in the theater. I've been watching these movies since childhood, some of them repeatedly, and have taken pleasure in seeing the sequel trilogy with my own kids.

Some *Star Wars* fans are much more involved than I am. As a child, I slept with a plush Chewbacca on *Star Wars* sheets, but I'm less engaged now as an adult. Some fans gather for intense discussion in online forums, attend conventions dressed as Stormtroopers, produce fan art or fan videos, and have a productive relationship with their fandom object, responding not only as cognitively active audiences making meaning of media, but as creative contributors (Jenkins 1992). Fans collect and organize their knowledge of media in wikis, they evaluate new installments of their objects of fandom with incredibly well-informed critical judgment, often following their objects of fandom across many media platforms (from movies and books to adaptations to other media like games, to merchandise and theme part experiences). Sometimes they compose their own stories from the world of the fandom (Coppa 2008). This kind of activity can offer us rich evidence of the meanings made from media by audiences, though we should be wary of assuming fans are typical users or spectators.

Fandom used to be more of a fringe activity among a small minority of audiences for some kinds of media. There was stigma involved in media fandom, which was often seen as nerdy and esoteric. That stigma lingers on sometimes, but in the 21st century the media industries have cultivated fandom and made it more mainstream. Audiences are often encouraged to see themselves as fans, as fans are such good media consumers. They're dedicated and passionate and will keep showing up to spend money on new products from the franchises they love. The explosion of comic book superheroes in movies, television, and other media is a testament to this. The latest installment in a series of *Avengers* films might not appeal to audiences who are unfamiliar with the comics characters, but to the fans who are engaged in the Marvel Cinematic Universe, every new release has the potential to deepen their relationship with a fandom object and community.

Since intense fans are a minority of audiences, we run the risk of missing the most typical kinds of audience activity if we take fan practices to be a norm for consumers of media. Another pitfall of taking fans as the model of the audience is that we risk defining audience activity too narrowly, setting too high a bar for what makes for an active audience. If your idea of the active audience is the hyper-engaged fan, writing comments online or making videos in expression of their fandom, the activity of the more casual and typical audience member starts to look more passive by contrast. We should recognize the many varieties of audience activity, and there is nothing deficient about the experience of audiences who do not identify as fans – which accounts for most of us most of the time. And while some kinds of media speak to fans and cultivate their engagement and participation, other kinds are made for more casual or distracted viewers, like the music playlists used as a background soundscape in an office or the TV shows keeping us company in waiting rooms and airports.

Researching Audiences

Even if they are exceptional, looking at the creative expressions of fans is one of the most interesting ways of accessing the meanings or readings of audiences. Fans make their readings public, which gives us a glimpse into practices of meaning-making. An example would be the fan practice of "shipping," a kind of fandom centered on desire for a pair of characters to be in a romantic relationship (Scodari and Felder 2000). Shipping shows us how some audiences relate to some media, especially but not only TV series. When fans of the show *Riverdale*, based on the Archie comics, ship Betty and Veronica, two canonically straight high school girls, they express a queer desire going against the grain of the text (except, when the creators seem to be acknowledging these fans, for moments that hint at an attraction or can be read that way by viewers looking for it). Their expressions of shipping in public online conversation spaces give us evidence of audience activity, of readings by some viewers of *Riverdale*. This kind of queer shipping has been one important way that LGBTQ+ audiences have taken pleasure over the years from mainstream representations that give them so little visibility.

But there are many other ways of accessing the activity of audiences (Stokes 2013, 170–200). Researchers can talk to audiences about their experiences of media. Researchers can interview them, giving them survey questionnaires, inviting them to participate in focus groups. Researchers doing ethnographic research with media audiences, whether face-to-face or online, observe their behavior, gaining insight into the way media is part of their everyday lives. For instance, Radway (1991) and Liebes and Katz (1990) developed their understanding of romance readers and *Dallas* viewers, respectively, by talking with them. Most of these types of research are qualitative and interpretive, which means that the researcher is working with ideas about how audiences experience media and what impacts media have on audiences, what role media plays in their lives.

In contrast, some research on media audiences is quantitative, which means that it involves counting numerical data (Jensen 2002). Some data is generated through experimental research in which subjects engage with media in a laboratory setting. Researchers might monitor their heart rate or sexual arousal, or observe their behavior after consuming media, such as observing children's play after viewing different kinds of television shows. This might be a way of finding out whether media leads to certain kinds of effects, such as increased aggression among children who watch violent television shows. Qualitative research can be done in social science or humanities traditions of media studies, but quantitative research tends to be a social science approach following the scientific method.

Media can surely cause a range of effects of different kinds, influencing opinions and behavior, and leading the way to social change. How strongly we believe that media has these effects should depend on the persuasiveness of research in the field. We should be wary of believing in media effects absent strong evidence, as ideas about these effects sometimes rely on wild overestimates of the power of media.

Research following these methods can help us understand how media impacts audiences in the present, but we might also want to look at its past effects, and researching audiences of the past can present challenges.

Experiences that occurred long ago can be hard to study. We can't go back in time to observe or talk to audiences. But there are ways of accessing past experience, such as reading letters audiences sent to media creators contained in archives. Oral history can be another way, which would involve getting research subjects to tell the stories of their past experiences. You might have done this kind of audience research for a school assignment if you ever had to ask someone what life was like before the internet, or if they remember 9/11 or the Kennedy assassination. We don't always remember everything, or remember everything correctly. But there are flaws in all kinds of research methods. Whether they're talking about the past or present, media audiences have much to tell us about how media work and what meanings and values media convey.

A Useful Fiction

An audience is a group, but our most strongly held beliefs about the effects of media usually pertain to individuals. If media can influence us, by convincing us to buy a certain brand of soft drink or to vote for a particular candidate for office, the influence happens one person at a time. The use of media for the persuasion of audiences goes back a long way, and while new technologies probably increased the persuasive powers of media, surely the potential of images, sounds, and stories to inform people's habits of thought and to change their minds has been around long before mass media existed.

No matter what kind of encounter people have with media (looking, listening, interacting), they're part of an audience. This audience is a construct, a fiction, as all of the people receiving a particular example of media content are not one body together that behaves as one. The idea that collections of individuals form an audience for media typically serves someone's agenda. It could be the industry's agenda of getting a desirable number and type of people to pay attention to something. It could be a researcher's agenda of understanding a particular kind of media's effects or significance. We think of individuals aggregated into an audience because it helps us think through what media is doing to us, and to our world.

Unlike the audience for a play or concert laughing or clapping all together, media audiences are typically more varied, more heterogeneous. Different members of the audience bring very different experiences and expectations to their encounters with media and their reactions can be divergent and contradictory. Their activities of taking pleasure, exercising judgment, making meaning, and possibly participating with media as users, prosumers, or fans will follow many paths. The differences among our readings of media is further evidence that an audience is a construction. It's one reason why many media scholars prefer to talk of *audiences*, plural, rather than audience, singular.

But whether singular or plural, it's a productive notion, a useful fiction. Without a concept of all of us doing something together, it would hardly be possible to generalize about how media shape human experience. And if there is any purpose to be found in studying media, it must include trying to understand that.

Discussion Questions

1. What are the differences and similarities between different concepts of the audience: readers, listeners, spectators, users, and audiences?
2. How might people think about audiences as passive or active? Why is this an important distinction?
3. Choose a media text and propose several different readings of it, including an oppositional reading and a negotiated reading.
4. How and why is the audience a fiction or a construction? What are the implications of thinking about it this way?

Note

1   This section draws on John Fiske's (1992) interpretation of Hall's three-part scheme of reading positions.

References

Acland, Charles. 2012. *Swift Viewing: The Popular Life of Subliminal Influence.* Durham, NC: Duke University Press.

Ang, Ien. 1985. *Watching Dallas.* London: Methuen.

Carey, James W. 2009. *Communication and Culture: Essays on Media and Society,* rev. ed. New York: Routledge.

Coppa, Francesca. 2008. "A Brief History of Media Fandom." In *Fan Fiction and Fan Communities in the Age of the Internet: New Essays,* edited by Karen Hellekson and Kristina Busse, 41–59. Jefferson: McFarland & Company.

Davison, W. Phillips. 1983. "The Third-Person Effect in Communication." *The Public Opinion Quarterly* 47.1 (Spring): 1–15.

Fiske, John. 1987. *Television Culture*. London: Routledge.

Fiske, John. 1992. "British Cultural Studies and Television." In *Channels of Discourse: Reassembled*, edited by Robert C. Allen, 284–326. Chapel Hill: University of North Carolina Press.

Hall, Stuart. 1992. "Encoding/Decoding." In *Culture, Media, Language*, edited by Stuart Hall, Dorothy Hobson, Andrew Lowe, and Paul Willis, 128–138. London: Routledge.

Jenkins, Henry. 1992. *Textual Poachers: Television Fans and Participatory Culture*. New York: Routledge.

Jensen, Klaus Bruhn. 2002. "Media Effects: Quantitative Traditions." In *A Handbook of Media and Communication Research*, edited by Jensen, 138–155. London: Routledge.

Lee, Michael J. and Leigh Moscowitz. 2013. "'The Rich Bitch': Class and Gender on *The Real Housewives of New York City*." *Feminist Media Studies* 13.1: 64–82.

Liebes, Tamar and Elihu Katz. 1990. *The Export of Meaning: Cross-Cultural Readings of Dallas*. Oxford University Press.

Martin, Jr., Alfred L. 2014. "It's (Not) in His Kiss: Gay Kisses and Camera Angles in Contemporary US Network Television Comedy." *Popular Communication* 12.3: 153–165.

Pooley, Jefferson and Michael J. Socolow. 2013. "The Myth of the *War of the Worlds* Panic." *Slate*, October 28, 2013. https://slate.com/culture/2013/10/orson-welles-war-of-the-worlds-panic-myth-the-infamous-radio-broadcast-did-not-cause-a-nationwide-hysteria.html

Radway, Janice A. 1991. *Reading the Romance: Women, Patriarchy, and Popular Literature*, rev. ed. Chapel Hill: University of North Carolina Press.

Ritzer, George and Nathan Jurgenson. 2010. "Production, Consumption, Prosumption: The nature of capitalism in the age of the digital 'prosumer.'" *Journal of Consumer Culture* 10.1: 13–36.

Schwartz, A. Brad. 2015. *Broadcast Hysteria: Orson Welles's War of the Worlds and the Art of Fake News*. New York: Hill and Wang.

Scodari, Christina and Jenna L. Felder. 2000. "Creating a Pocket Universe: 'Shippers,' Fan Fiction, and The X-Files Online." *Communication Studies* 51.3: 238–257.

Stokes, Jane. 2013. *How to Do Media and Cultural Studies*, 2nd ed. London: SAGE.

5

REPRESENTATION

Much of the action in Spike Lee's film *Do the Right Thing* (1989) takes place in and around Sal's Famous pizzeria, a restaurant decorated with a "wall of fame" of photos of notable Italian-Americans, celebrities like Frank Sinatra and John Travolta. Sal and his sons run the restaurant, and they are proud of their heritage. But the pizza place is in the middle of the Brooklyn neighborhood of Bedford-Stuyvesant, represented as a mostly Black ghetto, and one of the regular customers, aptly named Buggin' Out, demands that Sal include some African-American faces on the wall of fame. Sal points out that in his restaurant, he can put up whatever pictures he wants, but Buggin' Out argues that the patrons of the pizzeria are not Italian-Americans. They're Black folks like him from the neighborhood, and he agitates to get his community some *representation*.

Buggin' Out organizes a boycott of Sal's Famous, a campaign that instigates much of the drama in *Do the Right Thing*, and eventually leads to a climactic violent confrontation between Sal and another African-American customer, Radio Raheem. Radio Raheem refuses to turn down the volume on his boom box while standing inside the pizzeria demanding representation, and the loudness of Public Enemy's rap anthem "Fight the Power" coming from his speakers enrages Sal. He totally loses his composure, screaming horrible racial epithets and smashing the boom box with a baseball bat, symbolically silencing Radio's voice.

Violence escalates from here with devastating consequences, but the point of beginning with this example is to show how the inclusion or exclusion of

DOI: 10.4324/9781003007708-5

people of different identities and the presence or absence of representations – pictures, music and lyrics – matters so much to these characters that they struggle and sacrifice over it.

The faces on the wall and the sounds from the radio have symbolic significance in a community where Black citizens patronize a white-owned business yet have little economic power of their own. These faces and voices, these representations, stand in for identities. They function as extensions of people, of cultures. The Italian-Americans have pride in their accomplishments as an immigrant community whose success in business has helped them pursue the American Dream. The African-Americans, however, have endured a long history of suffering, of systemic racism that endures over generations, which motivates their commitment to "fight the power." As it is in Do the Right Thing, representation can be a battleground where social injustices are resisted and contested.

Let's examine this word representation and look at the parts that make up the whole. Starting at the end: -tion indicates a process. Representation is ongoing.

Presenta- is from ancient Latin praesentare, a verb meaning "to be present." To be present is to stand in front of, to have on hand, to be visible, to exist. Representation is about showing up and being recognized and acknowledged.

Re- is a common Latin-derived prefix. It often means "again" or "repeatedly."

Re-presenta-tion in media is thus a process of showing up again and again, a phenomenon of images and stories and ideas recurring in cycles and patterns.

A related meaning of representation has to do with one thing standing for another, as our representatives in government are elected to serve us, to look out for our interests as their constituents. In this sense, representation is a kind of substitution, and your representative is a delegate or stand-in for you. Instead of all of the people serving on a city council or student government, we choose leaders, voices, to speak for us all. A representation has that onus and responsibility of being the one that stands for many.

We often apply a similar logic to media representations, expecting them to stand for identities and communities with some degree of truth and even justice. For instance, the media representations of different social groups (e.g., religious faiths, people with disabilities, LGBTQ+ folks) shape the way many people think about individuals who share those identities, contributing to the shared meanings about them that circulate culturally. Any individual representation has some power to produce or perpetuate meanings about its contents, its topics and themes.

This makes representation an especially weighty topic not just for critics and scholars, but for the producers of media. If you are going to work in a media industry, you will bear some of the responsibility for representation. It will be on you and your co-workers to do right by the people and groups whom you will have the power to represent in the stories you tell. But even if this isn't going to be your professional path, even as a social media user, as someone who takes pictures or makes videos or shares comments with others, you are also a participant in media representation, and doing so more thoughtfully and with keen critical engagement can only help make for a more just and equitable world.

Reflecting, Constructing, and the Work of Representation

Think about your ideas and beliefs about the military, or about working in an office or a factory, or about what life was like during a time before you were born, or in a place where you have never been – maybe a different part of the country, or a far-away land. I have never been to the Caribbean, so I'm going to think about my ideas about who lives there, what the places look like, the sounds and smells and tastes and everyday experiences. Maybe some of these ideas come from personal experience or from stories we have heard from family members or friends, but many of them will have come from books and pictures, from advertisements, from television and cinema and the internet, from videos watched in school, from media of many different kinds. My sense of the Caribbean probably comes from the clichés of tourism advertisements, with their blue skies, tall palm trees, white sandy beaches, and beautiful people enjoying the sunshine, but also from coverage of natural disasters on the news, from books by Caribbean authors, and from listening to reggae, calypso, and Afro-Cuban music. Without having any first-hand knowledge, I still have a lot in mind.

We think of this relationship in terms of the real world, on the one hand, and media images of the real world, on the other hand. There is crime in reality, and there are stories (both fictional and true stories) about crime in the media, like on cop shows and news reports. Many of our ideas about crime are shaped by what we have learned from movies, TV, social media, and video games. We learn from the media that certain kinds of people commit crimes for certain reasons, that some kinds of crime are common or uncommon, and that police and the justice system deal with suspected criminals in particular ways. Our everyday understanding of crime is closely connected to representations of crime.

We can think of media representations as *reflections* of reality, and as in the mirror over the bathroom sink, we do see reality reflected in media of many kinds. The palm trees in my mental image of the Caribbean, like the ones you see in tourism brochures, surely resemble the real thing. Ancient Greek philosophers called this resemblance *mimesis*, which sounds a lot like some common English terms of today, such as *mimic*, *mime*, and *meme*, all words denoting *imitation*. A reflection is an imitation. Your mirror reflection isn't your face, but it sure looks like it.

A media representation can show us a true detail of something from the real world, and it can be honest and revealing. A photograph, a video, or a sound recording will be not just a reflection but a reproduction of reality, often with a fair bit of fidelity to the original (though no reproduction shows us everything, and there can be competing truths). Photographs, videos, and sound recordings are all made using tools that capture something of the physical world (arrangements of light and color, sound vibrations) so that we can save them and look or listen to them again, offering us fragments of what the world looked and sounded like in a particular moment. The fact that these image and sound recordings can be used as authoritative documentary evidence speaks to their power as reflections and reproductions of reality. Even if they never capture everything, we typically do believe that they capture something real. But the media also *produce* or *construct* images of reality, and ideas about the world around us. Every recording is the product of many decisions and constraints. Every representation includes some things and excludes others, and it gives emphasis to certain elements while others are harder to see. Every story comes from a point of view, is spoken in someone's voice. Every picture has frame lines beyond which we don't get to see anything, though we might have a sense of what has been left out. This frame is literal in the case of photographs and moving images, but it's also true as a metaphor: every story and image has a frame of reference, a perspective and a purpose. All of these factors are part of how a representation is made, so simple *reflectionism* can never be an adequate way of seeing a process that involves so much shaping of meaning. Some of this shaping is conscious and deliberate, but some of it is more a matter of conventions and constraints beyond the individual creator's power to determine, perhaps even outside of their awareness.

Routine crime reporting might reflect some fragmentary realities at particular moments, but in aggregate can give us a false impression of how much danger exists in our communities. Some crimes are covered in the news, and some are ignored altogether. Some are treated as causes for fear and anger, while others are treated as understandable responses to conditions, or are minimized or excused as no big deal. Some of the people who commit crimes are made out to be dangerous and deviant and some are painted in a more sympathetic light. Repeated associations between criminal behavior and certain kinds of people and communities can give us a false impression of what kinds of people commit crimes. Emphasis in the media on some kinds of crime rather than others can give us a false impression of what we should be concerned about. Representations can contrast some people and places framed as dangerous with others framed as safe or benign. So representation can mean the reflection of an already existing reality, but representation can also mean the *social construction of reality*, the production of ideas about the real world and the people who live there. In practice it can be impossible to disentangle reality from its social construction. Even if reality exists before its social construction, what do we know about it that isn't mediated through representation?

Let's delve into a different example to explore this dynamic of representation being both a *reflection* and a *construction* of reality. The covers of women's magazines like *Vogue* and *Cosmopolitan* have always conveyed an ideal of femininity. Cover images are carefully crafted studio portraits of a conventionally attractive model or celebrity posed in stylish clothes with perfect hair and makeup and a fair bit of flawless, smooth skin, projecting glamor and often sex appeal. While women of many ages and cultures appear on these covers, there is a premium on youth and – despite years of progress toward diversity – whiteness. These images are expressions of a society's ideals when it comes to femininity. They reflect a standard of beauty, a widely shared idea of what a desirable woman should look like. Very literally the photograph is like a reflection in a mirror, showing us the image of the woman as she appeared before the camera (though with the usual Photoshopping to make it more like a fantasy mirror than the one in your bathroom). You might also say the images on women's magazines are accurate reflections of a society's values when it comes to female bodies: their shape, their skin, their attitude, their posture and expression. They express an idea of what it means to be a beautiful woman.

But where did this idea about female bodies come from if not the covers and pages of women's magazines and other media? It's not simply human nature that certain kinds of bodies in certain kinds of poses and dresses and hairstyles are "attractive" or "beautiful." Some elements of beauty may be natural, but not all. These are cultural values that vary from place to place and by historical period. In earlier centuries, fat women were often seen as more beautiful than thin women, a cultural construction of beauty that was reversed during the 20th century. One reason why "Black is Beautiful" was an effective slogan of the African-American movement for civil rights and racial justice was that it called out the underlying unexamined whiteness of American notions of beauty. The images on women's magazine covers have played a significant part, along with Hollywood movies and television and other forms of media, in a particular construction of feminine beauty that values youth, whiteness, thinness, and sexual availability, and that differentiates feminine from masculine bodies and typically avoids too much androgyny or gender-bending. Every representation of this kind in some ways relays a set of values and ideals, with some potential for variation or subversion; but every instance of a women's magazine cover will be a participant in this construction of how a girl or woman should look.

This process of constructing reality via media has been called the work of representation: the productive quality of representations to make meaning rather than merely to convey, however transparently, an already existing reality (Hall 2013a). The work of representation, often seemingly invisible or hard to notice, is to make cultural values seem like natural properties of the world that just are the way they are because that's the way they are. Media studies offers us a particularly useful tool when it comes to representation: to identify and unpack this work and to reveal what might have gone unseen.

When you recognize how representations do work, you can become critically engaged in questioning media that often privilege some groups and disadvantage others, depending on where they fall within hierarchies of social power. The work of representation can make whiteness out to be an unquestioned norm, with every other racial or ethnic identity a departure from it, so that you might hear someone described as a *Latina entrepreneur* or a *Black violinist* but assume that an unmodified reference to an entrepreneur or violinist means a white entrepreneur, a white violinist. The work of representation can make gender appear to be a strictly binary quality of each person, defining each of the two genders with a set of core traits that seem natural rather than culturally constructed. The representations of boys and girls, men and women, are constantly reproducing a set of symbols and ideals that make up the social construct we call gender. The work of representation has often equated poverty with deviance, made queerness into a failure to conform to nature, made immigrants less deserving of basic rights, and made disability invisible. The work of representation is constant and ongoing in stories, in images, in fiction and nonfiction, news and entertainment, traditional media and social media. This work is done in the very language that we use to describe our daily experiences and the worlds we inhabit.

When we think of representation as a construction of reality, we can surround the often naïve question of realism, of whether the representation is accurate or true-to-life, with a more critical and sophisticated set of questions about the way the representation speaks to us. It's not that we shouldn't expect representations to be truthful or honest or to correspond with reality, though some are surely not aiming for a very close correspondence. Some representations, such as news stories and documentaries, are often rightly held to a standard of factual reliability, and you would obviously call out a journalist for getting things wrong. Some fictional stories, such as historical fiction, are to an extent also held to this kind of standard. But when we recognize the work of representation, we see that a better question than "is this realistic?" or "what does this get right and wrong?" is often "what reality is this constructing or reproducing?"

Visibility and Symbolic Annihilation

One of the reasons to care about representation is that we observe a correspondence between media images and their societal effects, and many people (not just media scholars) often hold strong beliefs about this. One version of this would be that the presence of media images leads not only to tolerance of difference but to an embrace of the struggle for equality and justice for all. This has been seen in particular with the history of LGBTQ+ representation on television over several decades from the 1970s to the 2010s. For many people who would not have known any LGBTQ+ folks in their daily lives (those out of the closet, anyway), the visibility of even fictional LGBTQ+ characters on people's TV screens has been said to have spread acceptance of causes such as marriage equality and workplace anti-discrimination policies. The cause of gay rights, according to this line of thinking, is more urgent if you or someone in your family or community suffers directly from the injustice of a heteronormative society. In the absence of such face-to-face relationships, LGBTQ+ representations on television and other media could make a difference (Bond 2015).

The slogan "representation matters" or its hashtag version #RepresentationMattters captures this perspective. The way it matters is that representation shapes the social world and changes people's minds and helps children grow up in a more equal environment. There are drawbacks and limitations to this rhetoric, but for now let's pause on the question of what matters about representation.

The identities that appear in media show audiences a picture of society. If everyone in this picture is straight, white, heterosexual, middle-class (or more affluent), suburban, American, and English-speaking as their first language, our image of the world not only erases the presence of all others, but is also one in which a particular identity is given as the norm and any deviation from it is marked as different, as non-normative or aberrant. It matters that a false sense of the social world would be the product of this, but *representation matters* is used in a way that goes beyond demanding that media offer an accurate image of the world. To young people in particular, seeing people who "look like yourself" is often a way of clarifying that representation has a connection to self-image and to expectations about one's future opportunities and stake in society as a citizen. Representation matters because you matter, whatever your identities.

Beginning especially in the 1970s, growing from the movements for civil rights, women's rights, and gay rights, Black, feminist, and gay authors mounted critiques of popular media like Hollywood films in terms of their histories of representation and the consequences of these images on marginalized identities. According to *From Reverence to Rape*, an influential account of women in Hollywood films by the feminist critic Molly Haskell first published in 1975, the big lie of American movies was that men are superior to women. Haskell (1987) analyzes the images of female characters and the women who played them through decades of cinema in support of her argument, showing patterns and themes prevalent at particular times.

In the history of American movies, Black characters have often been reduced to minor roles such as maids and porters, and stereotyped as happily subservient, or violent and dangerous, or simpleminded and comically ridiculous. The title of Donald Bogle's 1973 book captures this history: *Toms,*

Coons, Mulattoes, Mammies, & Bucks: An Interpretive History of Blacks in American Films.
Bogle (2006, 4) argues that the purpose of such demeaning representations
going back to Hollywood's early days was "stressing Negro inferiority." The
harms of such representations would surely matter in the way they circulated and perpetuated objectionable ideas, contributing to the ongoing
second-class status of African-Americans.

While some kinds of representation would appear in regular patterns,
other kinds of representation could be simply nonexistent. The feminist
media scholar Gaye Tuchman (1978) uses the term *symbolic annihilation* to
describe how a particular identity present in the social world can be absent
from media representation, effectively disappearing the people who get no
representation. In her key example, it was women who worked outside the
home. At the time, during the 1970s, there was fierce public controversy
around women's social roles, and, according to Tuchman, the media represented women mainly as homemakers caring for family and not as workers earning a living. Women working outside the home who did appear
on TV were denigrated, trivialized, or victimized. The refusal to represent
"working women" adequately and sympathetically was an example of this
symbolic annihilation. This pattern of representation has changed over
time, of course, but the concept endures to describe the power of absences.
Representation matters because the presence or absence of different groups
of people in media is recognized to carry symbolic power.

This is often similarly captured in the term *visibility*, an antidote to symbolic annihilation. In the history of LGBTQ+ representation especially, visibility has often been a key concern for activists and critics of mainstream
media. For decades, the LGBTQ+ characters who did appear in film, TV,
popular music, and other mainstream media were typically stereotypes
such as the sissy, a caricature of a feminine man who fails to conform to
heterosexual norms and is treated with contempt. These images and stories
made little space for a diversity of sexualities and reproduced a dominant
ideology of cisgender heteronormativity, which is to say, a worldview in
which everyone is assumed to be a straight person whose binary (male or
female) gender identity is the one assigned to them at birth.

Vito Russo's groundbreaking book *The Celluloid Closet* (1987), a history of
Hollywood's representations of homosexuality, begins by contrasting the big
lie about women (their inferiority to men) identified by Molly Haskell with
the big lie about gays and lesbians in movies: that they do not exist (xii).
There wasn't much visibility when it came to non-straight or trans identities,

with some exceptions often slipped into subtext, regardless of whether the representations that were visible were celebrated or found to be offensive. Since the 1980s in American film, television, and media more generally, the visibility of LGBTQ+ identities has been far greater than in the past, though some identities (e.g., white gay men) are still far more visible than some others (e.g., trans or bisexual persons, and LGBTQ+ persons of color). This visibility came as a product of many forces, including the activism of the gay rights movement and the recognition that to many media audiences embracing the struggle for LGBTQ+ equality was central to their identity and politics.

In the efforts at visibility, there are sometimes embarrassing missteps that show the limitations of simply having more representations of different kinds of people. Simply making different kinds of faces visible might answer the call to end the symbolic annihilation of some identities from media representation. The visual rhetoric of diversity initiatives, as in advertising and publicity imagery, is full of ensembles of people of diverse races and ethnicities. A college website or brochure that has pictures of students and faculty might, years ago, have used only images of white people (assuming a mostly white student body, as is true of more than a few American colleges). In the current climate, that would be deeply embarrassing as a representation of the institution producing those images, and almost certainly contrary to their stated mission. But in one notorious instance, a university was found to have edited images of students to drop one Black face into a crowd of white students at a football game. When discovered on the cover of the University of Wisconsin-Madison undergraduate application booklet for 2000–2001, this made the institution seem incapable of honestly representing the racial diversity of its mostly white student body. It was content to substitute a phony image of diversity for the real thing, an episode that speaks to the importance of visibility but also the need to go deeper than images in order to transform society's institutions (including its media institutions).

A somewhat less troublesome – though still problematic – practice when it comes to visibility is captured by the pejorative term tokenism. Rather than include more meaningful diversity in a representation, in instances of tokenism, some difference has been sprinkled in to anticipate criticism and deflect attention. A television series with no people of color might be asking for trouble, which is why we might see the occasional person of color in a secondary role. Perhaps this image of diversity is a white protagonist's sassy (Black) or nerdy (Asian) friend or roommate, or maybe the main character's therapist, a person whose social role carries some authority and prestige, but whose function in the narrative is still to listen to the white person's complaints and help the narrative of the white protagonist progress. This kind of tokenism gives some visibility to different kinds of faces and bodies without needing to deal with telling their stories.

Kristin Warner (2017) coined the term *plastic representation* to account for a certain kind of diversity in television and in movies that goes beyond tokenism but still has some of the same problems. In the practice of "blindcasting," i.e., of casting actors of any race or ethnicity for a role, and in many representations of Black characters in shows or films made by white creators who are eager to represent progressively, the color of the faces signals an investment in diversity of representation. But the representation is plastic in the sense that it's just a surface-level or cosmetic appearance of diversity, while the stories being told have not changed to accommodate cultural difference. Because being Black is about more than having dark skin, casting Black performers in roles that could have been played by actors of any culture diversifies in one way but fails in another. If representation truly matters, and diversity is a real goal of media industries, Warner argues, it needs to contain cultural specificity and not just an appearance of diversity. Media representations thus need to go beyond the plastic surface and represent the "histories and experiences" of African-Americans (37) and other historically marginalized groups.

These examples show some limitations of visibility and #RepresentationMatters. But they also support the point that representations construct rather than reflect reality. This is true not just in the literal sense of making up a fictional space in which a mixed-race crowd of students cheers together in the same stadium section, or a character of one racial identity seeks care from a therapist of another, but also in a deeper sense of the visual rhetoric of diversity constructing an ideal image of the social world. Whether or not the representation matches the reality, this image has become a default setting for what a modern social space ought to look like. This is true regardless of how successful any particular institution (e.g., a school or business) might be at achieving its diversity goals, and how much or how little is really changing under the diversity surface.

The Burden of Representation

The history of media representations is often marked by a struggle for visibility of one kind or another, but when we do have some visibility, especially if it's a circumscribed kind of visibility, the meager representations of some identities carry an unfair amount of weight. There are plenty of white representations to go around to the point that some audiences have trouble recognizing whiteness as such. But an Arab Muslim or a person with a disability or a trans person is often regarded differently, in a way that assumes they are standing for their group. They may be read as a statement on what Muslim or disabled or trans folks are like. And when there are so few representations of some kinds of people, the rare instances of visibility may be powerful in shaping mainstream perceptions of those identities. If the rare representations in American media of Muslims portrays them as zealous religious fundamentalists or violent terrorists, it can be seen as a statement on Islam, whereas a white Christian religious fanatic is unlikely to be read as exposing the pathology of whiteness or of Christianity, the faith practiced by the largest number of North Americans. This disparity is captured by the concept of a *burden of representation* (Mercer 1990). The burden is on the minority or Othered identity to represent, and the dominant or majority groups are by contrast free of such a burden. Any representation of the Othered identity is asked to stand for the entirety of that community.

A helpful way to appreciate this dynamic is by thinking about normative and non-normative identities. Normative, in relation to mediated social identities, means functioning as an unspoken social norm, and it's important to distinguish *normative* from *normal*, a problematic notion that often really means appropriate or acceptable according to the prevailing ideology. Normative identities are those "taken for granted" as typical or average, and the counterpart of normative would be Othered identities. The default assumption in many kinds of Western media has long been that characters are white, Christian, and native English-speakers, as well as able-bodied, cisgender and heterosexual, and typically middle-class (neither very poor nor very rich, though the normative identity is closer to rich than poor). Any representation of difference from this identity is routinely rendered as Other. The normative identity is by contrast unmarked. The cultural theorist Roland Barthes (2012, 249–254) called this *exnomination*: he wrote that the French bourgeois class (i.e., the upper-middle-class) has "difficulty acknowledging itself" and "completely disappears" into a kind of anonymity. *Exnominated* means *not named*, and there is a power and privilege in going unnamed.

Whiteness, masculinity, class privilege, and heterosexuality are probably the core of representational *exnomination* in modern Western media, though many kinds of difference can play into this dynamic. Insufficient diversity in media and a persistence of normative conceptions of identity both play into the burden of representation. While improving visibility would begin to address this, as we have seen, visibility by itself is unlikely to ameliorate the issue.

An additional problem with the burden of representation is that it puts the onus on a small number of alternative representations to be affirming and admirable. If white characters can be jerks without reflecting badly on whiteness, but Black characters need to be a credit to their race, it puts pressure on media producers to make their representations "positive," which is problematic in its own right.

Positive and Negative Images

Once we have visibility, the next question might be whether the images now visible are of the kind we want. Merely seeing different faces and bodies appear in the media cannot be adequate if representation really matters. Of course, there can always be multiple and divergent opinions about what is or is not desirable in a representation, and different audiences read things differently from one another. But in general, there is often a fairly wide agreement among groups of like-minded people that some images are bad, and others good – for instance, that racist caricatures are bad and that inspiring stories of courage in the face of injustice are good. Well, maybe. Sometimes racist caricatures are presented in a way that is meant to be critical of racism, exposing the potential harms of representations. Spike Lee's satirical 2000 film Bamboozled makes frequent use of hateful, racist language and blackface makeup as part of a sharp commentary on the representation of African-Americans in media. And sometimes inspiring stories are laughably shallow or corny, not to mention ideologically problematic, so there really is no formula for which kinds of themes and topics will read as positive or negative, and opinions may differ and shift over time. What seemed positive in the past may no longer seem so today. The media we feel good about now might not look so admirable in the future, and of course reasonable people may disagree about what's positive or negative.

Much of the concern about positive and negative representations is underwritten by some assumptions about media reception, in particular that representations affect audiences by encouraging admiration or imitation of what we see on screen, or what we read about. This can be especially worrisome in relation to children. Adults might worry about the influence of images and stories when representations of behavior are perceived to be inappropriate or undesirable, or when they include words that they prefer not to hear children say. Parents might want to see their kids emulate honorable characters and avoid dishonorable ones altogether.

The non-profit media advocacy organization Common Sense Media (CSM) publishes reports and guides to help parents choose appropriate media for their kids, and its reviews of video games, television shows, movies, and other media evaluate each text in various ways, including "Positive Role Models and Representations." For example, the classic TV comedy The Brady Bunch scores three out of five points for this category, with the explanation:

> The kids squabble and get jealous of one another sometimes (Jan is particularly envious of Marcia), but it always works out thanks to Mom and Dad. Very little racial/ethnic diversity. Each of the characters on the show has a moral compass and tries to do the right thing.

According to this perspective, being good and kind makes a character a positive role model, though a lack of diversity in representation is a drawback, perhaps costing a point.

By contrast, the video game Grand Theft Auto V scores a big fat zero in this category. CSM notes that "None of the protagonists or their associates serves as a decent role model" and that they "are driven by greed and self-interest." This is unsurprising, as part of the pleasure of this particular game is its subversive defiance of "positive role models." One movie that scores five out of five points on this CSM scale is Mr. Smith Goes to Washington, the story of a principled American politician who stands up for his values. CSM praises it as follows:

> Jefferson Smith stays true to who he is – an idealistic and honest man, and quite a patriot. When he's faced with corruption he calls a man a liar to his face, gets almost everyone against him, and is saved by his strong character and force of will.

It's almost as if screening movies like Mr. Smith is the surefire recipe for raising up citizens of good character (no mention is made of its lack of diversity).

Common Sense is a useful consumer guide, but some advocacy groups take on more of a role of watchdog or cheerleader when it comes to media representations. Civil rights groups such as GLAAD (which originally stood for Gay and Lesbian Alliance Against Defamation, and now is just GLAAD), NHMC (National Hispanic Media Coalition), and the NAACP (National Association for the Advancement of Colored People), engage in public efforts centered on the evaluation of media images of the communities they represent. All three of these organizations give annual awards for media that celebrate positive portrayals. The NAACP Image Awards, given annually in a televised ceremony, include categories across multiple media, including books, television, movies, and music. According to its website, the GLAAD awards "recognize and honor media for their fair, accurate and inclusive representations of the lesbian, gay, bisexual, transgender and queer (LGBTQ) community and the issues that affect their lives."

These organizations publicly honor what they regard as positive representations and admirable achievements by artists of particular identities, but they also sometimes threaten or organize boycotts of media organizations or particular television networks or programs or social media platforms whose practices either limit visibility or produce representations regarded as negative. The most famous and momentous of these efforts came early in the history of modern mass media, with the NAACP's campaign against the 1915 film The Birth of a Nation, a deeply racist film set during and after the Civil War that portrays the formation of the Ku Klux Klan in a sympathetic light and demonizes African-Americans as violent threats to white families. Much more recently, in 1999, the NAACP threatened a boycott of all of the major TV networks over a lack of representation of African-Americans in prime-time programs.

Conservative and religious groups also care about positive and negative representations, though they take positions often diametrically opposed to the civil rights groups like GLAAD, NHMC, and the NAACP. In 1997, the Southern Baptist Convention (SBC) organized a boycott of the Walt Disney Company over its tolerant and inclusive stance in representing sexuality and welcoming LBGTQ+ employees and theme park guests. The SBC objected to the ABC comedy Ellen, which famously had its main character come out as a lesbian, and to Walt Disney World for tolerating "Gay Days" organized by LGBTQ+ visitors each year (Myerson 1997). To many liberal television viewers, the coming out of the TV character along with the actor who played her, Ellen DeGeneres, was a positive representation, a step toward a much-needed visibility to become a key example supporting the idea that representation matters. To many conservatives in the American South, it was a negative representation that mobilized a backlash against gay rights (Becker 2006, 169).

It may be understandable that parents want a guide to navigating the many media options available for their children to consume, and as a parent myself, I've found CSM to be a regular source of useful recommendations helping me decide on films to watch with kids of certain ages. But as many critical media scholars have shown, reducing representation to a simple binary of either good or bad, positive or negative, misses a lot about what matters in the work of representation and reinforces a superficial or mistaken notion of how representation functions. Judging representation as either positive or negative, thumbs up or thumbs down, flattens the meanings of media texts for audiences, and misses the productive ways that many kinds of representations can be contradictory or ambivalent, and can engage audiences and give them meaningful pleasure (Gray 2004; Hall 2013a, 2013b; Hilton-Morrow and Battles 2015; Shohat and Stam 2013; Warner 2015). Racquel J. Gates (2018), for example, argues that representations of African-Americans in film and television are often judged as positive or negative based on dominant white terms that privilege images of "respectability." Such representations portray a certain kind of Blackness that is seen as unthreatening to mainstream society. She also shows a potential for "queer, feminist, and otherwise non-normative subjectivities" to be represented and addressed in so-called negative representations, such as supposedly trashy or "ratchet" reality TV (20). While the popular discourse around representation often fastens onto judgments of good or bad images, the work of critical media studies isn't to praise and blame any example of media in particular as it is to understand their meanings and their significance in the context of the social world and the history of representation. This is especially tricky when it comes to one kind of notoriously problematic representation: stereotypes.

Stereotypes and Regimes of Representation

The classic case of a "negative" representation is a stereotype that attaches to a social identity. Many of these go back a long way, preceding the rise of modern mass media. Live entertainment of the 19th century and early 20th centuries, including the theatrical format known as vaudeville, was filled with ethnic and racial humor and audiences instantly recognized the types: Italian, Irish, German, Jewish, and Black stereotypes (from blackface minstrelsy) would have been very familiar (Nasaw 1999, 52–53). Many of these characters were also present in literature (e.g., the anti-Semitic trope of a physically grotesque, greedy, villainous Jew appears in Shakespeare and Dickens), and were adopted in film, radio, and television comedy and drama in the 20th century. Gender and sexuality often overlap with race and ethnicity, so that many of these one-dimensional representations are specific to male or female types.

It's easy to be critical of racist stereotypes, but the story of stereotypes is often not so simple as routine condemnation. Audiences recognize stereotypes as comedic conventions that bend things out of shape rather than as efforts at social realism, so judging them as distortions often misses the point. Stereotypes are hard to distinguish from character types, and while these types might be unimaginative clichés, they're also reliable conventions of storytelling. Many stereotypes are used in a way that lets an ethnic group laugh at itself. Italian-Americans performing a travesty of Italian ethnicity for their fellow Italian-Americans is harder to fault than blackface minstrelsy in which white performers subject Blackness to cruel mockery. Ethnic stereotypes derive humor from exaggeration – of physical types, accents, language, group values. The humor is not necessarily unrelated to the experiences of the ethnicities represented, but it may also be recognized and appreciated as hyperbole, as pushing things a little far for the sake of comedy. Mockery can be vicious and dehumanizing, but it can also be affectionate. There surely is always a line not to be crossed, but the location of the line and where you are if you're stepping over it can be pretty subjective. In the same way that African-Americans can use language among themselves that I as a white person do not use, any ethnic or racial group might have permissible codes of speech and image that work differently inside the group than outside. Context matters, and meanings vary by audience.

Stereotypes are probably the most notorious negative representations, often singled out for being distorted and unrealistic and just plain bad. Taken one by one, negative stereotypes might seem merely unimaginative and pathetic, but they typically follow a familiar pattern. It might not seem like a big issue if the occasional Asian-American character were to be represented as a nerdy striver who's good at math and has overbearing parents who want them to be a doctor or engineer. The problem is worse if this is a painfully recurring image, feeding into a broader discourse. The idea of Asian-Americans as a "model minority" is based on stereotypes that are at their core based on racist habits of thinking, both assuming there is something deficient about other ethnic groups who don't measure up to Asians, and also erasing the diversity within Asian-American communities, conflating many nationalities and cultures into one predictable and dehumanizing trope.

If representations were all unique and isolated phenomena, it would make it much harder to talk about them and their meanings, but actually the opposite is true: they are highly conventional and systematic, occurring in regular, predictable patterns. (Think of this as the *re* in representation.) Over many decades of Hollywood cinema, male characters have appeared on screen more often and have spoken more lines than female characters, and men are more likely to be the main characters or agents of the narrative. This is a long-standing trend across many genres. At one point in film history, there was a popular American genre called "women's pictures," which was a damning giveaway that the rest of the film industry was on some level making "men's pictures," whether they were gangster films, westerns, musicals, or comedies. The women's picture genre is a thing of the past, but the concept lives on in the often-derisive term "chick flick" and similar potentially ghettoizing categories. This privileging of one gender over another is a systematic feature of representation, and it often goes unnoticed because it has become so conventionalized.

Stereotypes stand out as a clear example of the patterning of representation, because they are only recognizable as stereotypes as products of repetition, the same characters appearing over and over again. The stereotyped Black and gay characters mentioned earlier were part of the dominant patterns of representation at particular times, woven into the fabric of American popular culture. If one movie marginalizes one gender or contains a demanding representation of a racial or ethnic group, that may be cause for judging it to be "negative" in some ways, though a critical analysis will probably want to probe deeper than a simple positive/negative judgment. But if it participates in a broader pattern or system, that takes us to another stratum of analysis, as it then constitutes just one episode within a longer story.

This systematic quality is what Stuart Hall (2013b, 222) calls a *regime of representation*. *Regime* signals that we are talking about power dynamics, about representation as a form of politics. A literal regime is a dominant political force, as in a monarchy or dictatorship, that maintains unequal power relations in a society. Modern Western societies are democratic in their government, but still highly unequal. Their dominant social forces include a combination of capitalism, white supremacy, and patriarchy. The popular and pervasive representations in a society may accord with or resist or question the relations of power that structure the social world. In the case of popular media in the 20th and 21st centuries in many democracies of the global north, the corporate entities such as media conglomerates responsible for producing and distributing much of the media content have an interest in maintaining the status quo of social relations, as these are with rare exceptions large-scale capitalist enterprises under the control of rich white men. The power to represent is in their hands, and the regimes of representation they help produce are very often working to construct a reality that suits their economic and political interests.

A regime of representation is a web of meaning. Within the regime we find character types and stereotypes, narrative tropes and familiar situations. Iconographies are part of this too: the symbolic imagery that we associate with a particular genre, like the spooky old houses and disfigured monsters of horror. In a regime of representation, any particular story being told by a media text might be seen as the retelling of a familiar tale, drawing on the conventions already established. The western genre, which spans many media (books, films, plays and musicals, television, video games, comics, music) is made up not just of the character archetypes of the reluctant gunslinger hero, the Native American "savages," the virgin and the whore, but of a system of values about "civilization" on the frontier, about the "Manifest Destiny" of expansionist American ideology.

To do a critical analysis of any one text's representations could mean sticking just to the one text, but most analyses will benefit a good deal from attention to the context of these intertextual references – all of the ways that one text, one representation, is the product of many texts and representations, an interweaving of discourses and meanings. One representation never stands alone, and the power of representation often comes from its repetition.

There is politics in any regime of representation by virtue of the regime functioning to reassert dominant power relations, the inequality of social groups and the othering of those with less power. The examples above of the histories of women, African-Americans, and LGBTQ+ persons in Hollywood films are all grappling with regimes of representation that privilege some identities over others. But there is also a politics of representation in another sense: representation is a site of contest, of struggle. Lest a regime of representation seem like a top-down affair in which power simply reproduces itself, representations are very often opportunities for a kind of useful and productive discord over symbolic value. We might see representation as a staging ground for dominant and oppositional meanings to face off against one another. Representation can sometimes seem to speak in one clear voice, the voice of power. But a representation can also come across more like a dialogue between interlocutors of different positions and identities, or like a chorus of voices, voices talking back to one another or joining together in harmony or perhaps a combination of harmony and dissonance.

Modes of Address

Representations like westerns often seem to be speaking to some people in particular, and they adopt a style appropriate to that audience. In their case, we can think of the audience as white Americans or Westerners, aligning with the values of the settlers or lawmen against Native Americans or outlaw antagonists. The fans of particular media are often communities of people who share a particular age, gender, sexuality, or ethnicity, and while these are not necessarily those addressed by the representation, there is often some important correspondence. We can see representations speaking to audiences especially clearly in advertising. A commercial for laundry detergent will be designed to appeal to those people who are responsible for the washing. Because domestic labor like laundry is highly gendered, especially in households with children, the consumer typically addressed by detergent advertisements is a woman, more specifically a wife and mother. Some ads explicitly call her out as "Mom." A whole genre of radio and television drama, soap opera, was named after its sponsorship by detergent brands. Soap commercials and soap operas are both watched by gender-diverse audiences, but the ads and the daytime soaps speak to, they *address*, some viewers in particular.

Commercials might make explicit their address by being written in the second person, e.g., "You won't want to miss out on this once-in-a-lifetime offer!" But all kinds of representation are addressed to particular audiences, or have an ideal audience implied by their representation. The British art critic and novelist John Berger wrote a book called *Ways of Seeing* (1972), which was also turned into a television series, about how one dominant tradition of Western art — Hall would certainly call it a *regime of representation* — is addressed to a male spectator. This is the tradition of nude portraiture, paintings of women displayed for the viewing and ownership of men. Berger makes a compelling case that 20th-century advertising imagery, while not necessarily picturing nude bodies, perpetuates this same regime of women being displayed as sexual objects. As Berger writes, a message conveyed by this imagery is that "men act, women appear" (47).

Around the same time as Berger, the feminist film critic Laura Mulvey (1975) wrote an extraordinarily influential essay on representation and spectatorship in Hollywood movies called "Visual Pleasure and Narrative Cinema." Mulvey similarly argued that many popular media representations, including Alfred Hitchcock films like *Vertigo*, represent women as objects to be fetishized by a male character, and by doing so address a male viewing subject who identifies with this figure in the text. This regime of representation is similar to the nudes in *Ways of Seeing*, as both examples seize on women's sexualized bodies displayed for the gaze of men. It is from Mulvey that we get "the male gaze," a critical term that implies a strong connection between representation, looking, identity, and power. Her argument is actually not just that these films are made to be watched by men, in the same sense that soap operas are made to be watched by women. Mulvey goes deeper, arguing that whatever the sex of their spectators, the films position the viewer as a male subject. According to this theory, you occupy a male viewing position based on the way the representation addresses you no matter what kind of body or gender identity you have.

This power of representation to address or position a subject is trickier to think about and write about than some issues of representation, but it can be an incredibly useful critical angle. When you think about whom the representation is speaking to, even just implicitly, you have another way into thinking about its politics. This quality of speaking to some audiences or of constructing an audience can be called the representation's *mode of address* (Morley 1999, 267–268).[1] Like any analysis of representation, identifying a mode of address will be interpretive and subjective. Some representations make their mode of address more explicit, like advertising or news that tells you, "here's what else you need to know today." But many representations implicitly construct an audience of a particular gender or race or age, sometimes in subtle ways that can easily go unnoticed, and perhaps without the creators' conscious intentions.

Hollywood has often made films for a broad, general, global audience, the largest possible audience, which is suggested by the term "mass media." But this audience is often presumed to be white, middle-class, heterosexual, and American. Audiences for popular films like *Gone with the Wind* (1939) might not have always recognized that they were addressed to white audiences or

that the representations position the spectator as a white subject by center-
ing white characters, offering them up as sympathetic figures, and treating
people of color as inferior, subservient by nature. Critical analysis of the
representation of identity in a film like Gone with the Wind can point out its
overt racism in portraying the antebellum South in a romanticized positive light, showing the contented devotion of enslaved African-Americans
to their masters, and representing the southern Confederacy as a noble "lost
cause." It can also point out the way the story is addressed to a white audience encouraged to sympathize with this representation and take on the
concerns of the white characters at the center of the story. This isn't a way of
studying the audience per se, as the method is looking at the representation
as a text, reading the audience in the text.

Thinking about a representation's mode of address is a good way of moving beyond simplistic critiques of negative representations, stereotypes, or
failures of realism. Even if a representation strives to be accurate and positive and avoid distortions, there may be political and ideological implications to its address to audiences that could show complexity or ambivalence,
or the privileging of some over others.

Voice and the Power to Represent

As a critical concept, mode of address lets us ask: "Whom does this speak to?"
And there is a politics of address, of the way a representation constructs and
speaks to its audience. We can also think about this same dynamic from the
other direction: "Who speaks?" These questions often have similar answers.
Power speaks to itself and of itself. It constructs an audience that understands its language, the language of the dominant order.

Another way of posing the question of "Who speaks?" is "Whose story
is being told?" In some forms of media, it may be possible to identify an
individual author who speaks, who tells their story. Most commercial media
is collaborative, though, and has more corporate than individual authorship, so "Who speaks?" is not so much about identifying the genius artist or
original vision as it is about looking at where the power to represent resides.

Take a movie like the 1992 version of Aladdin. It is set in Agrabah, a fictional kingdom with some resemblance to an Arabian port city of some past
historical era (actually to the way an Arabian city looks in an older movie
set in a far-off past, the 1940 film The Thief of Baghdad). Aladdin is adapted rather
loosely from The Thousand and One Nights, a classic of Arab literature, though the

tale of Aladdin and his lamp is not part of the text of original Arabic versions, having been added by a French translator in the 18th century based on oral storytelling (Horta 2019). The literary story of Aladdin, then, itself comes via multiple authors of both the East and West. The Disney film's characters are Middle Eastern in appearance and in dress. You might say of a typical work of fiction that "who speaks" is its writer, its author, but this tale is oral literature, and has been passed down from one storyteller to another. And this version of the story makes answering the question even more complicated.

The film had several screenwriters, multiple producers, a lyricist and composer for the songs, and a cast of voice actors and vocalists who literally speak and sing. The film also has a director and in cinema the director is often singled out as the one who is credited as the author. But this is a less useful way of attributing authorship when it comes to animation of this type, which involves the labor of hundreds of artists. And Disney films in general, and Disney's animated features in particular, tend to be associated more with their production studio than with individual filmmakers. Many viewers undoubtedly see *Aladdin* as a Disney film, i.e., they regard Disney as its author, the one who speaks.

Aladdin is a story about the Middle East drawing on Middle Eastern elements (the genie is a version of a *jinn*, a supernatural being from Islamic and pre-Islamic culture). But *Aladdin* is also the epitome of Hollywood style when it comes to storytelling, with its conventional hero (hunky southern California looks, American accent) and villain (archly exaggerated, British accent), its clearly articulated goal and deadline (gorgeous Princess Jasmine must be married off by a certain date, and obviously we want the lucky guy to be our hero), and its integration of spectacle (musical numbers) into its storytelling. The people who made the film are by and large white men, with some exceptions, and the Middle Eastern characters are voiced by white actors. The musical style comes from the American stage musical, from Broadway via Hollywood, and the film was adapted into a successful theatrical production on Broadway.

So, while *Aladdin* is a representation of the Arab world and Middle Eastern people, and tells a story about non-white characters, it is also a film made by white people for US (and global) audiences of mainly white people. It tells a familiar and fairly predictable (though entertaining!) kind of story rooted in American traditions of entertainment, with an enchanting, exotic setting that adds visual interest and mystery, a quality of fairy-tale fantasy that affords American audiences a sense of escape into a dreamlike space of storybook romance and adventure. In other words, it's a Disney movie telling a Disney kind of story.

How does this figure into a politics of representation, and what work is being done here?

In appropriating a Middle Eastern, Arabian story and setting, Disney treats ethnic difference as a style to be tried on as a kind of Halloween costume or party theme, while underneath this surface telling a story that centers a normative American identity. This flattens Arab identity and drains it of its own symbolic meanings and cultural values. The work here is to make cultural difference into an image that may be pleasing to the eye, offering enchanting exoticism and romance, but without recognizing the full humanity and history of the Other.

This kind of representation of a Middle Eastern Other participates in the discourse famously named *Orientalism* by the Palestinian-American literary critic Edward Said (2000). Orientalism is a European and American perspective on the East that fixates on its otherness and its difference, and that defines the imperialist West in relation to the colonized East. Said calls it a "system of knowledge about the Orient, an accepted grid for filtering through the Orient into Western consciousness," and sees it as a product of Euro-American assumptions of superiority over Bible lands, India, and other Eastern places (75). A whole host of Middle Eastern stereotypes in popular culture are products of this mode of representing "the mysterious Orient" (90).

The purpose of connecting a popular Disney movie with this discourse isn't to point out that *Aladdin* is a particularly negative representation (though one can find much to criticize in its constructions of race, religion, and gender), but to look at the implications for critical analysis of the questions "Who speaks?" and "Whose story is told?" In *Aladdin*, despite its surface appeal, Western people, white people, Hollywood people speak, and an American story is told. The film appropriates an image of the Near East without really trying to understand the other culture being used as decoration or give it a meaningful voice. The film contains many delights and pleasures, and the storytelling is engaging, dramatic, and romantic. The musical number sung by Robin Williams as the character of Genie, "Friend Like Me," is remarkably clever in its musical and lyrical composition, imaginative and hilarious in its fast-paced and fantastical animation. It shows off Williams' comical talents as well as any performance in his career as a comedian and actor. But there is nothing particularly Middle Eastern, Arab, or Muslim in this representation except that his role, as a genie, is adapted from Islamic folklore into a shapeshifting Hollywood showman and supporting character.

Looking at it this way gives us another path into analyzing representation that lets us go deeper than superficial judgments of good and bad, positive and negative, realistic or distorted. When it comes to stereotypes in particular, these matters of voice are crucial, especially considering the stereotyping of one group by another, when the objects of caricature have less power than the ones who have the authority and the means to speak, to tell their stories. But *Aladdin* is not so much a caricature or stereotype of Arabs as it is a decorative façade of Middle Eastern imagery to dress up a conventional American text.

Ultimately, then, matters of representation are also matters of production of media. When media industries are owned and run by rich white men and rich white men are consistently advantaged and privileged in these industries, as they are in the broader society, the power to represent will not be equitable and just. It follows that "representation matters" should be as much about *who represents* as *who is represented*.

All Your Faves Are Problematic

If there is one recurring theme throughout this discussion, it's that representation is more complicated than it may seem. It's more complicated than simple reflectionism, and it's more complicated than judging media to be either positive or negative. Critical media studies ultimately will help you recognize that representation is a form of power, and that analyzing representation effectively means analyzing relations of power, of the dominant forces in society and those that resist them.

Representations are complicated because they are so often contradictory, speaking with more than one voice or articulating competing ideas, rival values. There are often undercurrents of resistance within a representation that on the surface expresses dominant ideals. Or there are undercurrents of dominant meanings within seemingly progressive texts. Progress is a powerful metaphor for representation in history, but we should be wary of seeing this as a perpetual motion in one good direction. Gains in representation are often counterbalanced by missed opportunities or steps sideways or backward, and even thinking of something as a gain or loss is bound to be relative and subjective, and to be localized in a particular place and time.

The popular idea of representations being *problematic* is a good way of capturing this dynamic. Sometimes this is used in a way that merely condemns, as if it were possible to ensure problem-free representation. But calling something problematic should be the beginning, not the end, of the discussion. All kinds of representations are problematic in one way or another, and one task of media studies can be to poke around in problematic sites of representation to explore and expose the implications of a representation along all of the lines suggested here: what *work* is it doing, what *regime* is it part of, *who speaks* and *who is addressed*, and what meanings, what reality is being *constructed*? The answers to these questions will often reveal multiple discourses circulating through a representation rather than a single clear message.

This multiplicity is exciting. It's where the action is when it comes to representation. While it may be satisfying to celebrate the positive or condemn the negative, it can also be intellectually rewarding to probe at contradictions. This is what critical scholars often mean when we say we want to "problematize" something. It's not that we want to make problems where they didn't already exist. Rather, we want to bring to light the problems that were previously hard to see.

Consider *Hamilton*, the stage musical and multimedia phenomenon, spawning music recordings, a 2020 movie version, and many other offshoots. One of its famous lines comes at the very end: "Who lives? Who dies? Who tells your story?" This is really another way of phrasing one of the key ideas that animates this discussion of representation: that the power of representation is not just in the text itself, but in the hands of the storytellers and image-makers, the ones who make media.

The creator of *Hamilton* is Lin-Manuel Miranda, a Puerto Rican New Yorker, who wrote the "book" (the text of the show) as well as the music and lyrics to its songs, adapting a popular biography of Alexander Hamilton by Ron Chernow, a white author. The musical was designed to be cast with actors of color, including African-American performers who inhabit many of the central roles. *Hamilton* tells the story of the founding fathers and the birth of the United States as an independent nation, so these performers of color play parts based on historical figures who were white: not just Alexander Hamilton, played originally by Miranda, but also George Washington, Thomas Jefferson, James Madison, Aaron Burr, and Angelica Schuyler, all of whom are written to be played by Black performers. Indeed, there are Black actors in Hamilton who play characters who in the true story of American history were enslavers. The descendants of enslaved Africans play characters directly responsible for perpetuating the horrors of slavery, and for founding a republic in which the brutal institution of chattel slavery would be at the foundation of its economic, social, and political systems.

Hamilton is a musical in which the styles of performance include hip-hop, R&B, and pop music. Miranda has said he was inspired to tell the story of Alexander Hamilton, an immigrant outsider (introduced in the show's opening line as a "bastard orphan son of a whore"), as a hip-hop artist rising up from the bottom of the social ladder on his talent and ambition. He adopts Black and Latinx styles of music to recast the story of America as diverse and multicultural. He has also said that he was inspired to become a musical theater writer and creator by the limited roles open to Latinx performers, so that there would be more than just knife-wielding Puerto Rican gang members in West Side Story for him to play (Gross 2020). Hamilton is an excellent example of a text that makes opportunities for performers of color contrary to the regime of representation that cast them in stereotypical roles and limited their visibility.

It's not so easy to pick apart what might be progressive or not in this representation, what is "positive" or "negative." If you are in favor of equity, it's good to have many juicy roles for performers of color. It's good to see American history made radically inclusive and modern. But many criticisms of Hamilton have faulted it for celebrating enslavers, for glossing over the inequalities of the late 18th century and early 19th century period depicted, for failing to represent any Black historical figures, and for participating in what has been termed "Founders Chic" (Monteiro 2016). The characters depicted belonged to powerful social elites, whose revolution was motivated not only by the quest for freedom and liberty (for land-owning white men like themselves), but also for their own enrichment as members of the moneyed class in the British new world colonies whose exploitation of those of lesser power (Native Americans, enslaved Africans, women), allowed them to pursue prosperity in the Americas. Miranda's version of history tells a good story about the American Revolution, about Hamilton's rivalry with Burr, which leads to his ultimate demise, about his love affairs, and his role in George Washington's cabinet. It excludes much of the context of the revolution, of European colonization of the Americas, and of the stark inequalities of revolutionary-era society, and it emphasizes the heroism and genius of its founding father characters.

I take pleasure from Hamilton and admire the artistry of its songwriting, storytelling, stagecraft, and performances. I really like it. I also find it problematic as a representation because of the way it imbues the image of the founding fathers with a new quality of edgy, glamorous cool by imagining them as Black and Latino hip-hop and R&B singers. But this is exactly what makes the show so fascinating, the clashing associations of official American history and contemporary popular culture with all of its diversity and its influences of Americans who have been marginalized by official historical accounts.

One could merely find fault with a representation that unproblematically shows George Washington, who enslaved more than 100 human beings, as a hero. But there is another way of reading this that makes the American narrative of the revolution and the formation of a new nation into a mythology available to all Americans, encouraging everyone to identify with the ideals of the nation as a place where "all men [sic] are created equal," and the tyranny of the monarchy is rejected in favor of self-determination. This kind of see-saw movement of finding fault while also finding something (or much) to admire is what we mean when we look at representation as problematic. We see that the work of representation needs to be interpreted and struggled over, and the admirable and questionable elements weighed against one another. This isn't some obscure process reserved for special cases, either. It's a routine of critical analysis to look for the problematic in every representation, including so-called positive ones, and acknowledge that pleasure in media and culture need not be spoiled by critical questioning. It can actually be enhanced by thinking deeply and meaningfully about how representation works and how it connects media with the social world that it both reflects and constructs.

Discussion Questions

1. What is the difference between seeing a representation as a reflection of reality and seeing it as a construction of reality?

2. Search Common Sense Media for examples that score high or low on the "Positive Role Models and Representations" scale. Do you agree or disagree with their ratings, and why? What does this tell us about judging representations as positive or negative?

3. What is a regime of representation? Identify your own example along with several media texts that are part of this regime. What work of representation are they doing?

4. Choose a media text and identify its mode of address. Whom is it speaking to, and how can you tell? Is the mode of address related to the voice of the representation?

5. Choose an example of a media text you feel ambivalent about when it comes to representation, similar to the way the concluding section looks at *Hamilton*, and explore what you both admire and find problematic about it.

Note

1 Some theorists might prefer to regard subject positioning as in Mulvey (1975) and modes of address as in Morley (1999) to be distinct dynamics in representation. Subject positioning is more of an implicit operation of media to create a sense of self for the individual viewer, while mode of address is more of a matter of interpreting the style and tone of a media text to indicate what audience it speaks to. I have collapsed these into *mode of address* to capture the way that media representations can be understood as relating to a particular conception of an audience.

References

Barthes, Roland. 2012. *Mythologies*, translated by Richard Howard and Annette Lavers. New York: Hill and Wang.

Becker, Ron. 2006. *Gay TV and Straight America*. New Brunswick: Rutgers University Press.

Berger, John. 1972. *Ways of Seeing*. London: Penguin.

Bogle, Donald. 2006. *Toms, Coons, Mulattoes, Mammies, & Bucks: An Interpretive History of Blacks in American Films*, 4th ed. New York: Continuum.

Bond, Bradley J. 2015. "Gay On-Screen: The Relationship Between Exposure to Gay Characters on Television and Heterosexual Audiences' Endorsement of Gay Equality." *Journal of Broadcasting & Electronic Media* 59.4: 717–732.

Gates, Racquel J. 2018. *Double Negative: The Black Image and Popular Culture*. Durham, NC: Duke University Press.

Gray, Herman. 2004. *Watching Race: Television and the Struggle for Blackness*. Minneapolis: University of Minnesota Press.

Gross, Terry. 2020. "'The Past Isn't Done With Us,' Says 'Hamilton' Creator Lin-Manuel Miranda." *Fresh Air*, June 29, 2020. https://www.npr.org/2020/06/29/884592985/the-past-isn-t-done-with-us-says-hamilton-creator-lin-manuel-miranda

Hall, Stuart. 2013a. "The Work of Representation." In *Representation*, 2nd ed., edited by Stuart Hall, Jessica Evans and Sean Nixon, 1–59. London: SAGE.

Hall, Stuart. 2013b. "The Spectacle of the 'Other.'" In *Representation*, 2nd ed., edited by Stuart Hall, Jessica Evans and Sean Nixon, 215–287. London: SAGE.

Haskell, Molly. 1987. *From Reverence to Rape: The Treatment of Women in the Movies*, 2nd ed. Chicago: University of Chicago Press.

Hilton-Morrow, Wendy and Kathleen Battles. 2015. "Visibility." In *Sexual Identities and the Media: An Introduction*, 69–99. London: Taylor & Francis.

Horta, Paulo Lemos. 2019. "Introduction," *Aladdin: A New Translation*, translated by Yasmine Seale, vii–xxii. New York: Liverlight.

Mercer, Kobena. 1990. "Black Art and the Burden of Representation." *Third Text* 4.10: 61–78.

Monteiro, Lyra D. 2016. "Review Essay: Race-Conscious Casting and the Erasure of the Black Past in Lin-Manuel Miranda's *Hamilton*." *The Public Historian* 38.1: 89–98.

Morley, David. 1999. "The *Nationwide* Audience: Structure and Decoding." In David Morley and Charlotte Brunsdon, *The* Nationwide *Television Studies*, 111–291. London: Routledge.

Mulvey, Laura. 1975. "Visual Pleasure and Narrative Cinema." *Screen* 16.3: 6–18.

Myerson, Allen R. 1997. "Southern Baptist Convention Calls for Boycott of Disney." *New York Times*, June 19, 1997: A18.

Nasaw, David. 1999. *Going Out: The Rise and Fall of Public Amusements.* Cambridge, MA: Harvard University Press.

Russo, Vito. 1987. *The Celluloid Closet: Homosexuality in the Movies*, rev. ed. New York: Harper & Row.

Said, Edward. 2000. *The Edward Said Reader*, edited by Moustafa Bayoumi and Andrew Rubin. New York: Vintage.

Shohat, Ella and Robert Stam. 2013. "Stereotype, Realism, and the Struggle of Representation." In *The Media Studies Reader*, edited by Laurie Ouellette, 205–226. New York: Routledge.

Tuchman, Gaye. 1978. "Introduction: The Symbolic Annihilation of Women by the Mass Media." In *Hearth and Home: Images of Women in the Mass Media*, edited by Gaye Tuchman, Arlene Kaplan Daniels, and James Benét, 3–38. New York: Oxford University Press.

Warner, Kristen J. 2015. "They Gon' Think You Loud Regardless: Ratchetness, Reality Television, and Black Womanhood." *Camera* Obscura 88: 129–153. doi: 10.1215/02705346–2885475.

Warner, Kristen J. 2017. "In the Time of Plastic Representation." *Film Quarterly* (Winter): 32–37, https://filmquarterly.org/2017/12/04/in-the-time-of-plastic-representation/

6

IDEOLOGY

Ideology is among the thorniest concepts in media studies and, more broadly, in the humanities and social sciences. It doesn't help that there are several ways of understanding ideology and that in different fields, and among different sub-groups within a particular field, there may be divergent traditions of thinking about it. Any attempt to define and unpack this essential term should start with some affirmations of humility and good faith. We will do our best to grapple with a topic that many – not just newcomers to media studies but graduate students and mature scholars – find hard to really figure out. Even if we might not arrive at a crystal clear understanding, we will shed some light and make some progress.

Whatever else we layer on top of an initial definition, an ideology is a system of ideas that many members of a society share. These ideas consist of beliefs, opinions, values, and whole ways of seeing and talking about the world and one's place in it. The ideas that make up an ideology have many sources, but a starting assumption for us will be that media are critical to their production and circulation in modern societies. Ideology is found in every kind of media, and media serve as a key vector for ideologies, alongside other institutions like schools, churches, and workplaces.

An ideology is more specifically a set of *political* ideas, and political is another term with several senses. It can be used broadly to include anything related to power, and not just the politics of political parties or of a political spectrum from right to left. This is where many media scholars part ways from some others who teach and research about ideology. In some

DOI: 10.4324/9781003007708-6

areas of social science and in mainstream journalism, ideology amounts to being liberal or conservative, or locating your politics within a schema that includes identities like libertarian, conservative, moderate, liberal, and socialist. Many other expressions could be added to this catalog of political terms (e.g., progressive, populist, authoritarian, centrist, reactionary, radical). The point is that some uses of ideology, or of political ideology, are specifically concerned with these ways of cataloging and categorizing identities. Groups defined by such political ideologies are constituted by a set of shared beliefs and priorities. While this particular sense of ideology being political is not the one we are talking about in critical media studies, let's not cast it aside entirely. There is something valuable in the idea that political identity is a matter of ideology, and that groups of people (or more specifically of citizens) organize themselves according to their political affinities.

As critical media scholars use the term, ideology is political in a different way that does not line up too neatly with a discourse of conservative versus liberal parties and policies. The political here is found in the structure of the whole society and the struggles between those with more or less power within it. It is the politics of global capitalism, of racial injustice, of inequality and oppression along the lines of gender and sexuality, disability, religion, and nationality. This politics is the terrain of all of these forms of power differentials intersecting with one another. To the extent that it is concerned with political parties, or with identities like liberal and conservative, this concept of politics sees them as serving either to advance or to contest broader and deeper workings of power in society, such as the power of multinational corporations and billionaire tycoons.

Ideology in this conception refers to systems of ideas that serve to justify and perpetuate the prevailing power relations in a society. These ideas are expressed in narratives, images, and other forms of culture. Ideas that help maintain and entrench the status quo of an unjust and unequal society are ideological to the extent that they function as obstacles to making progress on projects that would make the society better for the largest number of people. These ideas do the work of politics by supporting some groups with greater power at the expense of others with less (Becker 2018; Fiske 2011, 156–179; Storey 2009, 1–5; Williams 1983, 153–157).

For example, the ideal of the American Dream promises that anyone can succeed by working hard and pursuing their passions with great dedication. It is part of the conception of the United States as a meritocratic society in which your status at birth is not supposed to foretell your status for life. This ideal promotes values like individual determination and perseverance, and practices like entrepreneurship, and is supported by assumptions of America providing an equal playing field for all. A myriad of media texts, both fictional and nonfictional, have circulated these ideas about America being the land of opportunity where it's always possible to make a better life if, as the saying goes, you are willing to just "pull yourself up by your bootstraps."

The American Dream is ideological to the extent that it promises something that America cannot deliver, owing to the profound inequalities that structure the society of the United States. As the comedian George Carlin joked, "It's called the American Dream 'cause you have to be asleep to believe it." Impediments to class mobility in the US include historical racial discrimination that has produced a vast wealth gap between Black and other Americans, mass incarceration, and the school-to-prison pipeline. They include numerous practices that disadvantage individuals from lower socioeconomic status families, such as public school funding being tied to local property tax revenue and career opportunities being available only to those able to work at unpaid internships. Many barriers to the American Dream are insurmountable for many Americans. For them, believing in the American Dream means buying into a false narrative of how things work. This is an ideology that stands in the way of changing the situation for the better: why overturn a system that permits anyone to succeed if they just apply themselves? Ideology like this functions as propaganda for leaving things the way they are.

To call the American Dream an ideology is rather different from calling conservative or liberal an ideology. For one thing, both liberals and conservatives might promote the American Dream, so this sense of ideology as political ideas strikes a different note. For another, both liberals and conservatives might have no issue with their political identity being described as a political ideology. That just sounds descriptive. But to call it an ideology is to apply a negative connotation to the American Dream. This way of thinking tears down something that many Americans consider to be an article of faith or, perhaps, a sacred cow. When calling something an ideology or saying it's ideological, we often mean to criticize harshly, to cry foul and call out injustice. Criticizing the American Dream can sound like criticizing America, and that may be accurate. But Americans who are proud of their national identity can feel that this kind of argument cuts to the core of their sense of self. Analyzing ideology in the media often works this way: the purpose is to identify the ways that the media works to sustain some kinds of advantage or disadvantage while appearing to be just the way things are, and it makes it harder to change these things that have the appeal of being so seemingly ordinary or inevitable. Ideology is not just about ideas, then, but specifically ideas with a kind of oppressive power.

During the LGBTQ+ community's struggle for marriage equality, such powerful ideas were an obstacle to overcome. The assumption that marriage could only be between one man and one woman was deeply ideological in the sense that it was reinforced over and over again in so many kinds of storytelling and imagery, and was part of a wider set of ideas about normative gender roles and sexuality with deep historical and cultural roots. These ideas were harmful to LGBTQ+ communities. The opponents of marriage equality had on their side a kind of common sense notion of the way things are. "Of course, two women or two men can't get married," they might have thought or said. The location of ideology was in that phrase "of course," the taken-for-granted assumption that had so rarely been questioned, and which served to maintain the order of things.[1] Marriage equality under the law was achieved by challenging and undermining this ideology.

To circle back to definitions, then, an ideology is a system of ideas that is often taken for granted or seen as common sense that maintains unequal power relations among groups in society. Sometimes these ideas are called the "dominant ideology" or they are referenced as "hegemonic" (i.e., dominant). They often work by making themselves seem invisible or part of the natural order when in actuality they are just one way of seeing things. They circulate broadly in all kinds of media, including news and entertainment, non-fiction and fiction.

A further layer must be added to this definition that gets us even deeper into politics. In media studies, our concept of ideology comes via Marxism, from a critical tradition of social theory with a leftist political orientation. This tradition is concerned with modern capitalism and the social order that has been built upon global free-market economics. In Karl Marx and Friedrich Engels's concept of ideology, economics functions to condition a society's culture. This is the notion of the economic "base" giving rise to a "superstructure" built upon it. For Marx and Engels, the "bourgeois ideology" (the ideology of the ruling class in 19th century Europe) that supported the exploitation of labor by capital was a system of ideas that ultimately was the product of the economic system of capitalism.

Much debate has been waged over how much direct causality there is between the economic base and the ideology that is supposed to be a product of it, and which helps it to sustain itself. In Marx and Engels's famous formulation, "The ideas of the ruling classes are in every epoch the ruling ideas, i.e., the class which is the ruling material force is at the same time its ruling intellectual force" (quoted in Hall 1982, 84). Ideology, as critical media studies uses this concept, is working with and through this idea that ideology is an instrument of the ruling classes, or the dominant groups in a society.

This isn't to say that one must become a Marxist to use this tool in our toolkit. Hardly. For one thing, media studies sees race and ethnicity, gender and sexuality, and other identity categories to be no less crucial than capitalism and class in understanding ideology. For another, it should be possible to find a concept useful without buying into every assumption and investment of a particularly influential formulation of it. Critical scholars often reject the Marxist notion that ideology is simply determined by economics, and see a more complicated picture. Still, there is no question that this conception of ideology is political in a way that goes deeper than seeing politics in many places other than the workings of the state. Analyzing ideology can itself be seen as a form of political engagement from the left. It constitutes a criticism of the dominant social order from a position of opposition to its basic workings. When we regard media as an instrument of this dominance, as a form of political persuasion to perpetuate current configurations of power, we cannot imagine that we stand in a place outside of politics (as some social scientists or journalists might). So ideology is political in multiple senses, including one that acknowledges the critic as a participant in politics and not a mere observer of it.

Ideology Critique

Ideology, the critical term, can be regarded as the container for a theory of the relationship between media and society. The theory posits that society is structured in certain unequal and unjust ways, and culture (media) helps maintain those pernicious structures. When we analyze media texts to understand how they function as ideology, we can call it *ideology critique*, which is the practice of studying ideology in media. Criticism, as a more general term, often has a somewhat neutral meaning, and sometimes *critique* is used as its synonym. Criticism can be admiring or it can find fault, or it can be concerned with exploring meanings without engaging in praise or condemnation. Critique, and especially ideology critique, is different from regular criticism: ideology critique implies some negative judgment. Arguing that instances of media do the work of maintaining injustice cannot be neutral or admiring. While it does not necessarily see media as beyond redemption or as nothing but ideology, this mode of analysis is premised on discovering how media functions ideologically and intervening by calling it out.

Ideology critique also involves a process of peeling back the surfaces of things to reveal underlying political meanings. If ideology is a kind of false front, a practice of deception or distortion, critique unmasks or clarifies. The critique aims to show that the media text had a deeper purpose of misdirection and obfuscation. A Hollywood action-adventure movie like *Raiders of the Lost Ark* (1981) appears to have an admirable hero who fights for the side of the angels and ultimately prevails at saving the day. Sounds good. But an ideology critique can point out the ways the story centers the virile American white man as a godly savior. It can show how it uses racial and ethnic others as punch lines with amusing accents, scheming back-stabbers, or expendable sub-human enemies. How it privileges reckless individual heroism over collective action, and sexually objectifies its rare female characters, however much agency it grants them. These characteristics make the film into an ideological text that serves to justify dominant ideas about race, gender, and who really counts as American. None of these meanings are necessarily to be found on the pleasing surface of the text without being oriented toward looking for them. But once discovered via critique, they transform the text from an innocently enjoyable and diverting movie into something more problematic. Ideology critique strips away these pleasures in its work of demystification.

(By the way, I still like *Raiders* despite my critique of it, and I usually find it possible to think about media texts in multiple contradictory ways. I admire the film's humor and its thrilling action set-pieces, the way it evokes its historical era, and the performances by several actors in the film. Harrison Ford is in his prime and his scenes with Karen Allen sparkle with tension. The uplifting score by John Williams is emotionally engaging. I probably also get some pleasure from its sexism and Eurocentrism, and don't see myself as ever being free of these ideologies, or able to extricate myself entirely from their influence. I also have a fond memory of seeing it with my dad when I was nine years old, before I knew what an *ideology critique* was, and I like to tap into that childhood feeling of being astonished by what a movie can do to you. But I also cannot watch it now the way I did then.)

If ideology critique works by demystifying media, this implies something insidious about how media contain meanings. There is an implicit model of audience psychology hiding in this process: an idea about how media convey ideas and information about the world and how audiences receive these ideas and information. The Marxist concept of "false consciousness" captures this dynamic. According to Marx and Engels, ideology was a form of deception keeping the proletarian class from rising up and seizing control of political and economic power from the ruling class. Marx (1977) argued: "It is not the consciousness of men that determines their existence, but their social existence that determines their consciousness." That is to say, the exploitation of one class by another has produced this way of thinking and seeing. Ideology is a means of promoting the ideas that serve the dominant class's interest at the expense of the workers, inculcating in them ideas that run contrary to their interests. The Marxist agenda would be to replace bourgeois ideology and false consciousness with a revolutionary consciousness.

Many critics of this theory have pushed back by asserting that people are not so much duped and deceived by ideology as they are persuaded to consent to participating in the prevailing system of power relations, and that this is an ongoing process. This way of thinking about social differences shows the people in subordinated groups to have more agency in buying into hegemonic "common sense." But however we see the agency and the mindset of the dominated class, the critique of ideology often assumes that meanings are to be discovered through analysis rather than found on the surface level. Critique is a form of interpretation that draws connections between an example of media (e.g., a text) and a broader set of social forces, such as patriarchy and white supremacy. It discovers the meanings that support those forces in texts that might have been made without any conscious intention to be ideological. Because ideology is seen as an undercurrent in our habits of thought, it can be running constantly as a system of meanings that we might not consciously recognize but still buy into. Seeing it requires the work of active interpretation.

This kind of work can operate on the level of language, as when particular choices of words are serving to maintain the dominant power relations. Imagine a news report describing an episode of police violence as an "officer-involved shooting," or reporting that "an individual was struck by a gunshot during a routine traffic stop and died at the scene." These ways of speaking differ from a statement like: "a police officer shot and killed an unarmed Black man." Yet all three versions of this report might describe the same events in a way that is literally true. The ideological power of "officer-involved shooting" might not all by itself deceive anyone into thinking the police are blameless during these episodes, or that the officer was merely involved rather than responsible for an act of killing. But they advance one narrative about racial justice that is in competition with another, and contribute to the sense of police violence being legitimate. "Officer-involved" is also the language used by police spokespeople representing the agents of the state, and when news reports adopt their ways of speaking, their vocabulary, they are aligning with one side of an unequal power dynamic between the state and some communities of citizens. Critique of the rhetoric of "officer-involved shootings" unmasks the interests that underlie this kind of talk.

As in the case of crime reporting, this kind of media critique can be particularly powerful when applied to forms and genres that are presented in a way that seems neutral or objective, or as a realistic account of events. Nonfiction media like journalism adopts conventions of presenting a discourse that appears to be independent of personal interests or biases, free from any political agenda. But fiction often creates a similar appeal. The visual and storytelling style of much film and television is often taken to be transparent and invisible, and helps you focus your attention on the dramatic quality of the storytelling (the characters and situations), as if you are peering in on an existing reality. Film theorists have called this a "diegetic effect," referring to the sense of a narrative world that exists for you, as a spectator, to observe (Burch 1982). Or they have posited a cinematic "impression of reality" that produces a fictional representation that the spectator almost believes to be real (Metz 1974, 4), or an ideological effect of "illusionism" that deceives the spectator into believing that the image on the screen is a true picture of life (Kuhn 1982, 151–153). If media, whether fictional or nonfictional, present themselves as realistic, as "the way things are," media scholars can show that things are not necessarily this way, and that a particular set of interests and agendas go into making any kind of representation of reality.

Ideology critique can address many different kinds of objects for its analysis of how media supports dominant power relations. The typical examples would be texts: movies, television shows, video games, music, news, and other publications, etc. But this can be an expansive method of analysis of all kinds of cultural phenomena and expressions. "Text" is a capacious category that can include anything subjected to interpretation. Celebrities are texts that we can critique, as are technologies like smartphones and social media algorithms. One could do ideology critique of maps (conveying the perspective of Europe being the center of the world), pickup trucks (expressing brawny masculine individualism), and athleisure apparel (signifying productive work on the self even when worn just to drop off a kid at kindergarten and pick up some coffee). The targets of critique could include the objects themselves but also their representations and uses in advertising and other discourses.

Critique can also take as its objects genres or forms of media, or institutions within which media are produced. Indiana Jones is one character in one film franchise, but the action-adventure film of which *Raiders* is just one example is also ripe for ideological critique as a genre premised on conceptions of gender, race, and nationality in relation to heroism and villainy, which have been popular at particular moments in certain places and times (Jeffords 1994). Critique of "officer-involved" rhetoric seizes on one figure of speech, but crime and criminal justice reporting more broadly can be analyzed for the way it constructs perpetrators and victims in relation to official institutions of the courts and the police, often in ways that are highly racialized and gendered (Stabile 2006).

Media companies often address their products not to the largest possible audiences, but to narrower segments broken down by demographic characteristics like age and income. By seeking to attract more affluent readers and viewers, media institutions can privilege viewpoints aligned with higher socioeconomic status identities (the rich and upper-middle-class), while giving short shrift to working-class perspectives. News organizations regularly report on investment data like the daily changes in stock, currency, and commodity prices, matters of interest to only a narrow segment of the population that invests in securities and tracks global markets. By treating the stock indices' daily fluctuations as newsworthy, media organizations set priorities that align with the unequal power that the investor class enjoys. The very fact of "Business" being a major area of journalistic activity speaks to this alignment. It seems normal that newspapers have a Business section, which has been standard since the 1960s. As Noam Chomsky and others have pointed out, newspapers and other outlets have no Labor section focused on workers and the issues that matter to them (Chomsky 2011; Dugger 2000, 45). The ideological orientation of news organizations follows their market orientation as companies that benefit from making a product for people who would like to read about business from the perspective of managers and investors.

Unlike some textual analysis, then, ideology critique is always concerned with texts in contexts, and in particular social, cultural, and political contexts. By itself, a text is never adequate evidence for an ideology critique. The whole point is to make connections between individual instances of cultural expression and broader forces. One can only do this kind of critique with a notion of how power operates in a society, of how structures and systems maintain unequal relations among groups of people and stand in the way of social justice. To critique the American Dream requires not just a sense of how ideas about individual success and opportunity have circulated, but also how American society has actually functioned and how political and economic forces have kept the "Dream" from being realized for so many Americans. Ideology critique is always moving back and forth between media and the social world in which it is made, and in which it circulates.

Ideological Formations

When making connections between media and ideology, we are never starting from scratch. Every instance of media may be unique in its expression of particular beliefs and values, but ideologically, every instance will tap into broader discourses, to systems of meaning that relate to some elements of the unequal social structure. When thinking about ideological expressions about gender and sexuality, we are likely to understand particular examples in relation to *patriarchy*, an enduring structure of male dominance. When thinking about similar expressions of race and ethnicity, the structure in question is *white supremacy*, a doctrine that goes back hundreds of years to justify enslavement, violence, and discrimination. For Marxist critiques, *capitalism* is the structure, and can be seen as the deepest of the ideological forces as it works alongside and through the others. We can call any of these expressions of ideology as they occur across myriad sites and forms of media and culture *ideological formations*, and could name many others, including varieties of nationalism and religious fundamentalism. An ideological formation links particular forms of economic, political, legal, and social inequality with systems of ideas that perpetuate them. While some of these examples seem practically timeless, an ideological formation can work more specifically to capture the dynamics of power and the circulation of ideas in a particular era, a place and time.

A key example in media scholarship of the early decades of the 21st century has been *neoliberalism*, a concept that links economic and political developments with cultural values and norms (Brown 2003; Harvey 2005; Meyers 2019). Neoliberalism must be distinguished from *liberalism* as the kind of political ideology that sits opposite the spectrum from *conservatism*. Liberal economics is its own concept, but for almost a century the primary usage of *liberal* in many circles has been aligned with the policies of supposedly left-of-center political parties like the Democrats in the United States and the Liberals in Canada. Neoliberalism draws on the earlier sense of liberal as a philosophy favoring unconstrained markets and individual choice. That liberalism is the doctrine associated with 18th and 19th century economists Adam Smith and John Stuart Mill that is modified to become *neoliberal*. This helps identify it as a right-wing movement in contrast with the left-of-center connotations of *liberal* since the mid-20th century (McLean 2017, 51). Advanced or resurgent economic liberalism is a reaction against the growth of "welfare state" policies since the era of US President Franklin D. Roosevelt. These policies, such as payments to the aged and unemployed, apply the government's taxation authority to protect citizens from hunger and poverty and extend the purpose of government to include promoting the well-being of citizens.

To be neoliberal is to reject government programs and corporate regulations to make people's lives better and revive putting faith in markets to produce the best outcomes for all without the interference of the state. This is the key liberal economic principle of *laissez faire*: leaving things alone (though neoliberals might still favor state regulations that benefit corporate interests). To critics of contemporary capitalism, neoliberal is the term used to characterize the modern expression of market logic's supremacy. It names a broad movement, which has been advanced in many Western democracies by leaders from parties at different points on the political spectrum, to weaken or disassemble the policies and institutions of the state that provided a social safety net, public goods like education, and common resources like public media and public transit for the betterment of the whole society. Neoliberalism is more specific than simply capitalism, but it also names something broader. It merges a political and economic development with a set of principles and values that suffuse modern culture by normalizing a sense of individual responsibility and requisite self-care rather than a collectivist or communitarian spirit. It advances the causes of privatization of wealth and of public institutions in the name of "freedom" and "choice" and replaces an ethos of communities taking responsibility for their members with the mantra of self-empowerment. It is probably the most omnipresent and dominant ideological formation of our time.

Critics of neoliberalism see these forms of ideological discourse — these positive-sounding values like *freedom, choice, responsibility,* and *empowerment* — to be a cover for a deeper, hidden agenda of maximizing the private fortunes of the upper class who prefer not to surrender their wealth to confiscatory taxation. These discourses that place the onus on citizens to take responsibility for their own welfare tap into a long-standing Western culture of individualism. But such patterns of thought obscure the fact that many forms of critically needed change require collective action and the commitment of institutions that have the wherewithal to solve our problems. A neoliberal approach to fighting climate change might be to take personal responsibility for reducing your own carbon footprint, perhaps by carrying canvas grocery bags or driving an electric car. This kind of private solution to a grave public problem of a vast scale cannot be adequate without being paired with significant state action to curb carbon emissions by regulating corporations so that they will cease extracting and burning fossil fuels. But the ideology of neoliberalism promotes the primacy of individual actions alongside its agenda of corporate deregulation, effectively distracting us from the reality that our personal choices are inadequate or counterproductive. Being led to think you have addressed a problem that continues to fester and worsen is a great example of ideology at work.

One productive area of media research on neoliberal ideology has focused on the genre of reality television, which became particularly prominent in the first decade of the 21st century (McMurria 2008; Ouellette and Hay 2008; Ouellette 2016). Laurie Ouellette and James Hay (2008, 3–4) argue that reality TV programming is a form of education for the citizens of contemporary democratic societies in the values of neoliberalism, "a resource for acquiring and applying practical knowledge and skills" (14). The outcome of this entertaining televisual curriculum is to learn private self-actualization as the path to a good life. Across a variety of program formats, viewers are shown individuals in competition to succeed at work and in romantic relationships. Audiences are tutored in dressing with style, getting fit and looking attractive, caring for children, uncluttering and redecorating the home, and feeding themselves and their families. In all of these instances and many others, individuals are represented as the ones responsible for governing and asserting authority over themselves. Ouellette and Hay argue that "TV operates as a new form of neoliberalized social service, social welfare, and social management" (18). In other words, a neoliberal society trains citizens, using media, including reality television, to work on individual care and self-reliance. The model of a citizen in this world is an entrepreneur of the self, applying market logic to their own lives without the support of welfare state programs.

Among the central examples for Ouellette and Hay (2008, 99–133) is the makeover show, a subgenre of reality TV in which individuals are given a fresh look in order to succeed in their relationships and careers. These programs include *What Not to Wear*, *Extreme Makeover*, and *Queer Eye for the Straight Guy*, all of which build each episode around one person whose appearance is the problem to be solved by the closing credits. This is accomplished by getting a new hairstyle, a wardrobe refresh, cosmetic surgery, or some combination of these. Ouellette and Hay link the TV makeover to neoliberal concepts of the self, drawing a connection to the expectation under neoliberalism that paid work will be flexible and entrepreneurial, and that the individual is responsible for constant private labor in service of success getting and keeping a job. Self-fashioning, in the sense of working on one's appearance and abilities to optimize oneself, is promoted in neoliberal ideology as essential to economic security. Each made-over individual becomes a branded self, a commodity for exchange on the "unstable, youth-oriented labor market" (106). In this ideological environment, appearance is valued especially highly for women, as well as men in feminized spheres of work. Stylishness and looking young are a kind of currency. Essentially, the argument goes, these television programs train workers to participate in a flexible economy as individuals maximizing their personal benefit through self-fashioning, though ultimately the workers in such a system gain much less than their bosses and corporate overlords.

This same mode of self-branding has become absolutely essential to the social media marketing economy via passionate users who aim to leverage their online exposure for career success. Self-fashioning, entrepreneurship of the self, and constant work to appear attractive and youthful, are central to the construction of social media creators as workers with value for the digital economy, including Instagram influencers (Von Driel and Dumitrica 2021, 4). But here we can move from looking at the expressions of an ideological formation in texts like TV episodes to thinking about the production of media following neoliberal ideological imperatives that shape the content of online user-generated streams, feeds, and pages. As Brooke Erin Duffy (2017) shows in her study of fashion and lifestyle bloggers and other entrepreneurial online content producers, a "seductive" neoliberal "ideology of aspirational labor" (11) shapes a work environment in which passion and doing what you love are prized despite low rates of financial return on investments of emotions, time, and money. Aspirational labor is work undertaken in the present in hopes of reward in the future, mixing the joy of creativity with the desire of eventually seeing the work "pay off," which, unfortunately, it often does not (4–10).

One might view creators simply as some of the world's billions of social media users, but looking at their role as workers helps us understand their exploitation by an economic system that tilts the playing field against them. While toiling at self-branding, and at establishing relationships with commercial brands and social media audiences, these flexible online workers are taking on the risks and responsibilities that might otherwise be shouldered by employers or the state (e.g., providing health care, a pension, and other benefits) while enduring the insecurity of precarious self-employment. This variety of media work can thus be seen as an example of exploitation under the neoliberal "gig economy." If audiences for this content internalize the values of the entrepreneurial influencer or creator who trains them in fashioning an appealing self and blending passion and work, they are learning the lessons of an ideological formation that shapes the production of media no less than its content.

Identities and Ideologies

All of the ideological formations we have encountered have some things in common. They are all concerned with the way social structures are supported by forms of knowledge and cultural expression. For neoliberalism, the terrain is economic as well as political and cultural, but at the heart of the discussion is a distinction between different class positions: a dominant elite of ultra-rich and the ordinary working people who function under the flexible conditions of this way of imagining a society.

Two fundamental structures in modern Western societies are patriarchy and white supremacy. For the ideologies that support these unjust systems, matters of identity are a central issue. Ideological notions of gender or race are those that support unequal relations of power that oppress groups defined by their social identities, such as girls and women and Black, brown, and indigenous people. These are the kinds of differences we call "structural inequality." There are individual sexist and racist people who discriminate on the basis of identity, but as ideological formations, patriarchy and white supremacy operate at a different level from individual sexists and racists. These ideological formations make connections between material conditions – inequalities in wealth, income, and other forms of social power – and identity concepts, such as socially and culturally defined roles and characteristics. Ideological notions about identities, such as representations that naturalize or universalize racial or ethnic hierarchies, are present in many kinds of media and popular culture. Ideology critique can find very productive targets in these forms of media.

The identities in question here are to be understood as socially and culturally constructed. This isn't to say that your identity has nothing to do with you and your unique self. Rather, we all have social identities – our age, race or ethnicity, gender and sexuality, nationality, etc. – that are defined by social forces external to ourselves. These are group identities, widely shared with many others. Often the concepts that circulate about these identities seem like just the facts of life, but informed critique reveals them to be no such thing. For instance, race is not a biological or scientific category, though many people seem to believe it is. Their beliefs are ideological, and are products of many sources, including media representations and discourses.

Many media critiques directly address identity categories, especially those of race/ethnicity and gender/sexuality. Black and/or feminist scholars like bell hooks (1995) and Tania Modleski (2008) offer examples in studies often centered on the image of the Black or female body, on representations of otherness and the construction of difference. This could include ideas about the marginalization or invisibility of identities and their representation in stereotyped and demeaning ways. But ideology critique that focuses on identity can also productively consider the dominant constructions of gender or race more broadly and include whiteness and masculinity within these concerns.

This latter approach can seize on the term "hegemonic," a concept that often implies ideology critique. "Hegemony" is sometimes a synonym for "domination," so "hegemonic masculinity" can simply mean "dominant masculinity." But the term also carries some connotations and baggage from the theorizing of ideology among critics of the Marxist tradition. In the work of the 20th-century Italian communist Antonio Gramsci, hegemony means something more specific than dominance (Jones 2006, 41–56). It is part of a theory regarded as an alternative conception of ideology that replaces the "false consciousness" of Marx and Engels with a notion of different groups within society (Gramsci calls them "blocs") struggling over asserting their dominance on the terrain of ideas (Hall 1996, 40–44). Some of these groups are more powerful and some are less powerful, but the outcome of these negotiations is an ideological "common sense" that is produced with the consent of subordinated groups. Hegemony is the name for this dynamic wherein a bloc secures its dominance, as Stuart Hall (1982, 85) interprets Gramsci, "not by ideological compulsion, but by cultural leadership."

(An example in contemporary American discourse would be the way that a version of American nationalism intolerant of criticism of the US in its international affairs is asserted as common sense by a hegemonic bloc that includes people of diverse class positions: rich, middle-class, and working-class alike. The Gramsci/Hall position on this would be not that the working-class are deceived into fervent, flag-waving patriotism, but that they participate in it as an outcome of cultural leadership that speaks to them as common sense. This is how nationalism functions as a hegemonic discourse.)

So to speak of "hegemonic masculinity" as an identity suggests a dominant construction of gender, one particular type of masculinity that has more power than other gender identities. In the words of R.W. Connell and James W. Messerschmidt (2005), key theorists of the concept, hegemonic masculinity is a culture's dominant form of masculinity, which "require[s] all other men to position themselves in relation to it" and brings the benefits of patriarchy to all men, whether or not they conform to the hegemonic version of their gender. This dominant form of masculinity "ideologically legitimate[s] the global subordination of women to men" (832). Such a patriarchal structure can be seen as hegemonic in the way that dominance is "achieved through culture, institutions, and persuasion" and is "open to historical change" (832–833). Connell and Messerschmidt emphasize that there are many masculinities, that they are different in diverse historical and geographical settings, and they are open to being challenged under changing conditions. Such a concept of a dominant type of gender identity is highly productive for media scholars looking at the ways that media function as a persuasive form of culture.

As expressions of masculinity, sports and video games are two areas of media that overlap and have some common functions of maintaining gendered spaces and identities. E-sports, professionalized competitive digital gaming, has been studied as a highly gendered practice mixing expressions of an idealized "athletic masculinity" of sports with an ascendent "geek masculinity" typical of tech and gaming circles (Taylor 2012, 110–118). Looking at more than one version of masculinity is a way of capturing how ideological formations change and adapt, with "geek" identity having moved from a more subordinated status in an earlier moment to a more ascendant role within wider constructions of gender in relation to digital technology (112–114). As with the culture of video games more generally (Taylor and Voorhees 2018), e-sports can function as a male-dominated, patriarchal preserve while also allowing for multiple, complex masculinities to be negotiated within its spaces (Taylor 2012, 115–118).

A final critical point about ideology and identity concerns the interaction and layering of these different concepts and categories. An individual subject has many identities, and does not cease to occupy one when identifying as another. Black women are both racialized and feminized, not one or the other. The name for the way identities are multiple rather than discretely separated is *intersectionality* (Crenshaw 1991). An intersectional concept of identity understands that the operations of hegemonic masculinity and other hegemonic formations (whiteness, heterosexism, ableism, nationalism) are all acting at once, and that identity has multiple dimensions. It also recognizes that movements for social justice, such as feminist and antiracist organizing, often essentialize one identity (e.g., gender for feminism, race for antiracism) in ways that privilege certain identities (e.g., white women, Black men).

A revealing example of intersectional critique comes in Kimberlé Crenshaw's (1991) original formulation of the concept. The rap group 2 Live Crew was the subject of a notorious obscenity case in 1990. The group's lyrics on their 1989 album *As Nasty As They Wanna Be* had recently been found obscene by a judge in US federal court, and the group's members were arrested and charged with obscenity after a performance in Florida. (They were later acquitted, and the federal ruling was overturned.) The music is explicitly sexual, crude, and boastful, with women represented as participants in violent sexual acts (described using verbs like "busted," "cracked," and "rammed" and epithets including "cunt," "bitch," and "ho").

This episode was the occasion for a national media controversy and moral panic over sexual and violent imagery in rap music (Harvey 2021, 116–128). Ideologically, the case makes for a perfect illustration of how race and gender categories operate together but also in friction with one another. In Crenshaw's account, the group was undoubtedly singled out for attacks on the basis of anti-Black racism. There were white entertainers at the time whose acts were no less "obscene," and who were not targeted by the same kind of legal action and public outcry. But in defending the 2 Live

Crew from racist rhetoric and legal jeopardy, some commentators, including the African-American public intellectual Henry Louis Gates, Jr. (1990), challenged their sexism only with a gentle touch. According to Gates, the excessive lyrics in these songs was an act of parody, partaking in a competitive African-American tradition of "signifyin'" or "playing the dozens," in which participants try to express the most flagrant exaggerations. He saw their sexism as almost too outrageous to be taken seriously. Crenshaw, by contrast, saw the violent misogyny in the 2 Live Crew's music to be an invitation to violence against Black women, and to Black women "learning that their value lies between their legs" (1285).

Ideological expressions that invoke identity will often do so in complicated ways. For a Black woman like Crenshaw, intersectionality means being caught between two injustices: racism and misogyny. She describes her feeling at the time of the 2 Live Crew case as "being torn between standing with the brothers against a racist attack and standing against a frightening explosion of violent imagery directed at women like me" (Crenshaw 1993, 121). In approaching any ideology critique that engages with identity, it pays to consider all of the pertinent categories and their interactions. We all experience everyday life and popular media through the multiple dimensions of our intersectional identities. Being attentive to one form of privilege or injustice should not mean being blind to another.

Tensions and Contradictions

While ideology critique can proceed as a straightforward unmasking or condemnation, many examples of the popular media we might want to analyze contain tensions or contradictions between competing values or ideological positions, as in the case of the 2 Live Crew outrage. A persuasive critique would need to account for these. Media can function as hegemonic discourse and can also be counter-hegemonic and critical. But it may be unrealistic to expect very many examples of media to be purely one or the other. As an alternative to the ruling class's guaranteed manipulation and deception, we can conceive of ideology, in the Gramscian tradition, as a product of struggle over meanings, however unequal that struggle might be. Seen in this light, media critique can become an assessment and analysis of competing discourses.

Protest and resistance typically come from marginalized groups within an unequal society: women and LGBTQ+ folks, the young, the poor and working-class, and ethnic or racialized others. Whether their systems of ideas in opposition to hegemonic discourses should be considered ideologies is a matter for debate. Under the prevailing usage of *ideology* in critical media studies, movements that contest dominant political structures, like socialism and feminism, might not be described as ideological. But they are certainly systems of ideas freighted with political and social values, and some cultural theorists on the left (e.g., Eagleton 1991, 6–7) would describe such schools of thought as ideologies. Whatever we call them, they oppose in some fashion the workings of power under current arrangements. Many kinds of media tap into their systems of knowledge. Media criticism is often engaged not in demystifying ideological texts and practices but in celebrating the critical, progressive, or counter-hegemonic work that resists dominant discourses and promotes alternative conceptions of social arrangements. We see this, for instance, in queer studies of media such as film, TV, or games that articulate a cultural and identity politics that runs against the grain of mainstream, hegemonic media practice (Doty 1993; Ruberg 2019).

Another approach is to fasten onto the tendency of much media to contain ideological multitudes. When classic rock songs that had originally been understood as countercultural and defiantly opposed to business as usual are used in commercials for luxury cars or tax preparation services, as songs by Janis Joplin and The Beatles have, some audiences experience a jarring clash of meanings (Stevenson 2005). A sales pitch for Mercedes-Benz or H&R Block promotes ordinary consumerism, one of the essential facets of modern social structures. The significance of the music as protesting against the status quo might be drained away to nothing, but we might also hear a *tension* between the culturally dominant and countercultural values in such a text, a *friction* between competing values and worldviews. Texts often have unstable, multiple meanings and can be read in varying ways by different audiences.

We might see this as an example of a larger phenomenon of corporate media *co-opting* countercultural expressions as a way of borrowing its sense of legitimacy, its aura of cool that appeals to certain consumers. Mass culture can be seen as lacking in authenticity, but adopting styles that rise from the bottom up can offer an edgy, hip sensibility. This is sometimes known as *incorporation*: the process of mainstream media poaching alternative forms and styles, stripping away their critical hard edge, and packaging them as commodities. This concept has been applied to youth and working-class subcultures such as punk rock and its related expressions in fashion (Hebdige 1979, 90–106). In the various movements that have been called independent or indie media (music, film, television, comics, games), separation from the dominant media industries has sometimes appealed as a critical, oppositional dimension of a counter-hegemonic formation. Like punk rock, though, these styles can end up being absorbed by the mainstream media industries in a way that exhibits tensions between indie being an authentic alternative and indie being just another branding of commercial media addressing a niche audience (Newman 2011).

Such contradictory politics can be especially visible when corporate culture explicitly adopts the rhetoric and language of social or activist movements that oppose dominant practices. The conservationist goals of the movement fighting climate change include ending fossil fuel extraction. The fossil fuel industry has waged a campaign against this environmentalist agenda that involves various tactics. These include publicly appearing to answer the calling of "corporate social responsibility," to deflect from the reality that capitalist accumulation comes at the planet's expense. This gives them the "license to operate," a phrase suggesting that ideology is a key element of the fossil fuel industry's ability to persist in the face of climate science, policy, and activism (Miller 2018, 17). The public display of concern about climate change gives them a kind of legitimacy or credibility, allowing them to continue to follow the same practices that have led us to the brink of catastrophe.

A strategy that advances this cause for the fossil fuel industry is greenwashing, the adoption of language and rhetoric from environmentalism to cover for the reality of their continued polluting practices, emphasizing positive and hiding negative behaviors. Language in marketing and promotion like "go green," "save our planet," "sustainability," and the prefix "eco-" do this rhetorical work. Toby Miller (2016, 2018) shows how global sports institutions, including Formula-1 auto racing and Fédération Internationale de Football Association (FIFA) participate in this to give license to their own environmentally unfriendly operations by accepting greenwashing sponsorship from fossil fuel corporations such as BP, Shell, and Gazprom. These include tie-in promotions offering carbon offsets for ticket-buyers and claims of building "green" stadium facilities while staging global media events that involve considerable air travel and other pouting practices. In partnering with the extractive industries on such initiatives, these major sports, whose income is ultimately dependent on the billions of dollars in corporate advertising revenue generated by televised competitions, greenwash their images and appeal to audiences as good citizens of the planet.

Ideologically, the work of greenwashing fits neatly into a concept of dominant meanings, creating a mystification of reality that critique can uncover. But the rhetoric employed in greenwashing includes the knowledge that climate is changing at human hands, the need for us to see ourselves as conservators of a precious natural environment, an urgency to addressing carbon emissions, and a recognition that corporations as well as governments and individuals bear a responsibility to society. Here we might recognize ideology not just as a snow job obscuring the injustices of our power structure, but also as a contradictory mess of shameless corporate image management and the co-opted language of climate justice. This produces a common sense achieved through struggle between unequal forces of corporate capitalism and green activism.

Media need not be understood as either reflecting dominant interests or not. It can be ideological in a complicated way that mixes hegemonic and counter-hegemonic meanings and values, or that can be understood as conveying more than one political agenda at a time. This doesn't mean that politics is wide open and up for grabs, but it does mean that we can find nuance and complexity in the ideological workings of mediated images and stories.

The Whole Ideological Environment

As a tool in our toolkit, ideology allows us to make a critical contribution as media scholars. It gives us a conceptual grid for applying knowledge about the social world to the workings of media. It helps us make connections between politics, broadly understood as relations of power in society, and the many varied kinds of media. It also helps us appreciate how important media can be: ideologically, media has a function of keeping the dominant power structure in place, though it can also work to unsettle or challenge it. Media is part of the explanation for the way things work. Hegemony is maintained by the creation of a seemingly natural but always shifting common sense. In Stuart Hall's (1982) words, media have the power of "shaping the whole ideological environment: a way of representing the order of things which endowed its limiting perspectives with that natural or divine inevitability which makes them appear universal, natural and coterminous with 'reality' itself" (65).

We might pause here on a couple of keywords in Hall's formulation: "shaping" and "appear[ing]." To shape is to give form, to be a causal agent. But shaping is not the same as determining, and we know that the ideological environment can be shaped by other forces as well, that media can be one participant along with the other institutions of modern life. And to *appear* is to *seem* rather than *be*. The order of things that is the "reality" shaped by media, among these other forces, is but a projection of representations. Understanding how media works can include understanding how to look beyond its appearance, its façade of life as we think we know it. We can probe its correspondences with other things going on in the world: how identities are constructed, and how politics and economics shape the environment. We can also look closely at cultural texts of all kinds, and the ways they are made and used, training a critical, informed eye that has the power to see under appealing surfaces and behind engaging stories to the values and taken-for-granted assumptions always embedded in them. Ideology critique is ultimately empowering, not like the bogus empowerment of neoliberalism, but a different kind of empowerment that can facilitate, through keen attention and careful argument, the liberation of the mind.

Discussion Questions

1. What is the difference between ideology as used in critical media studies and the concept of ideology as a political identity such as conservative or liberal?

2. Choose any media text to critique, and analyze the way it functions ideologically, being sure to point out things that you find beneath the surface to demystify or unmask as political meanings.

3. Watch an episode of a reality TV show and consider the way it works (or doesn't work) as an example of neoliberal ideology. What is the show teaching the audience?

4. How is ideology connected to identity? What is an example from your own experience of a media text that seems especially relevant for understanding a hegemonic conception of identity (e.g., of gender or sexuality)?

Note

1   Stuart Hall (1984) describes the phrase "of course" as a kind of "ideological moment," or "the moment at which you're least aware that you are using a particular framework" (8).

References

Becker, Ron. 2018. "Ideology." In *The Craft of Criticism: Critical Media Studies in Practice*, edited by Michael Kackman and Mary Celeste Kearney, 11–22. New York: Routledge.

Brown, Wendy. 2003. "Neo-liberalism and the End of Liberal Democracy." *Theory & Event* 7.1. doi: 10.1353/tae.2003.0020

Burch, Noël. 1982. "Narrative/Diegesis – Thresholds, Limits." *Screen* 23.2: 16–33

Chomsky, Noam. 2011. *How the World Works*. Berkeley: Soft Skull Press.

Connell, R.W. and James W. Messerschmidt. 2005. "Hegemonic Masculinity: Rethinking the Concept." *Gender and Society* 19.6: 829–859.

Crenshaw, Kimberlé. 1991. "Mapping the Margins: Intersectionality, Identity Politics, and Violence against Women of Color." *Stanford Law Review* 43.6: 1241–1299.

Crenshaw, Kimberlé Williams. 1993. "Beyond Racism and Misogyny: Black Feminism and 2 Live Crew." In *Words That Wound: Critical Race Theory, Assaultive Speech, and the First Amendment*, edited by Mari J. Matsuda, Charles R. Lawrence III, Richard Delgado, and Kemberlè Williams Crenshaw, 111–132. Boulder: Westview Press.

Doty, Alexander, 1993. *Making Things Perfectly Queer: Interpreting Mass Culture*. Minneapolis: University of Minnesota Press.

Duffy, Brooke Erin. 2017. *(Not) Getting Paid to Do What You Love: Gender, Social Media, and Aspirational Work*. New Haven: Yale University Press.

Dugger, Ronnie. 2000. "The Corporate Domination of Journalism." In *The Business of Journalism*, edited by William Serrin, 27–56. New York: The New Press.

Eagleton, Terry. 1991. *Ideology: An Introduction*. London: Verso.

Fiske, John. 2011. *Introduction to Communication Studies* 3rd ed. Abingdon, Oxon: Routledge.

Gates, Jr. Henry Louis. 1990. "2 Live Crew, Decoded." *New York Times*, June 19, 1990.

Hall, Stuart. 1982. "The Rediscovery of 'Ideology': Return of the Repressed in Media Studies." In *Culture, Society and the Media*, edited by Michael Gurevitch, Tony Bennett, James Curran and Janet Woollacott, 56–90. London: Methuen.

Hall, Stuart. 1984. "The Narrative Construction of Reality: An Interview with Stuart Hall." *Southern Review* 17.1: 1–17.

Hall, Stuart. 1996. "The Problem of Ideology: Marxism Without Guarantees." In Stuart Hall: *Critical Dialogues in Cultural Studies*, edited by David Morley and Kuan-Hsing Chen, 25–46. London: Routledge.

Harvey, Eric. 2021. *Who Got the Camera? A History of Rap and Reality*. Austin: University of Texas Press.

Harvey, David. 2005. *A Brief History of Neoliberalism*. Oxford: Oxford University Press.

Hebdige, Dick. 1979. *Subculture: The Meaning of Style*. London: Methuen.

hooks, bell. 1995. *Reel to Real: Race, Sex, and Class at the Movies*. New York: Routledge.

Jeffords, Susan. 1994. *Hard Bodies: Hollywood Masculinity in the Reagan Era*. New Brunswick: Rutgers University Press.

Jones, Steve. 2006. *Antonio Gramsci*. London: Routledge.

Kuhn, Annette. 1982. *Women's Pictures: Feminism and Cinema*. Boston: Routledge & Kegan Paul.

McLean, Nancy. 2017. *Democracy in Chains: The Deep History of the Radical Right's Stealth Plan for America*. New York: Viking.

McMurria, John. 2008. "Desperate Citizens and Good Samaritans: Neoliberalism and Makeover Reality TV." *Television & New Media* 9.4.

Marx, Karl. 1977. "Preface." In Marx, *A Contribution to the Critique of Political Economy*. Moscow: Progress Publishers. https://www.marxists.org/archive/marx/works/1859/critique-pol-economy/preface.htm

Metz, Christian. 1974. *Film Language: A Semiotics of Cinema*, translated by Michael Taylor. New York: Oxford University Press.

Meyers, Marian. 2019. "Neoliberalism and the Media: History and Context." In *Neoliberalism and the Media*, edited by Meyers, 3–18. New York: Routledge.

Miller, Toby. 2016. "Greenwashed Sports and Environmental Activism: Formula 1 and FIFA." *Environmental Communication* 10.6: 719–733.

Miller, Toby. 2018. *Greenwashing Sport*. New York: Routledge.

Modleski, Tania. 2008. *Loving With a Vengeance: Mass-Produced Fantasies for Women*, 2nd ed. New York: Routledge.

Newman, Michael Z. 2011. *Indie: An American Film Culture*. New York: Columbia University Press.

Ouellette, Laurie and James Hay. 2008. *Better Living through Reality TV: Television and Post-Welfare Citizenship*. Malden: Blackwell.

Ouellette, Laurie. 2016. *Lifestyle TV*. New York: Routledge.

Ruberg, Bonnie. 2019. *Video Games Have Always Been Queer*. New York: New York University Press.

Stabile, Carol A. 2006. *White Victims, Black Villains: Gender, Race, and Crime News in US Culture*. New York: Routledge.

Stevenson, Seth. 2005. "What's the Worst Ad Song Ever?" *Slate*, June 6, 2005. https://slate.com/business/2005/06/songs-that-clash-with-the-ads-they-re-in.html

Storey, John. 2009. *Cultural Theory and Popular Culture: An Introduction*, 5th ed. Harlow: Pearson Longman.

Taylor, Nicholas and Gerald Voorhees, eds. 2018. *Masculinities in Play*. Cham, Switzerland: Palgrave Macmillan.

Taylor, T.L. 2012. *Raising the Stakes: E-Sports and the Professionalization of Computer Gaming*. Cambridge, MA: MIT Press.

Von Driel, Loes and Delia Dumitrica. 2021. "Selling Brands While Staying 'Authentic': The Professionalization of Instagram Influencers." *Convergence* 27.1. https://doi.org/10.1177/1354856520902136

Williams, Raymond. 1983. *Keywords: A Vocabulary of Culture and Society*, rev. ed. New York: Oxford University Press.

7

POLICY AND REGULATION

We have all experienced the effects of media policy and regulation even though these words might sound like something sure to be boring when you find out what they actually mean. This is one of those topics that becomes more interesting the more you learn about it and appreciate how much it shapes the world as we know it. For instance, if you live in the US, you are probably aware that there are some dirty words you are not supposed to hear on the radio and on TV (on some channels, anyway), and you probably know that children aren't supposed to be allowed in to see movies rated R ("Restricted") without a parent or guardian. Both of these examples show that media companies are constrained in what they say and how they operate. They are not free just to do whatever. *Media policy and regulation* refers to some of the most important forces that keep media companies from just doing whatever.

There are also constraints on media regulation itself. Americans are very proud of their First Amendment, which is a guarantee (among other things) of freedom of speech and of the press, and in particular freedom from state interference in matters of expression. Many other countries also protect press freedom with rules or laws. The Constitution of the United States forbids the government from censoring media, but for some reason (we will get to the reason in a little bit) it's okay for the US government, via its agency the Federal Communications Commission (FCC), to restrict TV stations from airing certain words that some people find offensive. These examples are just the tip of the iceberg of media policy and regulation.

DOI: 10.4324/9781003007708-7

Media companies, like companies in any industry, operate within legal frameworks governing their operations. Every nation has its own regulations, though some kinds of regulation also operate internationally, such as conventions that many nations sign onto agreeing to protect intellectual property. But not all media policy comes from the state. Companies and industries also regulate themselves, as in the case of the Motion Picture Association of America (MPAA) movie ratings system. The US government and state governments have not implemented regulations governing what kinds of movies may be seen by what age of theater patrons. It's not illegal to sell a couple of unaccompanied 10-year-olds tickets to an R-rated film. The Hollywood studios made up their own age-based regulatory system in the 1960s, which has been tweaked now and then over the years, because they thought it would be good for their business to do so, and movie theater operators enforce these voluntary rules (Lewis 2002). When an industry adopts its own regulations like this, we call it *self-regulation*. Unless we are talking specifically about self-regulation, you can assume any regulation that comes up here is being done by the state. (The *state* refers to the government and its agencies at whatever level – federal, state or provincial, regional, or municipal.)

Policy and regulation are similar and overlapping terms, but it helps to consider them individually. In everyday language, a *policy* is a plan of action, which might include specific goals and ways of achieving them. Policies are often matters for debate and struggle, and not all interested parties are likely to get what they want, so we can see policy as an arena in which different interests compete over resources and influence. This is true of how policy discussions often come up in political discourse: we associate political candidates and parties with their policies, such as a liberal party's policy of expanding access to social services or a conservative party's policy of cutting taxes, both of which ultimately are ways of managing shared wealth. In the language of political scientists, *public policy* constitutes all of a government's actions of whatever kind (Peters 2018). Such policies are extensions of values and beliefs and are taken to achieve particular outcomes. *State regulations* can be more specific, and refer to particular laws or rules, often adopted and enforced by a government agency tasked with overseeing certain types of business. The requirements that cars have seat belts or that restaurants serving alcohol have a liquor license are two examples of the great many regulations of business. Media industries operate under many kinds of state regulation, and these are specific applications of media policy.

Another side of regulation is *deregulation*, or the removal of constraints on businesses and other objects of regulation. If the government were to decide to get rid of rules concerning television content or automobile safety, that would be deregulation. The choice not to regulate something, or to remove regulations that previously existed, can be just as consequential as the choice to enact or continue regulations. When you think about it this way, everything that happens in the world of media is affected by the power of the state, whether that power is used to leave things the way they are, or to make changes by adding or removing regulations.

Public and Private Interests

Why does the government regulate industry at all, and why in particular does it regulate the media industries? Any reasonable answer would note that a good government exists to serve the people, and that a responsible democratic system should work to advance the best interests of the whole society. This is why, for instance, we have regulations that protect the environment: these measures should protect us all from harm and impose a responsibility on polluting industries that would benefit us all. Regulation is supposed to advance the common good.

In the media industries, there are some forms of regulation that are very directly tied to this ideal. From its founding in 1934 under the Communications Act, the FCC's stated purpose in regulating radio and later television broadcasting has included serving "the public interest, convenience and necessity." The FCC grants licenses to radio and television stations that permit the broadcasters to use the airwaves to transmit their signals, but in order to keep their licenses, every station has to follow the FCC's many rules, such as broadcasting a certain amount of educational programming for children, with limitations on how much of that time can be spent on advertising (Federal Communications Commission 2019). Some media policies are formulated to encourage economic development, such as subsidies or tax incentives for television or film production in particular locations, such as Georgia in the US or British Columbia in Canada, benefiting workers in those places. And some are aimed at addressing social or cultural goals, such as public media funded by the state to serve the informational needs of citizens.

We value the freedoms guaranteed by the First Amendment and similar basic guarantees of citizens' rights to the extent that they are good for individuals, but also for the whole society. When the government regulates industries by imposing health and safety standards, by setting price controls on goods and services, such as rent control and a minimum wage, or by approving or disapproving mergers and acquisitions of companies, it does so, at least in principle, in the public interest. In the US, an array of policies would stand in the way of one company controlling all of the television networks and cable channels in America. Imagine if Disney, Fox News, CNN, and Comcast were all acquired by the same incredibly rich individual. If someone tried to buy up all of them, the state could stand in their way. There are multiple reasons why this kind of situation would be contrary to policy, but one of them would be that the whole society might be better served by competition in the media industries. Policy like this is supposed to protect consumers and citizens and contribute to the welfare of us all.

Whether or not it achieves these goals is often an open question, if not a debatable proposition. Lawmakers and staffers of government agencies may be motivated by public service, but they are also working within an environment of intense lobbying on behalf of businesses that stand to gain or lose, depending on the outcomes of regulatory decision-making. Money has a corrosive effect on politics, and wealthy corporations often do their best to influence the policy environment for their own benefit, regardless of the impact on the whole society. In many industries there is a "revolving door" for lawyers and lobbyists who work in the public sector regulating the industries they previously worked for, or who leave public service for work in the private industries they once regulated. This is certainly true of the media policy world, where several chairs of the FCC have come from the telecommunications or cable television industries, and have returned to working in the industries they previously regulated after their terms at the agency concluded. Companies seek the most advantageous regulation or deregulation for their business, but the general public, the ones supposedly served by good government, are hardly represented among the lobbyists whose job is to produce policy outcomes favorable to the industries paying for their services.

When an industry achieves the power to dictate the terms of its own regulation by the state, economists and others who study business and the law call it *regulatory capture* (Carpenter and Moss 2014). The FCC is a frequent example in discussions of capture, as its regulation of broadcasting and internet services have often tended to pay lip service to serving consumers while advancing the economic interests of media companies (Esguerra 2007;

Kushnick 2013; Wheeler 2017). In the emerging area of the internet and specifically social media regulation, Facebook has been publicizing a pro-regulation stance, advocating for certain kinds of policies that might allow it to continue to be profitable without facing a threatening regulatory environment (Facebook n.d.). An advertising campaign called "It's Time" circulating in 2021 has advocated for regulation of election misinformation, privacy and security, content moderation, and data portability. Facebook appears to be aiming to influence the rewriting of internet regulation in a way that would favor its own economic interests at a time when some American politicians, on both ends of the political spectrum, have taken sharp anti-Facebook stances that might seem threatening to its future business.

A famous example of industry influencing media policy comes from the area of copyright law. A US copyright guarantees to the author of a creative work, like a book or a song, exclusive rights to publish and profit from that work "for a limited time." This phrase appears in the US Constitution, guaranteeing that no copyright is forever. This amount of time is called the term of copyright. Copyright is a form of regulation that restrains free expression for the common good. It gives authors an incentive to produce their work by granting them the exclusive right to publish it during the term of copyright. After the term expires, anyone may do so. That is why you are free to stage a production of Romeo and Juliet without getting William Shakespeare's permission: the work is not protected by copyright. You can't do the same thing with work still under copyright, like Harry Potter or Star Wars, without asking for trouble.

In the 1990s, the term of copyright in the US was 75 years from the date of publication for works of corporate authorship like a Hollywood movie. Under this law, the copyrights protecting many of the early films of the Walt Disney Company, including the first Mickey Mouse cartoons, would soon expire. Had this occurred, these classic films would have entered the public domain, which means Disney would have lost the exclusive right to profit from them. As it happens, the US Congress passed a term extension to expand the value of copyright for media companies like Disney to 95 years, giving the copyright holders a huge gift: 20 more years of exclusive rights to these and all of their other protected works (Lessig 2004, 135). The official name of this legislation was the "Copyright Term Extension Act of 1998," but it was widely mocked as the "Mickey Mouse Protection Act," indicating the power of lobbying by Disney and other American movie companies to shape media regulation favorable to their business interests.

In the area of copyright term extensions, the value to the whole society of having a robust public sphere of cultural works that belong to us all was secondary to the value to the media industries of protecting their revenue streams via their control over intellectual property. In such cases, we must ask whether policy and regulation are serving the public interest or the corporate interest, and where the balance ought to be between the production of wealth for private businesses and their shareholders, and the creation and maintenance of a popular media culture that belongs to us all.

Regulation of What?

Media policy can cover a myriad of different aspects of the business of culture and communication. Just looking at the examples introduced so far we see a wide variety of regulations, including regulation of what is or is not acceptable for particular audiences, regulation of the corporate structures of the media industries, and regulation of copyright. A chapter like this cannot hope to cover every possible instance of media policy and regulation, but it can identify some of the main types of regulation and look at some examples of each one. One way of managing this is to break these policies up into broad categories. These include regulation of media industry ownership, of media content, and of technical infrastructure.

Media ownership regulation refers to the ways that the state asserts control over corporate structures, regulating what kind of companies may or may not operate in the media business. In the US, if the owner of a television station wants to buy another TV station in the same Designated Market Area (DMA, i.e., geographical region, usually centered around a city), the FCC has rules they must follow to avoid excessive concentration of ownership. The FCC would forbid all of the television stations in a city being owned by the same company, and would also not allow two fifths or more of the stations in the whole country to be under a single owner. The FCC rules on Broadcast Ownership also cover radio station ownership and ownership of national television networks. It would, for instance, forbid NBC from re-acquiring ABC, which originated as a company in 1944, when the FCC forced NBC to sell off one of its two radio networks to ensure a competitive market in broadcasting. Until 2017, the FCC would not permit the owner of a daily newspaper to own a television station in the same DMA, but that rule was removed (i.e., this was deregulated) thanks to "the growth in the number and variety of sources of entertainment, news and information in the modern media marketplace" (Federal Communications Commission 2020).

The logic of regulating ownership of media is partly to ensure diversity, which is a key value that the FCC promotes by way of serving the public interest. Many owners of media companies should, at least in theory, represent a diversity of viewpoints and perspectives. A related principle is localism: the media are regulated to promote circulation of local content. In practice, the ownership of media tends to be concentrated in the hands of a small number of large, powerful companies owned or controlled by rich white men, so the impact of regulation in this area may be less diversity and localism than the public might wish. One-time media titan Ted Turner (2004), who created CNN among other companies, is among the critics who have called for the government to break up these enormous media companies to better serve these values of diversity and localism.

Another rationale for regulating ownership is to manage monopoly, duopoly, or oligopoly markets in which one company (a monopoly) or a small number of companies (a duopoly or oligopoly) has control over the market for certain kinds of products. Such control is widely regarded as bad for consumers and for innovation in industry, as all of the power goes to the company or companies who corner the market. Working against this power was the logic of splitting NBC into two networks in the 1940s. Around the same time, in 1948, the major Hollywood movie studios consented to divorce the movie theaters they owned from their production and distribution businesses as the resolution of a lawsuit brought by the US Department of Justice. The integration of all of these parts of the film industry within a small cluster of companies working in concert with one another had been found to be monopolistic and thus illegal (Borneman 1985). The studios were legally forbidden from owning theaters for the subsequent 72 years until the consent decrees were terminated in 2020 (Gardner 2020).

Not all monopoly power has been seen as problematic when it comes to media and communication. For many decades, the American telephone industry was dominated by a single company, AT&T (short for American Telephone and Telegraph). It operated as a "natural monopoly" with the blessing of the state, which allowed AT&T to corner the telephone market both local and long-distance as long as it maintained high-quality service available to all customers at prices regulated by the government. This arrangement lasted for most of the 20th century until competition in the telecommunication market and a shifting climate for industry regulation prompted a reconsideration of this arrangement. In the early 1980s, the government forced AT&T, also known as Bell (after founder Alexander Graham Bell) to be broken up, splitting the company into multiple "Baby Bells" offering local service while AT&T remained as a long-distance phone service. In 2005, one of these Baby Bells, Southwest Bell Corporation (SBC), acquired the company that had been its parent, and renamed itself AT&T. The regulatory climate changed over time to allow or forbid these different configurations of corporate power and consolidation at different moments in history (Wu 2011).

This area of public policy goes by the name *antitrust*, and is much broader than just media policy. The American antitrust laws date back to the 19th century, when "robber barons" in industries like railroads, steel, and oil, men like Andrew Carnegie and John D. Rockefeller, cornered their markets and consolidated power. A number of companies in a particular market working together to set prices and inhibit competition from newcomers may be known as a cartel or a *trust*, which came to be a catchall term for a big business that has since faded from usage. Antitrust law was written to force these industries into competitiveness by breaking trusts up into multiple companies in competition with one another. Antitrust is essentially a public policy favoring competition in industry (Sawyer 2019).

Since the late 20th century, we have seen the rise of massive media conglomerates like Disney and Comcast via merger and acquisition, and each deal along the way to their conglomeration had to be approved by the state's regulatory agencies. In the early 21st century we have seen the rise of the new media giants, including Google, Facebook, Apple, and Amazon, each of which in some ways functions as a monopoly. In 2020, the US Justice Department and many US states brought a number of antitrust suits against Google for its internet search and advertising practices, and its deals with phone makers to inhibit competition, actions likely to unfold over a period of years, which could result in fines or in Google being forced to sell off part of its business (McCabe, Kang, and Wakabayashi 2020).

Regulating ownership of media companies effectively to promote competition and protect against monopolies and cartels would, again in theory, be a way of serving the public interest by promoting diversity and competition and serving as a check on the power of these massively influential and profitable corporations. Whether this kind of regulation in the US in the 21st century accomplishes that goal is a matter of much debate.

Media content regulation brings us back to the words you can't say on TV or on the radio. Content is the product of media industries, what media scholars call texts, and any formal constraint on what content can or cannot be produced is an example of a media policy. If a word or phrase or name or idea is forbidden, that is content regulation.

Content is one area where we have to distinguish clearly between state regulation of media and industry self-regulation. The television industry includes both kinds. The FCC regulates the content of television broadcasts over the air from local stations, but the national networks also have self-regulating systems. Their "Standards and Practices" departments may be just as concerned about adverse publicity and advertiser displeasure as they are about the FCC's rules governing local stations. Ad-supported cable channels have the same concerns, and are not regulated by the FCC's content policies. Users of social media apps like TikTok and Facebook are also very familiar with the self-regulation of media content, as certain kinds of videos are regularly taken down for supposedly violating a standard set by the company, such as a policy against some kinds of nudity in photos and videos.

The history of media content regulation is partly a history of industries adopting their own systems of self-regulation as a way of avoiding trouble such as state censorship or audience boycotts or protests. This can mean formulating rules enforced in the name of morality and good taste that often serve to privilege some social groups over others, for instance, by adopting white, middle-class, Christian standards of decency to be followed by all. The Hollywood studios famously adopted a Production Code between the 1930s and 1960s that prevented them from using certain language (words like "damn" and "pregnant" once considered inappropriate), from representing criminals profiting from their crimes, screening explicit sexual activity, and various other kinds of storytelling. The Production Code Administration reviewed scripts before films were shot and had the power to intervene during the shooting and editing of films, as a means of avoiding local censorship of movies or public criticism of the movie industry (Bernstein 1999). Other American media businesses, including television and comic books, have also adopted restrictive content codes. Some have also used a ratings system or a system of warning labels, as in the recording industry.

In the age of the internet, new challenges have emerged in the area of media content regulation. A key issue facing the American social media giants of the 21st century, such as Facebook, YouTube, and Twitter, concerns their difficult choices regarding problematic content on their platforms. As the most popular social media sites have grown and gained influence, they have become our new public square, essential spaces for the circulation of ideas and for debate and discussion of politics and culture. They have achieved their amazing popularity by being very open, having few rules about what can and cannot be shared, and minimizing the resources they need to devote to content moderation. Dick pics and death threats might clearly cross the line (Chen 2014), and software might be able to detect some forms of problematic imagery, however imperfectly, yet a vast amount of internet content passes essentially unmoderated by human screeners unless flagged by users (Roberts 2019).

As a consequence of this hands-off ethos, they have been notoriously hospitable environments for abusive, harassing, and threatening speech, and for various kinds of propaganda and misinformation, most notoriously during national election campaigns. Their content algorithms, engineered to maximize user engagement, have a way of amplifying hot outrage and lies over cool expressions of reason and truth. None of them have found adequate solutions that maintain the freedom and openness they want to offer users in balance with protections from the harms that are visited on some by others. They have tried out policies like banning users or topics, or framing misinformation in disclaimers and warnings, but on the whole the solutions to their problems remain elusive. Critics of these new media giants often argue that they should be more aggressively regulated when it comes to content. In some instances, as with Facebook's "It's Time" campaign, the platforms themselves have invited this regulation.

Any kind of content regulation imposed by the state has the potential to raise concerns about government censorship. Censorship follows many different rationales, but one common thread is that powerful groups often police media content in order to maintain their power, like the school principals who have confiscated copies of their student papers to shut down the reporting of topics they didn't want to see publicly aired. In politics, this can mean shutting down information and ideas that the government does not want circulating among the people, such as opposition and dissent.

State censorship of media looks different in different countries. Western democracies pride themselves on having a free press, but there are many constraints on this freedom, such as laws in many jurisdictions preventing the publication of some kinds of news (e.g., information that could prejudice the jury in a trial, or that protects victims or minors), or criminalizing publication of sensitive information as in the American Espionage Act, which can be used to put journalists in jail for publishing state secrets. There are some topics that have been judged to be off-limits in certain places, such as Holocaust denial, which is forbidden in many European countries and in Israel. Whether this is a beneficial guard-rail against the return of fascism or a threat against individual liberties is a matter of much disagreement.

Authoritarian regimes typically assert much stiffer control over their media than we find in liberal societies. Chinese news organizations report little on certain matters we should consider gravely concerning about Chinese society, such as the state's persecution of minority groups. This censorship is omnipresent online, as internet search results are shaped by the interests of the government and foreign platforms like Google, YouTube, Wikipedia, and Facebook have been banned. This filtering system, the "Great Firewall of China," is the most extensive state censorship operation of the digital age. Chinese citizens do not have free access to media that citizens of many other countries would consider their right to be able to see and read and hear. Internet censorship is pervasive in a number of other countries, typically those with more authoritarian or theocratic regimes, including Russia, Iran, North Korea, and Saudi Arabia. Many countries that engage in repressive censorship also produce state propaganda campaigns to shape their information environment (Jack 2017). The state manages media much more aggressively in these countries than in most others.

We can also regard some forms of media content regulation that are not so much concerned with morality or decency, and that aren't what we would normally call censorship, such as rules about false advertising. A company is not free to deceive its customers about its offerings. Innuendo and suggestive messages are obviously permitted, but outright lies are not. In the US, advertising is regulated by the Federal Trade Commission, so while we think of the FCC as the American media regulator, other agencies also have a role in this.

Similarly, many rules constrain candidates running for political office, some of which cover content. In the US, any candidate's ad will include a brief voice-over indicating the candidate's approval of the message. This is included as a matter of policy, so that the candidate has to take ownership of their negative messages about their opponents. This is but one of the media regulations around elections that shape how money flows into politics and how voters can or cannot be addressed by candidates and other groups trying to influence the outcome of voting. Yet another state agency is involved here: the Federal Elections Commission makes these rules.

Another form of media policy that could be seen as content regulation falls in the area of libel and defamation. If you knowingly, maliciously spread lies about someone, or publish such falsehoods in the press, you can be taken to court. The lies themselves could be a form of media content that the state has seen fit to regulate by making it a civil wrong that can be legally actionable. The court could order you to pay damages to the person who has been so wronged. Different countries have varying policies on libel and defamation, as they do concerning all of the above issues. American courts have been more protective of speech when it comes to libel and defamation than those in other countries such as the UK, but the mere threat of a lawsuit can be chilling, and many media organizations are in constant consultation with lawyers to ensure that their exposure to legal actions over what they publish and broadcast is managed effectively to minimize their risk. Merely being sued for libel or defamation can be extremely costly even if the lawsuit is a baseless nuisance, so some jurisdictions also have laws that regulate the filing of bogus libel and defamation actions that can have a chilling effect on free expression.

These many different examples of media content regulation are strong evidence of the limits of the First Amendment and similar protections of free expression, where they exist. Such guarantees of freedom are always in tension with other principles: protection from harm, promotion of a democratic culture or of some particular set of values, or just the raw exercise of power.

Finally, *regulation of infrastructure* pertains to those forms of policy that cover the technologies and systems of media and communication, such as standards for transmission across electromagnetic frequencies. In the early 2000s, television broadcasting in the US and most other places switched over from analog to digital signals, an upgrade in technology mandated by policies of state agencies. A television set from several decades ago no longer receives broadcasts over the air without a digital converter because of the policy of adopting this new standard of transmission. Infrastructure policy applies in particular to the systems of communications technologies that make up modern information networks, including the telegraph and telephone systems, the airwaves or electromagnetic spectrum, and the internet as a network of cables, servers, and routers that connect many millions of computers around the world.

It also regulates how communication infrastructure may be used by media and telecommunication companies. For example, for more than a century, American policy has required common carriage over telephone lines. This means that your telephone company has to treat all uses of its lines the same way and not favor some users or uses over others, or refuse service to some customers. You can't be told that your telephone works only to call people on a list that the phone company provides, and may not connect to people on a no-call list. Rather, the phone company has to let you make phone calls to whomever you want. Common carriage is a principle from hundreds of years before the age of modern media, when it applied to transportation of goods rather than the communication of information.

In the area of internet regulation, common carriage has become a key issue, as the advocates of net neutrality have hoped that the internet would be treated as the telephone had been previously, and considered to be a common carrier. This would prevent internet service providers (ISPs) from favoring some kinds of internet traffic over others. It would be technically possible for your ISP to speed up or to slow down ("throttle") traffic to certain websites or for certain users. Comcast could make Netflix, its rival, work unreliably for its subscribers and Peacock, its own conglomerate's product, run more smoothly. A net neutrality policy would favor a regulation forbidding such a system of fast lanes and slow lanes.

Any policy requiring neutrality in this regard would be a regulation not of the ownership of media or of the types of content permitted or not, but of the infrastructure of media communication – in this case, internet servers and routers – and the uses of technology. There has been a fairly complex and tortured history of net neutrality policies being adopted and rejected under different FCC regimes, and the gains for net neutrality achieved during the Obama years were reversed under President Trump. Regardless, advocates of net neutrality have been instrumental in bringing to public consciousness how vital the infrastructure of the internet really is for a democratic society in the digital age (Pickard and Berman 2019). The power of the ISPs, and the conglomerates that often own them, to control flows of information should be a matter of grave public concern.

Why Broadcasting Is Different

In many countries' histories, we see much variation among the different media when it comes to how, and how much, they have been regulated by the state. Newspapers have been left alone much more than other media, though at certain times, such as periods of war, they have faced government censorship. Even so, the US's First Amendment specifies the print media – "the press" – for protection from state interference. For much of the 20th century, modern mass media did not enjoy the same freedom as the newspaper business did. In the US, state censorship of movies was legal for several decades as the Supreme Court had held in 1915 that the First Amendment did not extend to motion pictures, a decision overturned decades later, in 1952. Many state and local governments had censor boards empowered to ban films, or cut out portions deemed offensive (Wittern-Keller 2008). Obscenity laws at the state level in the US have led to many legal cases regarding pornographic or otherwise sexual or explicit texts, and while most pornography is legal in the US and many other countries in the early 21st century, child pornography is a serious crime and an uncontroversial major exception when it comes to free expression. American lawmakers and regulators have carved out many such exceptions to the First Amendment, which courts have supported. But by and large, the trend over the 20th century was toward more expansive understandings of freedom of expression, and laws curtailing that freedom have been harder to defend.

Policy covering broadcasting in the US has been a special case since the emergence of commercial network radio in the 1920s and the formation of the federal agency that regulates the airwaves in the US, the FCC. Radio was not invented to be a medium of mass entertainment, but developed in that direction in the early 1920s. It had been used for point-to-point communication, for instance, allowing ships to call the shore, and was a hobby of amateurs who used radio sets to send and receive signals across distances, taking pleasure from communicating by wireless transmission. The development of a commercial system of US broadcasting grew out of the electronics manufacturers like Westinghouse and GE, and retailers like urban department stores, seeking a market for their radio products (Arceneaux 2006; Douglas 1987).

Broadcasting literally means spreading out a message to the widest possible audience. It's the epitome of mass media as a single transmission received for free by anyone with a radio or television set who is within range of the signal. But it has always been a local media phenomenon. Broadcast signals over the air only reach so far, rarely more than 70 miles, which is why every city has its own stations and transmitters. National broadcast networks actually are providers of content for local stations affiliated with them, some of which they also own and operate. In the early days of US broadcasting, the content moved from networks in New York City, Chicago, or Los Angeles to local stations via telephone lines, and later this system was replaced with other technologies like satellite or internet feeds. There have never been more than a small handful of broadcast networks in the US, Canada, and many other countries, but every North American city has many local radio and television stations, some of which are network affiliates and many of which are independent stations or stations that are part of smaller chains. In the 2020s, the US still has thousands of local radio and television stations.

It's a key point for the topic of media regulation that broadcasting happens locally over the airwaves. When you turn on a radio, you receive a signal over the air that has been broadcast at a specific frequency. If I want to listen to a baseball game when my local team is playing, I tune my car stereo into the frequency of 620 kilohertz (kHz) on the AM band. When radio was a new medium, the commercial broadcasters were concerned about their ability to broadcast at a certain frequency without interference. If two or more broadcasters in a given location were to attempt to transmit at the same or at nearby frequencies, none of the signals would be clearly received. And there are only so many frequencies along the spectrum suitable for transmission of a radio signal. This condition of broadcast transmission is known as *spectrum scarcity* and it is one of the most basic rationales for media regulation (Aitken 1994).

The solution devised for managing spectrum scarcity was broadcast licensing. In the 1910s, anyone who procured the necessary equipment could send a radio signal over any frequency. With the formation of a regulatory agency to set policy for radio, it became necessary to get a license to transmit a radio signal. The broadcaster who airs my baseball games has a license to transmit in Milwaukee at AM 620. If I tried to set up a transmitter to broadcast at 620 kHz, I'd be running afoul of the FCC. But the airwaves across which radio and television stations transmit are a public good, and in exchange for holding a license to use the public airwaves that belong to us all, the broadcasters have to follow the FCC's rules, including rules that require them to serve the public interest.

In order to hold an FCC license, then, American broadcasters must submit to the agency's regulation. Since the national networks (now including Fox, ABC, and The CW in addition to CBS and NBC) reach their audiences via local stations, and local stations use the public airwaves, the national networks indirectly find themselves constrained by the FCC's content policies. The rules followed by FCC broadcast licensees that affect television content include forbidding broadcasting "indecent" material during the hours when children may be watching television (6 a.m. to 10 p.m.), which means they can't say the dirty words you seldom hear on TV. Stations are also required to offer equal opportunities to political candidates who appear on air. They must air a certain amount of educational programming for children, and to put the educate/inform "E/I" symbol in a bug on the screen during these broadcasts. Stations must offer closed-captioning and video description of most of their broadcasts for accessibility. These are just a few examples of the many rules that broadcasters must follow in the US (Federal Communications Commission 2019), and each national media policy agency has its own versions of such rules.

So here is how broadcasting is different: by using the public airwaves and needing to have a license to transmit over the air at a specific frequency, radio and television stations operate under much tighter constraints than other kinds of media outlets, including cable and satellite television, satellite radio, streaming platforms, and YouTube or Twitch. None of these alternatives to broadcasting need a license to transmit, so they are free of all of the requirements in the previous paragraph. This doesn't mean they are under no constraints at all. Being a commercial media service, whether supported by advertising or consumer spending or a combination of both, means working within many constraints. But for the broadcast media, having to maintain an FCC license layers more on top of the ones that any company faces. It also distinguishes television and radio from print media, which are basically unregulated by the FCC. Newspapers, magazines, and news websites operate more freely than television and radio stations when it comes to content regulation.

Most of the audience for television is no longer accessing TV via over-the-air transmission, but the structure of the network system remains, and local stations remain vital institutions. They are a critical source of local news for many citizens, and they have remained financially secure, thanks to political advertising, during a period of declining fortunes in the news industry (Pew Research Center 2021). Viewers who access their local stations via retransmission on cable, satellite, or streaming may not be using an antenna for over-the-air reception, but these retransmissions of local broadcasts are the only way for many viewers to access the television networks in the US as live television, and the power of the FCC's rules remains regardless of how you watch network TV.

Public Service Media

Media policy in a capitalist system, as in the United States, is typically a matter of regulating private industry. The rules that radio and television stations must follow are a means for the government to ensure that for-profit businesses use public resources (the airwaves) for the public's benefit. But there is another way of organizing media systems, which has more of a presence in many other countries than in the United States. This is to treat broadcasting in particular, but potentially other forms of media as well, as a form of *public service* that the state provides to the people. A state can follow the policy that it has no business being in the media business, but it can also set up systems – ideally in a way that would insulate them from political interference – that are public in funding and purpose.

The history of radio and television policy in the United Kingdom provides a sharp contrast to the American story. In the UK, radio and television did not originally develop as a private commercial industry as in the US with its network system. Rather than broadcast for free over the air, with the costs borne by sponsors paying to reach radio and television audiences with their advertisements, British radio and television broadcasting were established under the authority of the General Post Office. The British Broadcasting Corporation (BBC), established in the 1920s, is a government-owned entity that was granted a monopoly over broadcasting in the UK. It was financed by a special kind of tax, a license fee paid by every owner of a radio, and later of a television set. Broadcasting in the UK was regarded as a kind of utility, similar to electrical power and water, and carried no commercial advertising. Its mission was to provide educational and entertaining broadcasts, to spread knowledge and cultivate the taste of the public. It would also function to bring the nation together, uniting citizens of different classes and backgrounds in one common culture. Broadcasting was regarded, in the words of British media historian Paddy Scannell (2003), as "a kind of social cement binding people together" (215).

Public service broadcasting, as established in the UK, was the system adopted in many other nations, including those of the British Commonwealth following the BBC's example (e.g., Canada's CBC/Radio-Canada and Australia's ABC) and western Europe. Since the post-WWII era and especially since the rise of cable and satellite television around the 1980s and 1990s, public service broadcasters have seen rising competition from private commercial media companies, and the typical media landscape since then has been a mix of private/commercial and public service media. The BBC's monopoly over broadcasting long ago expired, though its mission continues. In the US, national public media got a relatively late start, with the formation of the Corporation for Public Broadcasting in the 1960s and the launch of PBS (TV) and NPR (radio) shortly thereafter. Neither of these broadcasters have ever had the robust support of the state enjoyed by public service media of many other countries, relying instead on corporate philanthropy and donations from viewers and listeners (Hoynes 1994).

However much public media organizations command attention in any particular country, the purpose of media as public service endures as a goal of media reformers looking for an alternative to for-profit commercial media (Pickard 2019). A media policy that puts public service ahead of corporate interests might address many of the problems of the prevailing systems, especially when it comes to news media, such as ratings-driven priorities, rising misinformation, and adherence to corporate ideology. The profit motive and the public interest are typically in competition with one another, and a system that strongly favors commercial media over public media makes the aspirations of public service harder to realize. While public media is not without its faults, including a tendency to favor elite values and views (Ouellette 2002), it has the potential to play a central role in reimagining media in a way that will make it serve all of the people in a democratic society.

National Cultural Policy and Canadian Media

Policy and regulation ultimately are supposed to serve the public interest, but defining the public interest is notoriously tricky. American media policy has never been terribly clear on what constitutes the public interest, but other countries have looked at things rather differently. Some nations have used their media policies for particular purposes that are distinct and specific in relation to the American version. Canadian media policy has privileged the promotion of a Canadian national identity as a desired outcome in a way that might make little sense to Americans unfamiliar with life in the country to their north. Unlike the US, Canada has a cabinet-level federal office responsible for culture, the Minister of Canadian Heritage (the equivalent of a US cabinet secretary). Their responsibilities include overseeing public broadcasting and public arts funding that includes film and television.

I grew up in Canada during the 1970s and 1980s, and was very familiar with Canadian cultural and media policy, even if I didn't have the vocabulary to analyze it in these terms. What I was aware of was called "CanCon" (short for Canadian content), which I knew to be a set of rules about what music could be played on the radio. Any attentive listener to Canadian commercial radio would have noticed that there were a lot of Canadian artists playing all the time. On the Toronto rock music stations I listened to that meant Neil Young, Rush, The Guess Who, and Bryan Adams, all of whom were globally popular acts who sold millions of records in the US as well as in Canada. I also heard a lot of music by artists with names less familiar to people who didn't live in Canada in these years, artists like Chilliwack, Kim Mitchell, and Blue Rodeo, who were rock stars at home but not very well known elsewhere. I heard plenty of imported pop music by international superstars like Led Zeppelin, Michael Jackson, and Madonna, but CanCon was part of the soundtrack of everyday life.

CanCon was a product of a nationalist cultural policy adopted in Canada in order to protect Canadian identity from the perceived threat of American popular culture (Edwardson 2008). Canada is an example of a small country (in population) with an exceptionally large and powerful neighbor, the United States. Movies, television, and music are among the US's most successful exports, and America is seen as exporting more than just goods when it sells its cultural products abroad – not just media but also Big Macs and Coca-Cola, Levi's and iPhones. It is seen as selling America's way of life, its ideals and its identity.

Canadian policy-makers saw this as something quite troubling for a country without the kind of robust entertainment industry present in the US. They feared that Canada could be without a distinct national character of its own, and thus lose a sense of cultural sovereignty. Canada adopted policy measures that would protect Canadianness from Americanization, and these included regulations governing how much Canadian music would have to be played on the radio each day. The government authority for broadcasters in Canada, the Canadian Radio-television and Telecommunications Commission (CRTC), established CanCon as a condition of broadcasting over the air. Similar requirements were established to require Canadian content on television as well, though these regulations did not forbid giving over prime-time hours to imported American series. These regulations have helped to support Canadian artists and creators, and stimulate a Canadian recording industry (Johansen 1973). They have certainly ensured that some of the songs and shows Canadians consume are Canadian. Canadian cultural policy also protects the French language in the majority-francophone province of Quebec through media institutions such as Radio-Canada, the French-language public broadcaster.

Canada also publicly funds a cultural sector of its economy to promote the production of Canadian media and the arts, with the express ambition of fostering a sense of national identity, a sense of Canadian values and ideals distinct from those of the United States. This is achieved through subsidies and other incentives and agencies like its famed National Film Board, which has produced decades worth of acclaimed documentaries and other films and videos, as well as other subsidies for Canadian media producers and artists. It also means an official policy of multiculturalism and funding to support the arts and media from indigenous communities. These varied forms of cultural policy serve many functions, one of which is to represent Canada to Canadians and produce images and narratives of the nation as its own form of public good.

Measures such as content regulations and state financial support may be good for promoting Canadian culture, but they also stimulate Canadian industry and create jobs, much as requirements that foreign automakers produce some of their goods in Canada have supported Canadian manufacturing (Wagman 2006, 205–259). We can also recognize the content requirements on Canadian media companies as a trade-off for economic security, which is helped by policy regulating foreign ownership of Canadian media companies. Such a nationalist cultural and media policy like Canada's is a form of protectionism in the global trade arena, a way of maintaining a position of some power in relation to competition from other territories. Sometimes this takes the form of incentivizing international media co-productions between producers of different nations, stimulating investment in multiple national industries. Many countries have practiced some form of cultural or media protectionism in the name of nationalism, such as many nations' movie quotas going back to the early 20th century. A motion picture quota might require that movie theaters program a certain percentage of their screens with local productions, a system that has protected film industries such as Britain's from Hollywood's dominance (Street 2009). There are many policy tools that can advance the social and economic agendas of cultural protectionism.

However successful it has been at constructing and maintaining a sense of national identity, Canada's media policy has shown how a concept of public interest can be shaped around the specific values and priorities of a particular nation, in this case a diverse country spread out over a vast landmass with a culturally dominant neighbor right in its backyard. It's also a reminder that American policy is only one version of how the media can be shaped by the agenda of the state.

Boundaries of Expression

The workings of regulation are often hidden from consumers of media, and matters of policy are often regarded as dry, bureaucratic, wonkish concerns. But the outcomes of media policy are of vital importance to our everyday lives. Policy and regulation ultimately determine what kind of media we have available to us. The decisions of state agencies constrain the companies and individuals that make media and the systems that distribute media. Policy and regulation dictate what is or is not possible in any given instance of media content. We may believe that in a free country we have freedom of speech and expression, and freedom of the press, but that guarantee of freedom is itself a form of public policy, and as we have seen, it comes with a myriad of exceptions and applies only to the actions of the state. Media companies may regulate themselves without being concerned about the First Amendment or any other similar law.

So to return to the words you don't usually hear on television: if they are forbidden, it is because either the state or a media company has determined that some interest is served by keeping them out of the ears of the public. As a tool in our toolkit, we can look at this constraint on media as an explanation for why media are the way they are. We can understand better that the words we hear, the images we see, the stories we receive have been shaped by a great many forces, by boundaries being drawn to mark off acceptable discourse from unacceptable violations. Many of these boundaries are the outcomes of media policy, of formal systems that make some things, but only some things, ok for public consumption, and that sanction the business practices and technological systems that deliver media to consumers. It's a matter of great public importance that these boundaries are drawn in ways that will maximize the benefit – and minimize the harm – to the whole society.

Discussion Questions

1. Why are media regulated? What are some costs and benefits of the state regulating media?
2. What are the different kinds of regulation? How has each of these shaped your experience of media?
3. Why is broadcasting different from other media? Do you think other media should be regulated in the way that broadcast TV and radio have been, and why or why not?

4. How do policy and regulation differ from country to country? How are the examples in this chapter of Chinese and Canadian media policy different from the regulation of media in the United States?

References

Aitken, Hugh G.J. 1994. "Allocating the Spectrum: The Origins of Radio Regulation." *Technology and Culture* 35.4: 686–716.

Arceneaux, Noah. 2006. "The Wireless in the Window: Department Stores and Radio Retailing in the 1920s." *Journalism and Mass Communication Quarterly* 83.3: 581–595.

Bernstein, Matthew. 1999. "Introduction." In *Controlling Hollywood: Censorship and Regulation in the Studio Era*, edited by Bernstein, 1–15. New Brunswick: Rutgers University Press.

Borneman, Ernest. 1985. "United States versus Hollywood: The Case Study of an Antitrust Suit." In *The American Film Industry*, edited by Tino Balio, 449–462. Madison: University of Wisconsin Press.

Carpenter, Daniel and David A. Moss, eds. 2014. *Preventing Regulatory Capture: Special Interest Influence and How to Limit It*. New York: Cambridge University Press.

Chen, Adrien. 2014. "The Laborers Who Keep Dick Pics and Beheadings Out of Your Facebook Feed." *Wired*, October 23, 2014. https://www.wired.com/2014/10/content-moderation/

Douglas, Susan. 1987. Inventing American Broadcasting, 1899–1922. Baltimore: Johns Hopkins University Press.

Edwardson, Ryan. 2008. Canadian Content: Culture and the Quest for Nationhood. Toronto: University of Toronto Press.

Esguerra, Richard. 2007. "The FCC and Regulatory Capture." *Electronic Frontier Foundation*, August 20, 2008. https://www.eff.org/deeplinks/2008/08/fcc-and-regulatory-capture

Facebook. n.d. "It's Time for Updated Internet Regulations." Accessed August 2, 2021. https://about.fb.com/regulations/

Federal Communications Commission. 2019. "The Public and Broadcasting," August 2019. https://www.fcc.gov/media/radio/public-and-broadcasting

Federal Communications Commission. 2020. "FCC Broadcast Ownership Rules," January 17, 2020. https://www.fcc.gov/sites/default/files/fcc_broadcast_ownership_rules.pdf

Gardner, Eriq. 2020. "Judge Agrees to End Paramount Consent Decrees." *Hollywood Reporter*, August 7, 2020. https://www.hollywoodreporter.com/business/business-news/judge-agrees-end-paramount-consent-decrees-1306387/

Hoynes, William. 1994. *Public Television for Sale: Media, the Market and the Public Sphere*. Boulder: Westview Press.

Jack, Carolyn. 2017. "Lexicon of Lies: Terms for Problematic Information." Data & Society Research Institute, August 9, 2017. https://datasociety.net/library/lexicon-of-lies/

Johansen, Peter W. 1973. "The CRTC and Canadian Content Regulation." *Journal of Broadcasting* 17.4: 465–474.

Kushnick, Bruce. 2013. "Regulatory Capture of the FCC – Time to Clean House." *HuffPost*, March 25, 2013. https://www.huffpost.com/entry/regulatory-capture-of-the_b_2936693

Lessig, Lawrence. 2004. *Free Culture: How Big Media Uses Technology and the Law to Lock Down Culture and Control Creativity*. New York: Penguin.

Lewis, Jon. 2002. *Hollywood vs. Hard Core: How the Struggle Over Censorship Created the Modern Film Industry*. New York: New York University Press.

McCabe, David, Cecilia Kang, and Daisuke Wakabayashi. 2020. "Google's Legal Peril Grows in Face of Third Antitrust Suit." *New York Times*, December 17, 2020. https://www.nytimes.com/2020/12/17/technology/google-antitrust-monopoly.html

Peters, B. Guy. 2018. *American Public Policy: Promise and Performance*, 11th ed. Washington: CQ Press.

Pew Research Center. 2021. "Local TV News Fact Sheet," July 13, 2021. https://www.journalism.org/fact-sheet/local-tv-news/

Ouellette, Laurie. 2002. *Viewers Like You? How Public TV Failed the People*. New York: Columbia University Press.

Pickard, Victor. 2019. *Democracy without Journalism? Confronting the Misinformation Society*. New York: Oxford University Press.

Pickard, Victor and David Elliot Berman. 2019. *After Net Neutrality: A New Deal for the Digital Age*. New Haven: Yale University Press.

Roberts, Sarah T. 2019. *Behind the Screen: Content Moderation in the Shadows of Social Media*. New Haven, CT: Yale University Press.

Sawyer, Laura Phillips. 2019. "US Antitrust Law and Policy in Historical Perspective." *Oxford Research Encyclopedias, American History*. https://doi.org/10.1093/acrefore/9780199329175.013.623

Scannell, Paddy. 2003. "Public Service Broadcasting: The History of a Concept" In *Television: Critical Concepts in Media and Cultural Studies* vol. 4, edited by Toby Miller, 212–226. London: Routledge.

Street, Sarah. 2009. "British Film and the National Interest, 1927–39." In *The British Cinema Book*, 3rd. ed., edited by Robert Murphy, 185–191. London: British Film Institute.

Turner, Ted. 2004. "My Beef with Big Media." *Washington Monthly*, July/August 2004.   https://washingtonmonthly.com/magazine/julyaugust-2004/my-beef-with-big-media/

Wagman, Ira. 2006. "From spiritual matters to economic facts: recounting problems of knowledge in the history of Canadian audiovisual policy, 1928–61." PhD diss., McGill University.

Wheeler, Tom. 2017. "A Goal Realized: Network Lobbyists' Sweeping Capture of their Regulator." *Brookings Techtank Blog*, December 14, 2017. https://www.brookings.edu/blog/techtank/2017/12/14/a-goal-realized-network-lobbyists-sweeping-capture-of-their-regulator/

Wittern-Keller, Laura. 2008. *Freedom of the Screen: Legal Challenges to State Film Censorship*. Lexington: University Press of Kentucky.

Wu, Tim. 2011. *The Master Switch: The Rise and Fall of Information Empires*. New York: Vintage.

8

CITIZENSHIP

Every chapter in this book, in one way or another, touches on the connection between media and politics. A critical approach to media studies takes this issue to be relevant to practically any discussion. *Politics* is the word we use to refer to relations of power in society, and politics can mean different things depending on the context. The politics of media representation or the politics of media technologies are not the exact same topic as the politics of political parties and elections, issues and campaigns, and movements and activism. This chapter more directly addresses the relevance of media to these latter kinds of politics.

Political systems vary by time and place. This discussion will be addressing the state of media in early 21st-century democracies, societies in which the people are given the power to determine their own leadership in free and fair elections. As a North American author, the view will necessarily be one shaped by my experience of Canadian and American media and democracy. But media in the early 21st century is thoroughly globalized, and the flows of media and ideas across the transnational networks mean that any individual's experience will likely share much in common with fellow citizens of the world in many diverse places. Many political movements are global, and many issues, such as climate change and public health, cannot be confined to a single nation or region.

The name for a political subject in a democratic society is *citizen*. There are many ways to define this term, and one way that will be useful here is that a citizen is a participant in political life. Citizens of democracies are

DOI: 10.4324/9781003007708-8

supposed to enjoy equal rights and privileges, such as the right to vote or run for office. The democratic system is premised, at least ideally, on citizen engagement and participation.

Citizenship is an identity, a way of seeing yourself. It is also a practice, a way of life. You have other ways of seeing yourself, other ways of being. Your citizenship overlaps with other identities and practices, such as your role in the family, the workplace, and other institutions such as schools and clubs. Citizenship is a public identity that you share with many diverse others. It connects you with the members of your community, the fellow citizens with whom you share an interest in public affairs and democratic governance. All together, you and your fellow citizens constitute a public. A democratic society functions effectively via the engagement of its citizens in public life.

In technologically advanced democratic societies, media, politics, and citizenship are tightly connected. Media is the source of much of our knowledge of politics and of global, national, and local affairs. It is also the channel through which we conduct much of our social interactions with fellow citizens. In a local community like a town or a neighborhood, we might see our fellow community members in person, face-to-face (though increasingly, even local politics plays out over social media and videoconferencing), but in a vast nation of millions or of hundreds of millions of citizens, our communications will be technologically mediated, and media are the essential site of our political expressions and activities.

Media have long been regarded as essential technologies for modern nations. As Benedict Anderson (2006) writes in his classic study of the origins of nationalism, Imagined Communities, the newspaper was essential to the establishment of modern nations with their multitudes of citizens. Anderson refers to daily newspaper reading in the early years of printing as a "mass ceremony" conducted by people across the nation, which he likens to the ritual of saying morning prayers. Newspaper readers would be aware of the same stories and topics, but also of multitudes of strangers whose simultaneous private reading occurs along with their own. He argues that this "community in anonymity...is the hallmark of modern nations" (35–36).

The introduction of new media has often been greeted as a promising development for citizenship. Broadcasting was heralded as a new way to unify the nation into one audience for the speeches of political leaders or the common simultaneous experiences of moments of national significance. In the 1920s, the new medium of radio broadcasting was regarded by some commentators as a tool to help immigrants to the US become part of the American melting pot, assimilating into their new community and becoming loyal citizens, producing one "well-knit" public in the United States (Boddy 2004, 16–20). The internet was regarded not so much as a force for greater nationalization as it was a herald of a newly energized citizenry who could use the new network as a platform for equal participation in "electronic democracy" (Friedland 1996; Rheingold 2000). Radio, television, and the internet all turned out to be rather different from what was imagined in their earliest days, but these optimistic visions are worth considering for the way they show us what people have imagined that media and politics could and should do for one another.

Media can be frivolous and fun, and can be a welcome diversion from everyday troubles. But media can also function as a forum for citizens, or an engine for spreading disinformation. We can use media to better our political knowledge and participation, but media can also harm our potential to engage as citizens by feeding our apathy and disillusionment, by distracting us from what matters, or by conveying lies and distortions in place of facts and truth. Media can shine a light on matters of crucial concern to citizens, but they can also trivialize politics by making it seem like a spectator sport or a fixed contest like pro wrestling. Mediated engagements over politics can be productive and informative, but they can also devolve into trolling and bullying, or they can be echo chambers for like-minded participants to affirm one another without considering divergent views. This is a high-stakes business, as the welfare of the whole society depends on democracy working effectively for the common good.

A well-functioning media is only one piece of a well-functioning democratic society, but it is undoubtedly crucial. Seen this way, media can be a form of civic culture, culture used to engage citizens in democratic experience and communication. When media addresses audiences as citizens, and when audiences engage with media as participants in democracy, that's civic culture (Dahlgren 2000).

Civic culture can be many different things, and some of the assumptions we might bring to thinking about this may be challenged along the way. For instance, it's obvious that journalism can be a form of civic culture, and online forums and social media outlets like Twitter are obvious examples, but we might miss many important instances if we see journalism and social media as the only important forms of political communication. Music, television, movies, comedy, and many other forms of popular culture have also functioned effectively as civic culture. In thinking about media and citizenship, we need to be willing to look in places we were not necessarily expecting to find it. And we should also be wary of using singulars when plurals are more important: there is no one public, but rather publics; no one civic culture, but rather civic cultures, and no one kind of political media, but many kinds.

The Public Sphere

Any informed discussion of media and citizenship needs to grapple with the key concept of the public sphere, which stands at the center of a theory formulated by the German philosopher Jürgen Habermas about the relationship between democracy and its citizens (Calhoun 1992; Habermas 1991). As a tool in our toolkit, the public sphere will help us to make some critical distinctions. It will also help us to grapple with problems that will need to be addressed if the media are to serve the citizens of a democracy most effectively for the good of the whole society.

The public sphere, according to Habermas, is a realm separate from the state (i.e., the government and its agencies) in which individual citizens engage with one another through a process of reasoned, critical deliberation and debate, and come to a consensus over matters of public concern. This arena for discussion is, crucially, separate from the state so that it can be critical of the state. Such conversation might occur in public spaces such as salons or coffee houses where patrons read newspapers and discuss the issues of the day. In this process, the best ideas, rather than the ideas advanced by those of high status, are those that prevail. In the public sphere, argument is conducted by citizens who share an equal stake in their outcome, and reason is the way to succeed in argument. The public sphere is a realm of discourse; talking among citizens is the way toward achieving the ideal political outcomes.

It is often pointed out that the public sphere of this theory excluded many more people than it included (a key example is Fraser 1990). It was a sphere of property-owning, elite white men. And as it's not clear if it ever functioned as described in the abstract, many scholars have treated it more as a metaphor or a utopian ideal than a reality. In the public sphere, the conditions of citizenship are activated by a discourse among equals over matters of common concern for the public. If the conditions of rational discourse, of equality of participants, or of access to the spaces of deliberation are not met, we don't really have a public sphere. But we can treat these conditions as aspirations, and hope that our systems of communication will come ever closer to achieving them.

Habermas is quite pessimistic about the public sphere in modern, technologically advanced societies. His model of the public sphere is found in European societies of the 17th and 18th centuries, before the rise of mass media, and eons before the internet came along. Many critics of mass media, including Habermas himself, have asserted that the domination of media systems by large corporations, and the monopoly enjoyed by mass media over the information that citizens can access, has meant that the public is fed more advertising, public relations, and propaganda than reasoned discourse (Habermas 2006; Papacharissi 2009). This is a matter reasonable people can debate. But regardless of where one stands on this, the shift from mass media to digital/ online/new media has produced new opportunities for civic culture in a networked public sphere that is rather different from the 20th-century landscape of mass media. The potential for these new platforms for political discourse to reinvigorate the public sphere has been treated as a hopeful promise of new media technology.

Journalism as Civic Culture

If any one type of media seems especially to fit into a concept of civic culture for an effective public sphere to function, it is surely journalism, also known as the news, the press, and sometimes just the media. Each of these terms has its own shades of meaning, but we often use them interchangeably. Journalism is the practice of gathering and publishing news, a product, while the press comprises the institutions of journalistic work, the newspapers, television and radio news operations, and online outlets. Once all journalism was print journalism, produced on a printing press, but after radio and television joined in, "the media" became a synonym for "the press."

Politics is not the only, or even the main, topic of the news. A typical daily newspaper might include recipes, movie reviews, sports scores, horoscopes, comic strips, and a crossword puzzle. But undoubtedly one of the key functions of the news is to inform the public about the workings of government, about politics and political issues, including the issues of concern to citizens that elected leaders might address in their work on behalf of their constituents. These range from the local, such as proposals for new bike lanes on city streets, to the national and global, such as policies to combat climate change. (Note that in these examples, the micro-level and macro-level issues are related.) To engage in the public sphere, citizens need good information. They can get it from many sources, but without a robust free press, it's hard to imagine how any modern democracy in which millions or hundreds of millions of citizens participate together as one public can hope to function.

The centrality of journalism to the public good is recognized in many ways, including the laws that protect the press from government interference. The US Constitution's First Amendment guarantees that Congress will not curtail the freedom of the press. This amendment is often misinterpreted to be a blanket protection of free expression, but if you read it carefully you notice that it specifically prohibits Congress, i.e., lawmakers at the federal level, from acting as a censor or constraint on the freedom of printers to publish what they wish. The state is supposed to keep out of the media business, which functions as an institution, autonomous from the government, holding elected politicians accountable by shedding light on their actions. (Old-timey newspaper names like *The Sun* and *The Star* suggest that the purpose of news is to illuminate.) Surely it was by this reasoning that Thomas Jefferson famously wrote: "Were it left to me to decide if we should have a government without newspapers, or newspapers without a government, I should not hesitate a moment to prefer the latter." (Jefferson followed that famous line with this bit, not as often quoted: "but I should mean that every man should receive those papers & be capable of reading them." We will come back to this.)

The modern profession of journalism has developed a self-image and sense of purpose that is closely aligned with the ideals of the public sphere. Not all journalists or news organizations subscribe to the exact same set of values, but the mainstream of journalism usually sees itself as doing something more virtuous than just producing a commercial product to earn a profit by engaging audiences and selling papers, subscriptions, or advertisements. Rather, journalism regards itself as producing a public good, a resource that serves the needs of a democratic society. This is evident in the "journalist's creed" that is cast in bronze on a plaque at the National Press Club in Washington, DC, which reads (in part):

> I believe that the public journal is a public trust; that all connected with it are, to the full measure of their responsibility, trustees for the public; that acceptance of a lesser service than the public service is betrayal of this trust.

To be a public trust, journalism functions alongside institutions of the state, separate from them but vital to their effective functioning. Anyone can inform their fellow citizens about what's going on in their community, but journalists make it a lofty mission, and the routines and conventions of their work often prioritize certain values such as reliance on facts, getting information first-hand from reliable sources, questioning and scrutinizing official communications, avoiding conflicts of interest, and maintaining a separation between reporting the news and giving opinionated commentary. Journalists like to think they are the ones to hold power to account and speak for the "little guy." As the old saying goes, a newspaper should "comfort the afflicted and afflict the comfortable." Journalists may fail to live up to these ideals from time to time, or even routinely, but the practice of journalism often depends on striving to meet these standards as a form of essential public service that cannot be performed by any other institution.

Journalism is sometimes called "the fourth estate," which is a way of asserting how important it is for society to function. The origins of this term are archaic, and can mean different things in different contexts. (I recommend you start with Wikipedia if you're interested to know more.) The way the term is generally used, it signifies that the press is an essential part of the political system without being an official branch or agency of government. Calling the press an "estate" signals its value and its traditional role of honor and esteem.

Politicians and others in positions of power might disdain the media or find journalists to be troublesome, to be advancing an agenda or searching for dirt where none exists, yet the system as a whole relies on a free press to hold leaders accountable by monitoring their work as the representatives of the people. Instances of journalism that have gained the most public honor and prestige for the press as an institution, such as the reporting of the Watergate scandal by reporters for the *Washington Post* and of the Catholic priest sex abuse scandal by reporters for the *Boston Globe*, are typically those that hold powerful people and institutions to account, unmasking wrongdoing and prompting reform. When Hollywood makes movies about righteous journalists, like the ones that tell these two stories in particular (*All the President's Men*, 1976; *Spotlight*, 2015), the reporters are portrayed as uncomplicated, dedicated heroes for having the courage to discover and publish the facts that reveal the true workings of power.

But despite being celebrated in movies like these, the press often fails to live up to our lofty ideals. Many news organizations are for-profit businesses supported by advertising and subscriptions. These organizations might be small, independent businesses, like local papers, but many are owned by large chains of newspapers or TV stations, or enormous multimedia conglomerates that see news as a profit-engine. Public media organizations are free of some of the constraints faced by commercial media, but they too need to worry about their revenues and expenses, and how well they do at attracting an audience. For commercial media in particular, there are many ways the incentives to please advertisers and keep subscribers satisfied can clash with the noble aspirations of journalism to be a quasi-sacred public trust. News that sells, and that captures the largest desirable audience's attention, is not necessarily the same thing as news that fulfills the ideals of a "fourth estate" to be a check on power and an essential resource to the citizen. Critics have faulted journalism for veering too much into sensationalized or trivial entertainment ("infotainment") and obsessing over scandals and personalities, for avoiding investigating topics that might alienate advertisers or offend management (e.g., going after the pharmaceutical companies that sponsor many cable news programs), or ever calling into question the very capitalist media system that produces its profits (Herman and Chomsky 1988; Lull and Hinerman 1997). Some question whether commercial, for-profit, advertising-supported journalism can serve the needs of a democratic society, and advocate for a more robust public media system (McChesney 2004; Pickard 2020).

And traditional journalism covering politics and other kinds of "hard news," journalism that isn't suffering from these problems, might often fail to be appealing to a broad enough public. In the later years of the 20th century, it was clear that traditional print news consumption was in decline. Fewer people were reading daily papers, and young people in particular were not as likely to be regular newspaper readers as their parents and grandparents. In 1940, the total circulation of daily newspapers in the United States was approximately 41 million. In 2020 it was 24 million, while the population of the United States had more than doubled over those 80 years (Pew Research Center 2021). For years it was television that was more likely to be their source of information than print publications, and then websites. To traditionalists, to people with a strong investment in the newspaper as an ideal vehicle for news that engages citizens, this would be cause for much concern, perhaps implying a decline in civic culture. In some accounts, rising "civic indifference" among the young has been a cause of concern (Rimmerman 2018), and a decline in Americans' civic engagement has been associated with various potential causes, including the popularity of television (Putnam 2000).

Many reasons have been offered to explain this supposed decline in engagement, which was often regarded as a crisis for civic culture (Dahlgren 2000). Perhaps young people raised on television didn't like to read, or were conditioned by TV to expect to be entertained all the time, and were consequently "amused to death" by a media system that prioritizes show business and fragments culture into digestible flashy images (Postman 1985). Perhaps television news coverage led to cynicism about politics, to a societal "videomalaise" that turned people off of caring about politics, of having faith in the legitimacy of political institutions and the trustworthiness of politicians (Robinson 1975). Perhaps the news was stuck in old-fashioned conventions that came across as too detached or untrustworthy, or journalists failed to put the news into a format and context that ordinary citizens would find credible and engaging (Merritt 1995; Rosen 1993).

Whatever the explanation, it was widely feared that a trend toward disengagement from politics and community life would have harmful effects on society broadly speaking by giving us a democracy without citizens who know or care enough to participate in it. There was undoubtedly an element of moral panic in this rhetoric. But it was true that newspaper circulation had been on a steady, long-term decline well before the internet became a venue for news (Pew Research Center 2021). And while political engagement is hard to measure objectively, one metric would be voter turnout, especially in non-Presidential elections. In the US, voter turnout had been declining since the 1960s and barely half of the eligible voters turned out for the November election of 1996, when Bill Clinton won a second term. In that election, as in many presidential contests, the people who didn't vote outnumbered the people who chose either one of the major party candidates. It's hard to pinpoint cause-effect relationships when there are so many factors shaping the interests and behaviors of millions of people, but many observers saw a troubling connection between these trends.

Pop Culture Is Civic Culture Too

It's convenient to divide up media into two crude categories: information and entertainment. We will want to trash this distinction because there is just too much overlap in these categories, but for a moment, let's use it as a prompt for thinking about the potential of different kinds of media to be politically engaging.

News contains essential information. This is true in particular of political news and reporting of topics that are serious and consequential, like energy policy, public health and medicine, and war and famine. One essential element of civic culture is that it is informative, so naturally news is relevant to this discussion. We might wonder, then, if entertainment belongs elsewhere and not here in this chapter.

When we think of the media of entertainment, we might think of Hollywood-style movies and TV series, pop music, video games, sports, and social media platforms like YouTube and TikTok. An old-fashioned name for this kind of media is showbiz, which suggests pleasing the audience, leaving them eager for more, and making a buck. Showbiz hails from the circus and the variety theater, the concert hall and the picture show. Some of its audiences might prefer their entertainment to be free of politics and seriousness. Maybe what you're looking for in a game is fun, and what you're looking for in music is a groove you can dance to, and what you're looking for in a TV show is an intriguing story with relatable characters. Many of the people whose work is making these kinds of media are not particularly interested in contributing to a robust civic culture. There was a saying in old Hollywood: "If you have a message, call Western Union." (In those days, you'd call Western Union to send a telegram.) This was a way of complaining that movies should avoid preaching and social commentary and just tell a good story.

Of course, movies, television, and many other kinds of popular culture are often informative in a way that appeals to people's curiosity about the world and their investment in social issues. This can be true of fiction or nonfiction. Many viewers have learned about the government from shows like The West Wing and Parks and Recreation and movies like Mr. Smith Goes to Washington and Bulworth. The police are agents of the state, and much of what we know about how they work comes from an endless succession of cop shows and movies (which almost inevitably portray them sympathetically). Movies like Selma teach us about the history of social movements, and television series like Law & Order dramatize the criminal justice system with stories "torn from the headlines." Fictionalized representations may not present a wholly truthful or realistic picture, but audiences understand that dramas take license, even when adhering to the contours of a true story. Despite variations and embellishments for the sake of dramatic engagement, we do learn about the world from fiction and fictionalized storytelling. The techniques of good storytelling can make these representations broadly appealing by being vivid and colorful, emotionally engaging and deeply pleasurable.

Politicians also appropriate popular culture, and invoke its characters and themes to appeal to their publics. A notorious example of this occurred in the early 1990s, when the Vice President of the United States and a fictional sitcom character became engaged in a political debate about "family values." Murphy Brown (Candace Bergen) was the protagonist of the popular television comedy *Murphy Brown*, set behind the scenes of a TV news program. In the fictional storyline, Murphy, a professional single woman, decides to become a mother. The 1991–1992 season follows her pregnancy and the birth of her child.

While giving a speech in the summer of 1992, Vice President Dan Quayle criticized the series for making it seem okay for unmarried women to have children and thereby questioning the importance of fathers, seizing this example to further the right-wing rhetoric, common at the time, in defense of the traditional nuclear family. Quayle offered this as a case of Hollywood elites corrupting their audiences by promoting a vision of the family that conservatives deplored.[1] The conflict blew up during the 1992 US presidential campaign, and landed Murphy/Bergen on the cover of *Time* magazine, among other publications. And this episode was merely one flashpoint within a broader, long-term culture war between left and right in which popular media have often appeared as a bugaboo of conservatives who oppose its influence (Fiske 1994, 21–74). There have been many instances over the years of politicians (of the left and right) picking on pop culture for promoting values they don't like, whether movies, comic books, video games, television, or popular music.

The creators of *Murphy Brown* may not have intended to pick a fight with the Vice President, but pop culture does regularly intervene directly into politics by speaking to current issues and struggles. Popular music has the power to engage listeners as citizens, and might do a better job than some aspects of the news at contributing to the public sphere by tapping into deep wells of feeling and first-hand experience. Songwriting has long functioned as protest, commentary, and a call-to-arms for movements and countercultures. The 1960s counterculture is unimaginable without the music of protest against war and racial oppression. Many social movements have embraced popular songs. Sam Cooke's 1964 "A Change Is Gonna Come," inspired by an episode in which Cooke was turned away from a hotel because he was Black, became an anthem for the civil rights movement of the 1960s. Its words are simple and direct, revealing feelings of despair ("I thought I couldn't last for long") turning to hope and a sense of purpose and faith in progress ("I know a change is gonna come").

These words, and the music they are set to, were taken up by the African-American struggle for dignity and equality under the law and has become a touchstone of the continuing effort to achieve racial justice in America. It has been covered by more than 500 artists. Barack Obama quoted the song on the night he was first elected President, and it was performed at his Inaugural Celebration. Popular songs like this are so much a part of our experience of citizenship that it's hard to believe anyone would say pop culture is all "just entertainment." Protest songs, union songs, anti-war songs, songs about exploitation and oppression, have been some of the most powerful examples of popular music. American popular music in particular has roots deep in the history of African-American suffering and resistance.

Perhaps the most compelling reason to reject the division of media into entertainment and information is that so much political media outside of the sphere of traditional journalism is presented in a way that methodically blurs these two categories. I'm thinking here in particular of nonfiction media about politics, especially ironic or satirical takes on news and political affairs that combine humor and criticism in a way that offers audiences an alternative to traditional journalism. Memes and other user-generated content posted on social media would be one version of this. Memes are typically humorous and ironic, and they depend on shared knowledge among members of a community. They only make sense and make you smile if you recognize their references, including the format of the meme and the object of the humor (Shifman 2013; Milner 2016).

For example, a Twitter user named Travon Free posted a tweet on August 2, 2020, that has been "liked" more than 300,000 times, a sure sign of strong virality. It was a "quote tweet" of a photo posted by The Lincoln Project, a political action committee of conservatives opposed to President Donald Trump. The photo was a portrait of three of Trump's adult children, Ivanka, Don Jr., and Eric, with the caption "Name this Band." The format of this tweet invites users to respond with amusing or clever ideas of band names that would effectively make fun of the subjects of the photo. (Sometimes the caption in this meme is "Name this band. Wrong answers only." By the time this tweet was posted, the second part could be merely implied.) Travon Free's wrong band name was "Lady Anti-BLM," a pun on Lady Antebellum, the former name of country music trio Lady A, and the short form for the Black Lives Matter movement, which had been organizing protests against police brutality for much of the spring and summer of that year across the US and around the world. Earlier that summer, Lady Antebellum had announced their name change, signaling their reckoning with a history of racial oppression in the American south. ("Antebellum" is a term used – often problematically in former slave states – to describe the pre-Civil War era in the US.)

This is just one tweet, but it captures a dynamic of humor and political critique being inseparable. The joke depends on several levels of "getting it": the format of "name this band," the Trump children as scions of a political leader identified with white nationalism, and the band name that was changed as a product of a growing recognition of American racial injustice. This kind of social media humor is political to its core, and it speaks to a community of people who understand its language and share common values. It also comes out of a very long tradition, running through a history of political cartoons and other forms of satire that we can trace to ancient times.

As it turns out, Travon Free is no average Twitter user. He is a writer for satirical television shows, one of the key examples of politics and entertainment being merged into one form of media. He has worked on *The Daily Show* and *Full Frontal with Samantha Bee*, two examples of the trend of entertaining politics on American cable television (Jones 2009). These shows feed off the news and react to contemporary developments, offering commentary and criticism in a comical style that mixes parodies of news reports, standup comedy-style monologues reacting to recent events, and interviews that often probe into contemporary issues. Satirical news programs are joined by many other kinds of TV that blend entertainment with critical political engagement, including the broad political impersonations and mock newscasts of *Saturday Night Live* and the raunchy spoofing of *South Park*. The late-night talk shows on the major US networks (*The Tonight Show*, *The Late Show*, etc.) have also been regular venues for political humor over most of the history of American TV. Poking fun at politicians and other powerful figures were their bread and butter before most of us were even born.

Satirical news programs can be found on television channels around the world, and have become an enduringly popular genre in the United States, United Kingdom, and Canada (Thompson, Jones, and Gray 2009). A boom for shows like these began in the US with Comedy Central's *The Daily Show* (1996–) under its second host, Jon Stewart, who appeared from 1999 to 2015. These programs share some key qualities with satirical print publications like the late British magazine *Punch*, which began its run all the way back in 1841, and the American newspaper-turned-website *The Onion*, which started publication in 1988. Satirical newspapers and magazines exist around the globe, and a number have been in print for more than a century. Whatever their medium, these publications typically mimic the format of news and the tone of news writing, but the content is filled with sharp put-downs, absurd exaggerations, and outlandish made-up stories. The best examples at once savage typical news conventions and also travesty the subjects of much of the news. Satire exposes the folly and vice of powerful people and institutions, and exposes them to ridicule and criticism. It is a form of political humor, often expecting its audience to be familiar with its targets. It shares with journalism not just a focus on the government and current affairs, but an audience or readers or viewers with an interest in being informed about the issues of the day and in being offered insight and perspective on them.

At first, programs like *The Daily Show* might have been seen as amusing diversions or acerbic commentaries, and their presence on channels like Comedy Central suggested that they belonged in the category of entertainment rather than news. But as Jon Stewart became extremely popular, especially among younger audiences, and as *The Daily Show* came to occupy a central place in America's political culture during the early-to-mid 2000s, scholars began to look at it not just as a form of entertainment but as an instance of "alternative journalism" that engages audiences as a form of civic culture. As the media scholar Geoffrey Baym (2005) argues, "*The Daily Show* can be understood as an experiment in the journalistic" that "uses satire to interrogate power, parody to critique contemporary news, and dialogue to enact a model of deliberative democracy" (261). He means here that despite not appearing to be conventional journalism, comedy shows like this can do the same kind of work as the news by engaging citizens in a discourse about politics in a democracy. This would occur during the segments in which Stewart mockingly summarized recent events, sprinkling in insults and swears, but also in the interviews he would conduct with authors, politicians or candidates for office, and celebrities. Shows like this might do an even better job than conventional journalism at engaging citizens thanks to their strong appeal, especially to younger viewers who by the early 2000s were increasingly uninterested in being traditional news consumers.

Around the time when Jon Stewart passed the hosting role over to Trevor Noah, his Daily Show successor, data from the Pew Research Center showed that the program's audiences were relying on it as a source of news (12 percent of Americans said they got their news from The Daily Show, roughly the same percentage as got their news from the national newspaper USA Today). The audience for The Daily Show (median age 36) was considerably younger than that of more conventional public affairs programs such as NBC Nightly News (median age 52), suggesting that for many younger Americans, satire might substitute for straight journalism, or be a complement to it (Gottfried, Matsa, and Barthel 2015). A poll by the Pew Research Center (2007) found that viewers of The Daily Show were as well informed about national and international affairs as readers of daily newspapers, and that they were better informed than viewers of network and local news programs, as well as CNN and Fox News. These statistical data about viewers of a satirical TV show hosted by a comedian on a channel known for its cartoons and sketch comedies capture a blurring of boundaries, and prompt a reconsideration of what "counts" when it comes to civic culture.

Journalism and popular culture are often regarded as separate and distinct, but The Daily Show and many other shows like it have offered strong evidence that the separation doesn't hold up too well to scrutiny. Politics takes many forms, and so does knowledge. Citizens need more than just facts; they need a context for understanding them and a reason to care about them. Entertainment often supplies these conditions, drawing audiences in and giving them pleasure. Many kinds of media have the potential to serve the civic needs of a democratic society. As Sarah Banet-Weiser (2004) puts it: "Forms of popular culture and, more specifically, commercial entertainment, are not outside the realm of 'official' politics; on the contrary, it is often within these realms that our understanding, resistance, and acquiescence to 'official' politics are constituted" (222).

The Internet as Democratizing Media

Since the middle of the 1990s, when the internet became integral to everyday life, media scholars have seen it as one of the most crucial topics in understanding media and citizenship. Computer networks afford some new and different kinds of relationships to communication and culture than other kinds of media. While it can be used for many varied purposes, one of the key contributions of the internet to the public sphere has been its platforms for users to engage and participate with other users.

This has been described in a number of ways, such as transitioning from a "read-only" culture (think: print books or movies) to "read/write" experiences with online forums and social media sites that afford us not only an experience of consuming, but also of producing and contributing to media with our own voices, images, and stories (Lessig 2008). This has also gone by names like "Web 2.0" – a version of the web that emerged in the early-to-mid 2000s that invited users to be creative and share online – and more commonly in scholarly discussions, "participatory culture." Participatory culture means the audience members are also potentially creative collaborators in media, taking part in the conversation rather than just looking or listening. As Henry Jenkins (2006) puts it: "Rather than talking about media producers and consumers as occupying separate roles, we might now see them as participants who interact with each other" (4).

One reason to prefer "participatory culture" is that it bridges online and offline realms, as it has a lot in common with oral and folk cultures that existed long before the rise of mass media. But it has flourished in an age of blogs and Twitter, social networking sites and apps, message boards and forums, and community platforms like YouTube and Twitch. It may often be the case that a minority of users produces the majority of the content even in these networks, but the scope of participation and potential for engagement is still so much greater by comparison to earlier media forms, with their more meager feedback opportunities (e.g., newspaper letters to the editor).

If the public sphere is a space for citizens to participate in discussions of community concern, the participatory culture characteristic of the internet would seem like an exciting opportunity for engaging people in civic culture in a way that might solve some of the problems of pre-internet communication like TV and print media. The internet permits communities to form across many borders and divisions. It's always on and, with some exceptions, global. It's not difficult to access, though it does require resources in a way that excludes users on the wrong side of the "digital divide" between richer and poorer communities. It has often seemed to be a promising democratizing force, though some critics have questioned this assumption (e.g., Papacharissi 2009).[2]

Democratizing here doesn't necessarily mean spreading democracy to countries that have other political systems, though the internet has been seen this way sometimes (Tufekci 2017). It is more centrally concerned with a process of expanding access and participation to more people, working to level off the distinctions between elites and other groups with less official or political power. Democratizing media ideally means that *all* of the people get to have a voice and a seat at the table.

It is tempting, having lived with this participatory internet for a couple of decades, to be cynical about such a utopian notion of technology that would democratize media. We now know that participatory culture is often appropriated by trolls, abusers, and propaganda merchants (Phillips 2015). The problems of the offline world don't magically melt away when we move our communications online. But we should be able to see both the good and the bad, and the participatory potential of the internet really has opened access to cultural creativity and civic discourse to huge numbers of people. Just because it hasn't been all good news doesn't mean it hasn't been good news at all.

Participatory culture might not always engage directly with matters of politics and citizenship, which is fine. But civic culture has often been energized by digital platforms and their consciously political cultures. When this happens, we can see online media serving as hubs for *networked publics* and *counterpublics*. A networked public might be another name for an online community, but the term may also invoke the civic potential in participatory cultures, along with new possibilities for spreading knowledge and organizing collective action that networked digital technologies offer us (Varnelis 2008; boyd 2011). A *networked counterpublic* would be a public that is premised on its opposition to another dominant or mainstream public. For example, a counterpublic could be any social movement agitating for justice in the face of inequality, including women's rights, LGBTQ+ rights, indigenous rights, disability rights, workers' rights, and civil rights movements. Religious minorities, such as European Muslims, may form a counterpublic. The Occupy movement was explicitly positioned as the expression of the majority's rejection of capitalist exploitation (its slogan: "we are the 99%"), while around the world, activists for democracy have challenged repressive and authoritarian regimes. A counterpublic is political to its core, positioning itself in relation to a more powerful public, and contesting its dominance (Fraser 1990).[3]

Two examples here can illustrate some of the ways that networked publics and counterpublics function as mediated civic culture. The first is a politically engaged fan community, and the second is a protest movement.

A fan is an individual, and the identity of the fan is defined by a strong passion for some object: a celebrity, a sports team, a media franchise, perhaps a brand or consumer product. Media fandom is hardly solitary, though, and fans have long sought each other's company in various forms of community, offline and on. Fans share their objects of interest and take on common pursuits, combining their knowledge and resources. Many fans like to meet one another at conventions and other gatherings, where some dress up in tribute to their fandom objects ("cosplay"). In forming communities around their fandoms, these media audiences are one model of participatory culture. They go beyond reading, listening, and watching to organizing and making their own media, from commentaries and videos to fan art and fan fiction (Hellekson and Busse 2006; Gray, Sandvoss, and Harrington 2017).

Online platforms have been one of the critical catalysts for an explosion of fandom in the 21st century. The TV fan might once have been seen as a marginal figure of overinvestment in popular culture. But during the early years of the participatory web, fandom became much more mainstream. Media industries began to cultivate fandoms as a way of speaking to audiences eager to seek out their products amidst a cluttered media landscape. The ease of gathering online and sharing fan objects on message boards, social networking sites, and other networked platforms was central to this explosion of media fandom.

Fan communities thus became fixtures of the online experience. An online community is a public, and in many ways the organization of fandoms runs parallel to the communities of citizens that we call the public sphere. A fandom is akin to a nation: the members of the fandom have similar experiences of allegiance and belonging as citizens have to the nation as a community. (Sports fans often describe themselves this way: Red Sox nation, Liverpool nation, etc.) For many younger fans, this experience of going online and participating in fan cultures could serve as an entryway to civic culture as a practice of community engagement. Fandoms are not democracies, but they have many qualities in common with other kinds of publics, including political struggles over who is in or out of the group and what its values or policies should be. They also engage in forms of activism related to their fandom, such as campaigns to save television shows from cancelation. This practice goes back to the attempt to save *Star Trek* in 1969, among the first of many such fan efforts (Guerrero-Pico 2017). The skills required of effective fan and citizen communities are not all the same, but they both include sharing information, engaging fellow members in discussion, and making common cause on matters of shared values. Jenkins (2012) makes an explicit bridge between civic and fan cultures when he argues that "fandom may represent a particularly powerful training ground for future activists and community organizers" (paragraph 2.6).

Some fan communities have made this bridge into a more direct, intentional connection between media and politics. The Harry Potter Alliance (HPA) is a nonprofit organization founded in 2005 around fandom of the HP franchise. Ashley Hinck (2012) argues that this group in particular shows the overlap of fan and citizen activists: "Fandom can function … as a way to come to see oneself as a member of the public, capable of civic engagement" (paragraph 1.4). The HPA is an activist collective whose membership has participated in campaigns to raise money and awareness of global issues and exert political pressure. HPA's politics are progressive, and participants in the community have drawn inspiration from themes of the HP stories and characters in addressing the real-world issues they care about, referring to themselves as "Dumbledore's Army." Hinck focuses in particular on the HPA activism around the genocide in Darfur (which began in 2003). In 2007 podcast episodes, the HPA engaged in traditional political organizing, motivating community members to take part in a letter-writing campaign and to circulate petitions calling on corporations to cut ties to any entity doing business with Sudan, whose government was responsible for the violence in Darfur. HPA activists encouraged membership to call their elected representatives and "to engage in expressive and creative acts, demonstrating support and expressing their political position and identity" (paragraph 5.3).

Long before the emergence of the internet, there were numerous examples of celebrities inspiring activism and participating in traditional political events like campaign rallies. But we have seen some bold examples of fandoms organizing online in response to calls from their objects of worship, effectively blurring entertainment into civic culture. A more recent example is the fan culture around the K-pop band BTS. This group, known as ARMY, have mobilized as activists for progressive causes, including Black Lives Matter, for which they have raised considerable funds. As Laura Springman (2020) describes, these stans use their digital media savvy to make trouble for groups they oppose, flooding alt-right hashtags with BTS memes, "drowning out the hateful rhetoric these hashtags intended to foster." K-pop stans gained wide notoriety during the US presidential election of 2020 when they organized massive online requests to attend a rally in support of President Trump, which turned out to be embarrassingly sparsely attended.

Hinck (2012) argues that participation in the HPA made political activism meaningful to members of the group as they felt anchored in a community of others who shared their same concerns and interests. So while most fan communities might not be so explicitly identified with politics in the form of specific projects and activism, we can see that the conditions for civic engagement are often met within online fan communities. This has often been welcomed as a promising sign of new media's potential to overcome some of the perceived shortcomings of mass-mediated societies, such as a creeping apathy, passivity, and civic disengagement. Obviously fans are citizens like anyone else, but fan communities can also be a model of engaged citizenship.

However engaged some citizens might be, the Habermasian public sphere has some shortcomings as a concept of how civic culture works in a modern democracy. The most critical drawbacks are its exclusions. The idea of a single public, of one sphere of political conversation among equals, was premised on the public sphere belonging to one minority of the people: bourgeois (upper-middle-class or affluent) European (white) men (presumably straight and cisgender). In reality, there has never been such a public that is broadly inclusive and equal. We live in a highly stratified society, with many kinds of inequality structuring relations among different social groups defined by class, gender and sexuality, race and ethnicity, and other markers of identity all in intersection with one another.

Rather than one community, scholars of the public sphere have asserted that there are publics, plural, including counterpublics positioned in relation to other publics (Fraser 1990; Jackson, Bailey, and Foucault Welles 2020). Many examples of networked counterpublics are online communities based around a specific form of activism, an agenda for change. Networked counterpublics have organized online via platforms and technologies like Twitter and hashtags. Their ability to drive attention to urgent social justice campaigns and effect meaningful change has been one of the remarkable developments of the era of participatory culture. They court allies to their causes and attract the notice of mainstream media, which has long been a gateway through which protest movements have achieved wider participation and legitimacy.

In the social media age, a successful movement needs hashtags. It might even be named for its hashtag: e.g., #MeToo or #BlackLivesMatter. A hashtag functions to organize data and communication. Social media users have adopted hashtags to serve diverse functions, but their fundamental usage always comes back to building and maintaining community. Tweeting using the hashtag, or including it in a post to Facebook, Instagram, or another platform, includes the new content in a collective expression organized by the community. The hashtag serves to bring the public together, to constitute participation as a member of the public, and to collect the expressions and arguments of the public under a common label. Hashtag activism, according to Sarah J. Jackson, Moya Bailey, and Brooke Foucault Welles (2020), is the effort to use this tool "to make political contentions about identity politics that advocate for social change, identity redefinition, and political inclusion" (xxviii).

Black Lives Matter (BLM) is a civil rights movement that overlaps with Black Twitter. Marc Lamont Hill (2018) describes Black Twitter as an example of a counterpublic, a community of critical resistance, a site for African-American users online to "negotiate oppositional identities" (287) in a kind of online version of the barbershop, church, and other traditional spaces of Black community. In looking at the discourse around BLM on Black Twitter, Hill identifies in this community a practice of critical public pedagogy. That is, he sees Twitter users educating one another – and the broader public – about race, politics, identity, and state-sponsored violence.

This discussion comes in reaction to Twitter conversations in the aftermaths of a number of highly publicized episodes of unarmed Black men being killed by police officers. BLM discourse is most prominent in these moments of trauma and rage that lead to protest and organizing. Hill notes that in these times, BLM activists often engage with a discourse known as the "politics of respectability," which they reject. The contested assumption behind respectability politics is that Black people have some responsibility for their own oppression. "Respectability" thinking says that racism can be overcome if African-Americans conform to "middle-class" expectations of conduct and appearance and adopt mainstream values to win the favor of white America. When this politics is invoked in relation to the killing of Black men, Hill argues, it fastens onto "imperfect victims" as if to blame citizens for their own unjust deaths. Michael Brown, a Black teenager killed by a police officer, might have robbed a convenience store; Eric Garner, a Black man killed by a police officer, was selling unlicensed cigarettes on the street; Walter Scott, a Black man killed by a police officer, was fleeing from him. Hill notes that the BLM movement is anti-"respectability" when it argues that Black Lives Matter, however perfect or imperfect they may be, as they are human lives deserving of the same love, dignity, and respect as any others.

The pedagogy came into play in one particularly revealing episode in 2016, when BLM activists on Twitter engaged with reactions from a well-known pro athlete to the killings of two Black men, Alton Sterling and Philando Castile. Hill describes this exchange:

> In response to the killings, NBA basketball player Damian Lillard tweeted that Black people "have to take better care of each other [sic] … We do harm more often to our brother/sister than anyone else." He continued, "Change is needed on our behalf NOW … And then the battle can go further in demanding that we be treated better from others" (original emphasis; Lillard 2016a, 2016b). Rather than criticizing the officers who killed Sterling and Castile, or acknowledging the structures that normalize extrajudicial state violence, Lillard criticized the Black community writ large for its own behaviors.
>
> (294–295)[4]

Hill describes that following these posts, Black Twitter responded forcefully by arguing against Lillard's position, defending their conviction that Black people are not to blame for their own victimization and that change needs to come from the institutions of the state that perpetrate this violence. Following this criticism, according to Hill, Lillard showed contrition and openness to learning from the online activists. This exchange gave BLM and Black Twitter an opportunity for teaching not just one celebrity, but a much broader online community about its values, in particular its resistance to respectability politics, and to defining the value of Black lives on the dominant public's terms.

This episode is but one moment in a daily struggle among counterpublics to engage in debate and deliberation over the terrain of politics and their position within it. Ultimately, this story speaks to the ways we *talk* online about politics and identity, and talk really is the essence of civic culture and the public sphere. Hashtag activism is sometimes put down as "slacktivism" or as somehow disconnected from real politics on the ground and in legislatures and parliaments. But media are crucial for any kind of modern movement, and social media have given activists a powerful tool to connect with one another and convey their messages to a broader, engaged public.

Citizenship as Belonging

Citizenship is a set of formal rights, a legal concept, but it is also a matter of identity, a concept we use to think about ourselves in relation to our communities. We can be citizens of many publics: of our neighborhoods, towns, and cities, states and provinces, and countries. We can be citizens of other kinds of communities as well: workplaces and schools, and groups we join out of passion and affinity or allegiance to a cause. Citizenship, ultimately, is about our sense of "social belonging" to something greater than ourselves (Canclini 2001, 20).

Media of various forms and genres are where we often find this belonging. We find it by connecting with media texts, with their information, with their stories, their characters, their themes and meanings and their vision of a world. We find it as readers and spectators and listeners. We find it when we connect with our fellow citizens around objects of shared interest, with the members of our publics and counterpublics. And when, increasingly, we use media as authors as well as readers, as participants in online (and offline) communities.

Media have this crucial role, and our critical eye should scrutinize how well they perform it. I promised to come back to Thomas Jefferson, who said he would choose newspapers over government, but only if "every man should receive those papers & be capable of reading them." Expanding our concept of civic culture well beyond newspapers to include many kinds of journalism and entertainment, and many forms that blow up the distinction between them, we should still demand as Jefferson did that media be accessible, and that the public – better yet *publics* – be endowed with the literacy and resources to engage robustly with one another in expressions of civic culture. The welfare of a democratic society depends on it.

Discussion Questions

1. How do journalism and entertainment engage citizens? Choose one example of each one and make the case that it is or is not an effective example of civic culture.

2. How does the internet function in relation to civic culture? Do you see important differences between online and offline examples of media that engages citizens?

3. What does it mean to you to be a citizen? Do your everyday experiences with media either facilitate your participation in civic culture or distract you from it?

4. Choose a political issue that you care about, and think about how your interest in this topic developed. Were media important for this and what kinds of media have factored into your investment in this issue?

Notes

1   For a much more elaborate discussion of these cultural politics, see Fiske (1994, 21–74).
2   For a critical interpretation of the idea of the internet as a democratizing force, see Papacharissi (2009).
3   Fraser (1990) refers to these as "subaltern counterpublics." *Subaltern* is a synonym of *subordinate*, and is often used as the opposite of *hegemonic* (sometimes defined as *dominant*).
4   Hill cites two tweets by Damien Lillard from July 6, 2016.

References

Anderson, Benedict. 2006. *Imagined Communities: Reflections on the Origins and Spread of Nationalism*, rev. ed. London: Verso.
Banet-Weiser, Sarah. 2004. "'We Pledge Allegiance to Kids': Nickelodeon and Citizenship." In *Nickelodeon Nation: The History, Politics, and Economics of America's Only TV Channel for Kids*, edited by Heather Hendershot, 209–240. New York: New York University Press.
Baym, Geoffrey. 2005. "*The Daily Show*: Discursive Integration and the Reinvention of Political Journalism." *Political Communication* 22: 259–276.
Boddy, William. 2004. "Wireless Nation: Defining Radio as a Domestic Technology." *New Media and Popular Imagination: Launching Radio, Television, and Digital Media in the United States*, 16–43. Oxford: Oxford University Press.
boyd, danah. 2011. "Social Network Sites as Networked Publics: Affordances, Dynamics, and Implications." In *Networked Self: Identity, Community, and Culture on Social Network Sites*, edited by Zizi Papacharissi, 39–58. New York: Routledge.
Calhoun, Craig. 1992. "Introduction: Habermas and the Public Sphere." In *Habermas and the Public Sphere*, edited by Calhoun, 1–50. Cambridge, MA: MIT Press.
Canclini, Nestor Garcia. 2001. *Consumers and Citizens: Globalization and Multicultural Conflicts*. Minneapolis: University of Minnesota Press.
Dahlgren, Peter. 2000. "Media, Citizenship, and Civic Culture." in Mass Media and Society, 3rd ed., edited by James Curran and Michael Gurevitch, 310–328. London: Arnold.
Fiske, John. 1994. *Media Matters: Race and Gender in U.S. Politics*. Minneapolis: University of Minnesota Press.

Fraser, Nancy. 1990. "Rethinking the Public Sphere: A Contribution to the Critique of Actually Existing Democracy." *Social Text* 25/26: 56–80.

Friedland, Lewis A. 1996. "Electronic Democracy and the New Citizenship." *Media, Culture & Society* 18.2: 185–212.

Gottfried, Jeffrey, Katerina Eva Matsa, and Michael Barthel. 2015. "As Jon Stewart Steps Down, 5 Facts about The Daily Show." Pew Research Center, August 6, 2015. https://www.pewresearch.org/fact-tank/2015/08/06/5-facts-daily-show/

Gray, Jonathan, Cornell Sandvoss and C. Lee Harriongton, eds. 2017. *Fandom: Identities and Communities in a Mediated World*, 2nd ed. New York: New York University Press.

Guerrero-Pico, Mar. 2017. "#Fringe, Audiences, and Fan Labor: Twitter Activism to Save a TV Show from Cancelation." *International Journal of Communication* 11: 2071–2092.

Habermas, Jürgen. 1991. *The Structural Transformation of the Public Sphere: An Inquiry into a Category of Bourgeois Society*. Cambridge, MA: MIT Press.

Habermas, Jürgen. 2006. *The Divided West*. Cambridge: Polity.

Hellekson, Karen and Kristina Busse. 2006. *Fan Fiction and Fan Communities in the Age of the Internet: New Essays*. Jefferson: McFarland.

Herman, Edward S. and Noam Chomsky. 1988. *Manufacturing Consent: The Political Economy of the Mass Media*. London: Vintage.

Hill, Marc Lamont. 2018. "'Thank You, Black Twitter': State Violence, Digital Counterpublics, and Pedagogies of Resistance." *Urban Education* 53.2: 286–302.

Hinck, Ashley. 2012. "Theorizing a Public Engagement Keystone: Seeing Fandom's Integral Connection to Civic Engagement Through the Case of the Harry Potter Alliance." *Transformative Works and Cultures* 10. doi: 10.3983/twc.2012.0311

Jackson, Sarah J., Moya Bailey and Brooke Foucault Welles. 2020. *#HashtagActivism: Networks of Race and Gender Justice*. Cambridge, MA: MIT Press.

Jenkins, Henry. 2006. *Convergence Culture: Where Old and New Media Collide*. New York: New York University Press.

Jenkins, Henry. 2012. "'Cultural Acupuncture': Fan Activism and the Harry Potter Alliance." *Transformative Works and Cultures* 10. https://journal.transformativeworks.org/index.php/twc/article/view/305

Jones, Jeffrey P. 2009. *Entertaining Politics: Satiric Television and Political Engagement*, 2nd ed. Lanham: Rowman & Littlefield.

Lessig, Lawrence. 2008. *Remix: Making Art and Commerce Thrive in the Hybrid Economy*. New York: Penguin.

Lull, James and Stephen Hinerman. 1997. *Media Scandals: Morality and Desire in the Popular Culture Marketplace*. New York: Columbia University Press.

McChesney, Robert W. 2004. *The Problem of the Media: U.S. Communication Politics in the Twenty-First Century*. New York: Monthly Review Press.

Merritt, Davis. 1995. *Public Journalism and Public Life: Why Telling the News Is Not Enough*. Hillsdale: Lawrence Erlbaum Associates.

Milner, Ryan M. 2016. *The World Made Meme: Public Conversations and Participatory Media*. Cambridge, MA: MIT Press.

Papacharissi, Zizi. 2009. "The Virtual Sphere 2.0: The Internet, the Public sphere, and Beyond." In *Routledge Handbook of Internet Politics*, edited by Andrew Chadwick and Philip N. Howard. London: Routledge.

Pew Research Center. 2007. "Public Knowledge of Current Affairs Little Changed by News and Information Revolutions," April 15, 2007. https://www.pewresearch.org/politics/2007/04/15/public-knowledge-of-current-affairs-little-changed-by-news-and-information-revolutions/

Pew Research Center. 2021. "Newspaper Fact Sheet," June 29, 2021. https://www.journalism.org/fact-sheet/newspapers/

Phillips, Whitney. 2015. *This Is Why We Can't Have Nice Things: Mapping the Relationship between Online Trolling and Mainstream Culture*. Cambridge, MA: MIT Press.

Pickard, Victor. 2020. *Democracy Without Journalism? Confronting the Misinformation Society*. New York: Oxford University Press.

Postman, Neil. 1985. *Amusing Ourselves to Death: Public Discourse in the Age of Show Business*. New York: Viking.

Putnam, Robert. 2000. *Bowling Alone: The Collapse and Revival of American Community*. New York: Simon & Schuster.

Rheingold, Howard. 2000. *The Virtual Community: Homesteading on the Electronic Frontier*. Cambridge, MA: MIT Press.

Rosen, Jay. 1993. "Beyond Objectivity." Nieman Reports 47.4: 48–53.

Rimmerman, Craig A. 2018. *The New Citizenship: Unconventional Politics, Activism, and Service*, 4th ed. New York: Routledge.

Robinson, Michael J. 1975. "American Political Legitimacy in an Era of Electronic Journalism: Reflections on the Evening News." *Television as a Social Force: New Approaches to TV Criticism*, edited by Douglas Cater, 97–139. New York: Praeger.

Shifman, Limor. 2013. *Memes in Digital Culture*. Cambridge, MA: MIT Press.

Springman, Laura. 2020. "'It's Army Versus The U.S. Army': K-pop Fans, Activism, and #BLACKLIVESMATTER." *Flow*, August 3, 2020. https://www.flowjournal.org/2020/08/its-army-versus-the-army/

Thompson, Ethan, Jeffrey P. Jones, and Jonathan Gray, eds. 2009. *Satire TV: Politics and Comedy in the Post-Network Era*. New York: New York University Press.

Tufekci, Zeynep. 2017. *Twitter and Tear Gas: The Power and Fragility of Networked Protest*. New Haven: Yale University Press.

Varnelis, Kazys, ed. 2008. *Networked Publics*. Cambridge, MA: MIT Press.

9

CONSUMERISM

The Price Is Right has been a popular daytime game show on American television for half a century. Its premise is simple and durable: members of the studio audience are called to the stage ("come on down!") to compete in pricing games. The contestants can win products – from inexpensive grocery or drugstore items to new boats and cars – if they can guess their retail prices most accurately. A raucous studio audience cheers them on and screams advice. The game show rewards its contestants for their knowledge about the value of consumer products, and sends them home not just with prizes but also with the experience of having shown their skills on national TV.

The Price Is Right is a fun competition, with upbeat brassy music, a riotously colorful set, and contestants energized by the opportunity to be on television, encouraged to jump and shout, to scream with pleasure when they see what they have been given a chance to win. The most energized, most excessive moments come as a contestant reacts with obligatory hysteria when given the chance to win *a new car!* This is how *The Price Is Right* celebrates consumerism, as it gives ordinary people the opportunity to profit from their familiarity with what things cost. It shows consumer products to be highly valued and much desired, and displays them alluringly for the viewers watching at home, with sexy models smiling at the camera as they show them off.

Like most broadcast television, *The Price Is Right* is also advertising-supported. The show integrates advertising into the main text and also pauses for advertising in between its pricing games, breaking for pods

DOI: 10.4324/9781003007708-9

of 30-second spots. It is totally saturated with commercial, consumerist appeals, and so it epitomizes one of the core functions of modern media. Episode after episode, from beginning to end, it *sells*. It entertains by selling and sells by entertaining. Children of the 21st century may have trouble seeing a consumer society as only one possible way of living, and a break from the past. As the saying goes, *fish don't know they're in water*. Consumerism has been the water in which we all swim for more than a century. If we try to imagine how human beings lived before the consumer society came along, it might help us see our own lives through fresh eyes.

For almost all of human history, most people lived in small communities as either hunter-gatherers or farmers. A small minority led different kinds of lives, but these were not the average folks. Humans found, hunted, grew, and prepared their own food. They made their own shelter and tools. They made and mended their clothes. Their culture was homemade too, and passed down over generations: stories, songs, dances, religious rites. Few people were literate, so the transmission of this culture from one generation to another was largely oral.

These conditions might sound prehistoric, but many of these conditions persisted for many populations well into the 19th century, and even into the 20th and 21st. In the novels of Laura Ingalls Wilder, set in the American prairie and Midwest in the mid-19th century, some special objects are described as "boughten," meaning they were purchased in a store. Most of the products in the home were made by members of the family, as was the home itself. (Well into the 20th century, American homes were often built by their first occupants.) The family was an economic unit, growing and making the things it needed, and trading or buying and selling with others to make up for what it could not produce on its own. People had a lot of children so that there would be plenty of hands to do the work. Production was the business of the family in the home, and those items not made by the family might be exchanged by neighbors and local craftsmen and artisans. Surplus food from a successful hunt or harvest might be traded for tools, or shoes and boots might be bartered for other kinds of handiwork. People were rarely involved in buying and selling for money, and what they did buy and sell would have neither branding and packaging, nor advertising arousing desire for it. Global and national brands so familiar to us now, names like Quaker Oats and Coca-Cola that we identify closely with a particular kind of product, scarcely existed before the 19th century (Ohmann 1996, 62–63).

The shift from this kind of pre-industrial society to a modern capitalist society was profound, and it was shaped by many forces and developments. Mass production of goods like textiles, sugar, and cigarettes by industry required workers, who earned a wage for their labor. The production of these goods led to a complex system of distribution over land and water coordinated across telegraph and then telephone lines. It required a system of relations between producers, wholesalers and retailers, bank financing and credit, and commodity and stock markets. The increase in production would lead to a corresponding increase in consumption. For consumption to spread and become a normal feature of everyday life, a public campaign of mass persuasion helped people adjust to this new reality. The people who had formerly produced their own goods would need to be invited and instructed how to be consumers of "boughten" clothes and foods and cleaning products, of leisure-time amusements like magazines and records and radios, of household appliances like sewing machines and refrigerators, of bicycles and automobiles. This whole process was the rise of a consumer society alongside the rise of the modern mass media. The two were linked together at the time of their emergence. They have been so ever since.

Media has a layered relationship with consumerism. On the first layer, the advertising that pays for many kinds of media is propaganda for consumption. Advertising's purpose is to persuade us to consume particular products and services. But many other kinds of media, from movies and TV to video games and social media posts, are also promotional in the ways they engineer our desires for consumer experiences. If you have ever thought it would be cool to look or dress like someone you follow on Instagram or TikTok, or like a character in a movie or TV show, you know about this first-hand. When I was a kid, my home was filled with *Star Wars* merchandise and I deeply desired the skateboard Michael J. Fox rides to school in *Back to the Future*. These movies were not literally advertisements but they were the inspiration to millions of people's consumer behavior.

On another level, media themselves are consumer products, and the consumption of media is one of the values promoted by media. Sometimes one media product is advertised by another (e.g., a billboard for a movie), and Netflix advertises on cable television, its rival for our attention. Whether offering products for sale like video games or services like subscriptions to Spotify, the media industries are a consumer-facing business that survives by separating us from our money. The rise of a consumer society was accompanied by the rise of mass leisure-time pastimes like coin-operated arcades,

amusement parks, traveling shows, world's fairs, professional sports, vaudeville, and motion pictures, which were all sites of commercialism and consumption (Nasaw 1993). Modern audiences in turn have long used media
consumption as a way of defining their identities: as fans of certain kinds of
movies or games, or collectors of certain kinds of media products like comics and records. We have also grown accustomed to shopping itself being a
mediated experience, as Amazon and other e-tailers offer their own kind of
screen-based leisure activity.

Consumer, consumerism, and consumption are terms inextricably linked with
a cluster of close cousins that also start with a C: commerce (and commercial),
commodity (and commodification), and ultimately the most important of all the
C-words: capitalism. A consumer society is a world in which commodities
(goods) and commodified experiences (services) are bought and sold, i.e.,
commercially exchanged, within a market, i.e., a capitalist economy. The
consumer economy is one of the most critical components of modern capitalism, as fortunes and everyday well-being often rise and fall with consumer spending, also known as shopping. Consumerism is thus one way we
can understand media's most essential functions within our prevailing economic system and the social order that goes along with it.

A consumer society is practically impossible to imagine without a media
system supportive of consumerism. The institutions of our media system grew up around consumerism to become what we know them to be.
Newspapers and magazines, radio and television, movies and video games,
search engines and social media: all of these influential media forms are on
some basic level thoroughly commodified commercial products or invitations to consumption more broadly speaking, and some of them are both.
The media system and the consumer society fit one another like symbiotic
organisms. They shape our society together, in concert.

Advertising Then and Now

The branch of media most overtly engaged in the promotion of consumerism is the advertising industry. Also known as Madison Avenue after the
New York City thoroughfare where many American ad agencies have been
located, this industry is the conduit of much of the funding for media online
and in print, in podcasts and on the radio, on outdoor billboards, and on
TV screens. Advertising agencies serve their clients, usually private, for-profit
corporations, who hire them to create ad campaigns and place ads in media.

These clients, sometimes known as *sponsors*, use media in order to communicate with consumers, or what media industries call *audiences*. In advertising-supported media, including radio, television, newspapers, magazines, and much online media, the audience's attention is attracted by the content of media, and bundled and sold to the advertisers. The advertising industry often speaks of "CPM" rates, which stands for "cost per mille" (i.e., per thousand) reached by an advertisement. They think in terms of how many consumers they can capture and what it will cost.

This kind of thinking requires audience measurement, which is an essential component of the advertising trade. The audience attracted by media must be desirable to the advertiser in order for the content to be commercially viable. It can be desirable by being an especially large audience: among the millions of people who pass through Times Square each year or watch football on Sundays, there are probably some potential consumers for practically any product. But advertisers might prefer to spend their budgets reaching smaller, concentrated audiences of more likely buyers. Advertisements for diapers are made to address a different potential customer than advertisements for beer.

On social media platforms like YouTube and TikTok, audience measurement is built right into the interface, as we recognize popular content by metrics like views and subscribers. Television ratings are one version of audience measurement that goes deeper than just how many people are watching. The Nielsen Company has been sampling television audiences for decades, recruiting "Nielsen families" to have their viewing monitored on "peoplemeters" that track who in the household is watching what, in and out of the home. This (in theory) representative sample of the American television audience allows Nielsen to determine approximately how many people watch particular programs, and how these audiences break down by demographic categories: gender, age, race and ethnicity, household income, and location. For you as a television viewer, the purpose of media is to be entertaining or informative, or part of a shared experience with others. From the perspective of the advertising industry, the purpose of media is to assemble desirable audiences (i.e., potential shoppers) together at a particular time and place to be exposed to commercial appeals. For you, a YouTube video might be just for your pleasure, but for the advertiser, a YouTube video is an opportunity to sell you something.

The content of this advertising is highly varied. Advertising includes national campaigns for major brands of cleaning products, foods, restaurants, apparel, insurance, airlines, consumer electronics, and automobiles. Think: Super Bowl commercials. These are often expensive and elaborate productions that are made with extensive crews of skilled professionals. Ads like these reach massive audiences. It also includes regional and local campaigns for businesses like supermarkets, hardware stores, and personal injury attorneys, which might be made more inexpensively and on a smaller scale. Think: local TV news and radio over the air. Increasingly, advertising is tailored to narrow slivers of the population. On social media, our location and other data about our individual profiles feeds into this targeting, and our internet activity is routinely tracked. One time I searched online for coffee beans, and upscale coffee ads have been "retargeting" me for months in my web browser. This has become a standard technique of Facebook advertising: users who have previously interacted with a brand can be addressed as a "custom audience." Whether audience appeals are broad like Super Bowl commercials or narrowly targeted to shoppers who previously had a brand's product in their cart, the dynamic of advertising, media, and consumers is the same: an exchange of money for attention.

The agenda of any kind of advertising is thus to sell particular products and services to particular consumers, and to promote the brand identity of those goods. But ads also have a deeper purpose and a more fundamental role in society. However effectively they sell Snickers bars or Subarus, advertisements as a whole field of media practice promote consumerism as a way of life. Advertising promises us to deliver the solution to our problems and the fulfillment of our fantasies in the products and services for sale. Advertising creates needs for consumerism to satisfy. It sows fears for brands to relieve. It fashions utopian ideals of self and society that it promises to deliver as the outcome of commercial transactions. In a media landscape blanketed by advertising, consumerism is presented as a way of living, a mindset, an identity.

It was not always so. Advertising existed for hundreds of years before the rise of a national mass media around the beginning of the 20th century, but it was more like the classifieds connecting buyers and sellers of particular products or services. Ads in newspapers were a way for people engaged in commerce to connect with one another. They were typically all text, and even if they were advertising products for sale, would be unlikely to include a brand name. At the turn of the century, especially in magazines with national circulation, pictorial advertising emerged that we would recognize as the same kind of consumerism familiar from our own media.

The products advertised were nationally branded merchandise like Ivory soap and Gillette razors, for sale in stores all around the country. The advertisements had pictures – drawn or painted illustrations or photographic halftones – and text addressing the magazine reader. As Richard Ohmann (1996, 180) describes this phenomenon: "the newer visual advertising set out to ambush the reader's attention, produce affect quickly, and lodge in the memory."

Techniques of these early mass-market brand advertisements are still familiar to us in the 21st century. As Ohmann (1996, 201–210) describes, they appealed to a consumer who wants to appear youthful, healthy, and attractive. Advertisements would flatter the consumer by demonstrating how the product being sold would show off their true qualities to their best advantage. Advertisements would instruct consumers on how to be modern and up-to-date by adopting the latest technologies and fashions. The objects for sale, then as now, would be the shiny new thing that you absolutely must have. Along with this appeal would come the promise of high social standing. Aspirations to class and distinction have been a selling point for as long as mass-market advertising has existed. Ads would also represent the warmth of community and family relationships, and would often present what the advertising historian Roland Marchand (1985, 165–167) calls "social tableaux," scenes of people in comfortable settings enjoying each other's company and presenting a model of the good life.

Advertising early in the 20th century was also notorious for its invention of questionable problems. The most famous of these was "halitosis," a scientific-sounding synonym for bad breath used in advertisements for Listerine mouthwash beginning during the 1920s (Ewen 2001, 46). Such appeals made it seem as if social popularity, high-class status, and success in romance would be impossible to achieve without the regular use of consumer products. Campaigns like these were made to appeal to recent waves of immigrants eager to become "Americanized," instructing them that fitting into their new social world would require careful consumption of the right products (43). They preyed on consumers' fears and appealed to their vanity, making up novel problems that only consumerism could solve (45–46).

The link between advertising and its intended or desired effects has never been absolutely clear, and to some critics appears to be rather dubious (Schudson 1986, 9–12; Stole 2001, 83). In a consumer society, it would be good for shoppers to have a source of reliable and helpful information about products they might purchase, but advertising does not privilege an agenda of being informative. It tends, rather, to offer suggestive connotations about products and their effects, and to work on the level of fantasy as much as reality. As an industry in which such large sums of money are spent, it would be good to know how effective advertising is at selling products, but this is also hard to quantify. Advertising rarely leads directly to sales, and much of it is avoided, ignored, or disdained. Michael Schudson (1986, 11) calls advertising "the art form of bad faith" as it "features messages that both its creators and its audience know to be false." Audiences are well enough informed to see commercial appeals for what they are, and routinely avoid paying attention to them. In the digital age, media audiences have found more ways of shielding themselves from the annoyance and interruption of advertising, whether by paying more for ad-free content, clicking the "skip ad" button, recording content and fast-forwarding past commercials, or seeking out media that has no advertising at all.

So taken together, these points make advertising seem suspiciously ineffective, and yet it shows no signs of going anywhere. Advertising spending is enormous by any standard: globally, more than half a trillion dollars is spent annually, and more than 100 companies spend $1 billion or more each year on advertising in the early 2020s (Ad Age 2020a). While spending dips during economic downturns (e.g., in 2008 during a recession and in 2020 during a pandemic), the general trends are toward increased spending. And the media of advertising have been shifting over time from print and television to digital and mobile. As consumers spend more time online and engage with their phones seemingly at all moments of the day and night, advertisers find more ways to reach them where they are. By the early 2020s, spending on digital advertising was greater than spending on television, radio, newspaper, magazine, and outdoor advertisements combined (Ad Age 2020a).

These shifts might make things seem like they have changed significantly with shifting media technologies, but the basics of the culture of advertising have remained quite consistent. Advertising is seen as a necessary business expense in particular in certain kinds of markets. Big advertising spenders tend to be companies in oligopoly markets in competition over market share (Stole 2001, 85–88). An oligopoly is an industry dominated by a small number of large companies, often selling similar or interchangeable products. They differentiate their offerings from those of competitors more on the basis of branding rather than the distinctiveness or price of the products. Many of the heavily advertised products in advanced consumer societies, from laundry detergents to soft drinks to SUVs, fit into this model. Companies are loath to compete on prices to risk a price war in which everyone loses revenue. They are more eager to protect or increase their market share. And expensive advertising budgets can be among the ways that industries effectively bar entry to newcomers, protecting themselves from competition.

When we look at the biggest advertising spenders, we see just this kind of situation (*Ad Age* 2020b). One of the companies that has famously been among the top advertising spenders for generations is Procter & Gamble, which produces numerous name-brand retail products (Pampers, Tide, Charmin, Tampax, Cascade, Crest, Olay). These items are not dramatically different from their competitors and are often sold on the basis of brand appeals as much as informative or price-based appeals. In recent years, many of the top advertising spenders are companies in intense market share competition in oligopoly markets where products or services really are extremely similar: telephone and internet providers (Comcast, AT&T), insurance agencies (Geico, Progressive), and automobile manufacturers (Ford, Chevrolet). Amazon has become the biggest spender on advertising, which befits an internet-age company that has attained an astonishingly dominant position vis-a-vis consumer activity (*Ad Age* 2020b). Amazon's competition includes the mega-retailers like Walmart and the technology and media giants like Apple and Google, all of which are likewise major spenders on advertising.

Another internet-age development, in response to user trends, has been a creative solution to audiences' ability to avoid advertising. Many brands have integrated themselves into media content so that the brand promotion and the media product are the same thing. Sometimes this is called "native advertising" and other times "branded entertainment." On news sites, a native advertisement might be a story that resembles a regular news story in basically every way but is marked "paid post" or "Story from [name of sponsor]." Typically, this kind of news story would in some way show the sponsor in a positive light. On a spectrum from "hard sell" (direct call to action, overt persuasion) to "soft sell" (a more subtle and understated appeal to the savvy), native advertising tends toward the more suggestive soft end.

Branded entertainment is a broad term that covers many kinds of media, both fiction and non-fiction. A viral video from 2013, "Dove Real Beauty Sketches," was part of a broader campaign for the soap brand to establish a brand identity associated with self-esteem and body positivity. It doesn't sell any product in particular but works to create a positive aura around the brand. Shareable, spreadable media content is an ideal way for brands to overcome audience advertising avoidance. When users engage with advertising on purpose and make it a topic of conversation, brands undoubtedly benefit.

A more elaborate example of branded entertainment is the 2021 HBO documentary *The Day Sports Stood Still*, a film sponsored by Nike that chronicles the experiences of elite athletes amidst the COVID-19 pandemic and Black Lives Matter movement. A news story on this film as part of the broader phenomenon of brands making movies to reach consumers notes that it "is infused with Nike's ethos but carries none of the traditional branding audiences are used to seeing" (Sperling and Hsu 2021). As advertising historian Cynthia B. Meyers (2014) has pointed out, this is actually a new version of an old strategy: before television networks changed things up, radio sponsorship worked the same way as branded entertainment. Radio programs were often named for their sponsors (e.g., *Kraft Music Theater, Campbell Playhouse*) and were produced by an advertising agency. Advertising in radio was often integrated into the program, with the host reading the sponsor's copy on the air and lending his or her authority and credibility to the commercial appeal. Many podcasts have revived this audio practice, with hosts giving personal testimonials about their sponsors' mattresses and meal kits. Some brands have also made podcasts promoting their products, such as #LIPSTORIES, from Sephora.

Consumers might disdain or avoid it, but advertising has followed them as they have migrated from traditional print and broadcast media to the internet, and it shows no signs of going away. Advertising in our mobile apps and social media feeds can be almost unavoidable. The most influential new media companies are either major beneficiaries of advertising spending, like Facebook, are big spenders on ads, like Apple, or are both, like Google. The online economy is thoroughly integrated with advertising, and while subscription services do pose a threat to advertising's claim on audiences' attention, ad-supported alternatives promise to keep competing for audiences whose media budgets are strained by so many monthly bills. Advertising for national or global brands has paid for much of our media for well over a century and has shaped identities and values over generations. Its claim on consumers' consciousness has been moving to new platforms and formats, but has hardly diminished in the 21st century.

Pop Culture and Gendered Consumerism

In a famous scene in the 1990 Hollywood comedy *Pretty Woman*, the protagonist Vivian (Julia Roberts), a sex worker hired to spend a week with a businessman in a posh Los Angeles hotel, goes out shopping. She has been to a particular Beverly Hills boutique in an earlier scene, where she was treated with insulting disdain for looking trashy. She returns later armed with her escort's credit card and the hotel's personal shopper, who promises to "spend an obscene amount of money." The salespeople have no choice but to show her respect. In a montage set to the upbeat Roy Orbison song of the film's title, we see Vivian acquiring expensive clothes to wear while on the arm of her new man, and along with her appearance we observe a transformation in her identity. She goes from being a cash-strapped prostitute dressed to attract clients to an elegant lady who will be accepted in the society of fancy garden parties and outings by private jet to the opera. In this pop culture fairy tale of a woman's makeover in image and class status, consumerism plays a critical role. Vivian becomes a new woman by acquiring that kind of person's clothes.

The idealized image of the movie star has been an object of desire for almost the whole history of filmmaking. Hollywood studio publicity manufactures stars as commodities for audiences to adore and admire. They establish ideals of beauty and models of the good life in a way that blurs their onscreen and offscreen images. Stars are also a direct inspiration to consumerism. Like celebrity culture more generally, popular movies and television like *Pretty Woman* are essential nodes in the transmission of ideas about fashion and cosmetics, about beauty culture, and about the values written onto our bodies.

This dynamic is highly gendered. While masculinity is critical to how it works, the link between consumerism and femininity has been most elaborate and profound. This is true of advertising as well, as so many campaigns address women as the society's primary shoppers and serve to construct girls and women as consumers of products and services that will produce for them a socially acceptable gender identity. The association between consumerism and girls and women has produced an unfortunate linkage between femininity and some of the negative values often ascribed to consumer culture, such as shallowness, gullibility, and materialism. But modern masculinity is defined via consumption as well, though different kinds of products are typically marketed to men and boys more than girls and women (e.g., beer, trucks, video games). The binary (male/female) gendering of consumerism suffuses popular culture, including social media and movies and TV.

It might be tempting to see movies as a medium clearly distinct from television, and to define this difference in terms of consumerism. Advertising has always been part of television in the US and it has become strongly associated with broadcasting in many countries. Commercials have made television into one of the most thoroughly consumerist influences in modern societies. But while movies do not have the interruptive commercial breaks that TV shows often have (unless they're shown on television), movies are a consumerist form of popular entertainment through and through, and always have been. Movies are constantly selling themselves, their stars, and their fantasies of fine living. Blockbuster franchise films are intended to be tentpoles of a whole host of ancillary consumer products: soundtrack recordings, adaptations as comics or video games, spinoffs and sequels in various media, licensed merchandise from lunch boxes to Halloween costumes, and tie-ins like McDonald's Happy Meal toys. Eventually, a successful film franchise might lead to a theme park ride, a pinnacle of the consumerist cinematic experience.

Feature films also integrate consumer products in one way or another, like James Bond's iconic Aston Martin DB5 in *Goldfinger* (1964) and the trail of Reese's Pieces candies that advance the plot of *E.T. The Extra-Terrestrial* (1982). We typically call this product placement or integration, and it extends beyond film to TV series and the "sponcon" (sponsored content) and brand partnerships of social media postings. Like branded entertainment, product integrations are a way of inserting consumer appeals that audiences cannot avoid by skipping commercials or paying for an ad-free version.

These integrations of consumer goods into films go back a long way, and have also been known as "tie-ups" and "tie-ins." They certainly precede interruptive television advertising. Hollywood emerged in the 1910s and 1920s as a powerful consumerist force alongside print magazines, anticipating radio and TV. As the film historian Charles Eckert (1978, 4) has described, movies in the early decades of Hollywood functioned as "living display windows for all that they contained." For instance, sophisticated comedies of the late 1910s and 1920s directed by the legendary director Cecil B. DeMille contained scenes in the bathrooms of affluent characters' homes with modern fixtures like tubs and towel bars and ostentatious décor like ornate moldings and floor tiles (Higashi 1994, 142–178). Images like these made a strong impression at a time when many American homes lacked even bathtubs. Many such Jazz Age films were spectacles of wealth that mirrored the magazine advertising and department store windows of the same time, showcases for bedroom furnishings and table settings. They were like instruction manuals for consumerism. Marchand (1985, 198–200) refers to such films set in high society as offering "modest housewives and working-class girls a glimpse of the life of the rich" and functioned to shape a mass audience's fantasies of attaining the pleasures of social status.

Hollywood has showcased many kinds of consumer goods in its films, from housewares and furniture to appliances to automobiles. The US has been a major source of films in foreign markets for more than a century, and American cinema has been one of the key vehicles promoting consumption of American manufactured goods on a global scale. In the golden age of the Hollywood studios, movies worked in tie-ups for cosmetics, fashions, perfumes, and jewelry, and fan magazines instructed their readers, mainly girls and women, how to duplicate the attractive presentation of stars in motion pictures in their own appearance. Department stores featured the clothes worn by characters in movies. Macy's Cinema Fashions Shop offered specific items from particular films, like the gown worn by the actress Carole Lombard in the 1935 film *Rumba*. As Eckert (1978, 20) argues, American popular films "did as much or more than any other force in capitalist culture to smooth the operation of the production-consumption cycle by fetishizing products and putting the libido in libidinally-invested advertising." And as these examples indicate, the appeal of this consumerist rhetoric was strongly gendered female, addressing girls and women most directly. The department store product collections named for 21st-century celebs like Lauren Conrad and Jennifer Lopez are one recent version of this venerable star-powered marketing technique.

Popular cinema and television have hardly eased up on this appeal to consumerism in fictional, scripted representations. But television in particular has also developed genres of non-fiction entertainment overtly tied to consumerism, in particular cooking shows and home decorating shows. These have existed in various forms for much of TV history, including public television programming, but came to new prominence in the 1990s with the rise of two cable channels, Food Network and HGTV. Along with makeover shows like *What Not to Wear* and *Queer Eye for the Straight Guy*, cooking and decorating content comprise *lifestyle TV*, which overlaps with forms of print and online *lifestyle media*. Lifestyle media appeals broadly, but addresses middle-class women as a primary audience and presents them with instruction and inspiration in historically feminized pursuits of the domestic sphere. As Maureen Ryan (2018) describes it, "lifestyle media frame tasks that have historically fallen to women – housekeeping, home design, entertaining, beauty, childcare, and food preparation, among other repetitive practices of personal and domestic betterment – as richly rewarding pursuits and sites of inspiration on aesthetic and emotional levels" (2–3).

One of the key appeals of lifestyle media is how it offers its audiences a vision of an ideal life and an ideal self, an aspirational vision of an identity marked by the good taste modeled by the host of the show. Images of the perfect results achieved in a successful home renovation or a well-executed set of recipes to create a meal offer a vision for the viewer: you could live here, you could serve and eat this food. Consumer goods, whether paints and countertops or ingredients and kitchen tools, are the essential items in realizing these outcomes. As Ryan (2018) describes this appeal of consumerist lifestyle media: "It is not simply that there are more goods, in more styles, available than ever before; it is also that we increasingly think of our tastes as expressive of our core selves" (6). And the visions of self on offer from this media are almost as a rule affluent and class-privileged, a vision of aesthetic quality that merges taste and wealth.

This is evident in the Food Network series *Everyday Italian* with Giada di Laurentiis, a "dump-and-stir" cooking show that debuted in 2003, in which an alluring celebrity chef both instructs audiences how to prepare Italian dishes, and demonstrates a domestic aesthetic of authenticity and refinement. As I have argued (Newman 2020), there is a contrast in this show between the kind of food prepared on screen, like ice cream made from scratch using ricotta cheese, or fennel roasted with *Parmigiano-Reggiano*, and the packaged foods advertised during commercial breaks, like ranch dressing and frozen pizza. Giada offers viewers invitations to pleasure and flatters them by addressing an audience with the discernment to appreciate authentic preparations made with gourmet ingredients. The show also merges the appeal of her sexually desirable image with "food porn" close-ups of ingredients and finished dishes. This sells and promotes Giada as a celebrity who has books and product lines for sale along with the literal consumption of certain kinds of food promoted in both the content of the show and the commercials in between its segments.

Lifestyle TV like *Everyday Italian* entertains its audience with fantasies of desirable and even attainable commodities. It pays viewers the compliment that they are deserving of the same sensory pleasures as they see realized on screen, which they might actually achieve with the knowledge gained from lifestyle media. This kind of TV implicitly promises that via consumption you may become the kind of person such shows were made to address. This type of audience appeal may also be found in advertising, but many other kinds of media do similar cultural work without being as obvious and interruptive, without being so forward about their intentions to sell you something. Advertising may seem like the quintessential form of consumerist media, but consumerist media come in many other genres.

The Citizen-Consumer

Commentators on consumerism often recall that shortly after 9/11, political leaders encouraged the American people to come together and serve their country by going shopping (Zukin 2004, 1; McGovern 2006, 2; Shaw 2010, 6). This would have been a way of "returning to normal," to the comfort of the ordinary, after a profoundly shocking event. It was also a way to bolster the nation by supporting its economy, linking patriotism and prosperity, citizenship and consumerism. Critics of the American government at the time under President George W. Bush might have regarded this call to shop disdainfully as a sign of how out of touch leaders were with the people still suffering from the trauma of the attacks, or as a distraction from reckoning with America's foreign affairs that contributed to conflict with Islamists from the Arab world. Yet by 2001, the welfare of the nation had been thoroughly enmeshed with its consumer economy for at least a century.

Consumerism has had its share of detractors over the years, who often see it as manipulative and inauthentic, as a distraction from more important concerns, and as a cause of waste and environmental degradation. On the left in particular, it's hard to find anyone who would express unqualified enthusiasm for consumerism. And critical rhetoric often positions consumerism in contrast to citizenship.

Consumer and citizen are both identities. A consumer is a shopper, one whose interests and desires focus on commodities, and who realizes their full, true selfhood via consumption. A citizen is a political subject, a member of a community whose equal participation in governing is supposed to be guaranteed by free societies. Of course we can be both consumers and citizens, even at the same time. But to consumerism's detractors, our modern societies frequently privilege an emphasis on consumption at the expense of a robust civic life. They see the two identities engaged in a competition that citizenship seemingly never wins.

As far as media are concerned, we might think of how audiences are addressed, or which identity is being invoked by media texts. Are media made to serve the interests and needs of consumers or citizens? Are we invited to take notice of products and services for sale? Are we invited to care about social and political issues and the workings of government? Are we being offered appeals to buy, or information and knowledge of public concern? Where is the balance or emphasis between these different forms of audience address?

The harshest critics of consumerism might see these identities and these ways of addressing audiences as stark alternatives. William Croteau and David Hoynes (2006), authors of several media studies textbooks, argue that "In market-oriented societies such as the United States, the consumer identity looms very large, often crowding out notions of citizenship" (224). Croteau and Hoynes are generally critical of private, for-profit media systems, and are eager to see more public service media emerge and gain support, media that would prioritize a civic culture. In their vision of a better system, "mass media should 'serve' ... citizens rather than 'target' potential consumers" (22). They find market-dominated media systems to be inadequate to the extent that they prioritize consumerism, and they consider this to be a betrayal of the role that the media should perform in a democracy (26–29).

Some cultural scholars of consumerism and media have taken a rather different perspective (McGovern 2006; McGovern 2008; Banet-Weiser 2007; Banet-Weiser and Lapsansky 2008). Instead of seeing citizenship and consumerism as necessarily opposed, these scholars have looked at how they have been intertwined in popular imagination. They see the "consumer-citizen" as a key identity adopted in modern capitalist societies, and investigate – in both historical and contemporary examples – how consumerism and citizenship have worked together and informed one another. These critics are no fans of capitalism, but they do recognize that under a market economy structured thoroughly around individuals' consumption, citizenship can hardly be separated from it. In her book *A Consumer's Republic*, the historian Lizabeth Cohen (2003) identifies this dynamic particularly sharply in discussing the post-World War II period in the US: "Rather than isolated ideal types, citizen and consumer were ever-shifting categories that sometimes overlapped, often were in tension, but always reflected the permeability of the political and economic spheres" (8). Her book's title, merging the economic and the political, is a good way of thinking of these terms in relation to one another. One senses the friction between *consumer* and *republic* even as they are married together in one neat phrase.

There are several related ways that the dynamic of the consumer as a citizen can be understood. Most basically, mass consumption is often represented as a benefit to the nation. This occurs in the post-9/11 rhetoric of shopping as a patriotic activity, and it has important precursors in the 20th-century US New Deal and Cold War eras. When society's prosperity depends on a healthy consumer economy, there is civic virtue in promoting consumption. Periodic campaigns to encourage consumers to "buy American" have been premised on this recognition that individual purchasing has an impact on the fortunes of the nation. Defining nationalism in terms of consumerism gained relevance in a postwar American society defined by the freedom of the market in contrast to the communist Soviet Union. The 1959 "kitchen debate" between American Vice President Richard Nixon and Soviet First Secretary Nikita Kruschev, widely seen on television, made clear the contrast between an American society characterized by its wealth of branded consumer goods like household appliances and the Soviet society that lacked them. It was staged at a model American house built for a cultural exchange in Moscow, a media event that positioned the domestic consumption of American families at the heart of national identity.

In a hyper-commercialized world of ubiquitous brands, the sense of people belonging to one common community is surely bolstered by consumerism. Many modern nations are made up of massive populations comprising different cultural groups spread out over a vast territory. Unifying nations of this kind can be accomplished in various ways, and consumer brands are central among them. As McGovern (2008) asserts of American consumer culture in the first half of the 20th century: "Mass culture and commodities offered a common experience in an otherwise diverse and fragmentary society. People have used the products and rituals of commercial culture to fashion themselves as full citizens and to reshape a social order that recognizes them" (192–193). We continue to identify ourselves by our brands of choice, e.g., Apple or Android, Converse or Vans, Mountain Dew or Sprite. These can extend to media brands like Disney and Nintendo and sports brands like our favorite leagues and teams. We might not usually think of these in terms of politics, but they provide points of connection across many kinds of difference and unify disparate populations in an experience of commonality, which is one of the most crucial elements of being a citizen.

There are specific forms of consumption that are more consciously, more intentionally citizenship-focused. Some consumer behaviors are premised on ethical choices or efforts to serve an interest beyond yourself, or to advance a cause or movement. Brands solicit this kind of consumer behavior when they position themselves as virtuous agents serving the common good. Some do this by supporting philanthropic activities, e.g., donating a percentage of proceeds to charity. And consumers seek out brands and products that fit their values, often in a way that connects to broader issues. This has been called "commodity activism," linking shopping with values that conjoin expressions of identity with investments in politics.

Rupalee Mukherjee and Sarah Banet-Weiser (2012) argue that "consumer-citizens increasingly practice moral and civic virtue principally through their pocketbooks" as practices of "ethical consumption" (12). Examples of this kind of practice might include choosing foods raised sustainably and humanely, boycotting a brand made by a company that mistreats workers, or choosing to patronize minority-owned businesses in your community. Brands solicit these investments in socially conscious consumerism when they use marketing appeals to activist-minded shoppers like "fair trade" labels or promises of being "carbon neutral."

Shopping as activism has its detractors, who point out that the onus for achieving social justice cannot rest solely on the shoulders of individual consumers and that institutions (e.g., corporations and governments) have much greater agency to make meaningful change. We might also question how much of "ethical consumerism" is a product of cynical branding by companies eager to take advantage of consumers' desires to fit their purchasing to their progressive identities. For instance, the annual breast cancer awareness campaign that paints pink ribbons on a vast array of consumer products and media campaigns has been criticized as "pinkwashing," i.e., attaching a virtuous facade of support for a good cause to what is really just marketing to certain consumer demographics that actually does little to advance gender equity. The pink apparel worn by American football players in televised sporting events as part of this campaign in the early 2000s might have been more of a performance of activism to attract female fans than the real thing (Jones 2014).

The movement toward ethical consumption might thus be compromised in many ways, but its existence speaks to the centrality of consumerism to the identity of the contemporary citizen. When thinking of your role as a citizen, it's not so easy to cast aside the other roles you inhabit in your everyday life. Your sense of belonging to something greater than yourself, your participation in communities of shared interest, and your investment in advancing the common good may often coincide with your identity – and your behavior – as a consumer.

Social Media and the Branded Self

As with many of the central topics in media studies, ideas about consumerism were formulated in an era of mass media. National advertising in print and broadcast media, and dominant cultural industries like the major record labels and the Hollywood studios, offered one-to-many communication. But in the internet age, audiences have become producers and participants in media. Audiences have alternatives to legacy mass media in online platforms that offer "relatable" personalities, whether celebrities or just ordinary folks, or ordinary folks who have become social media celebrities. The rise of popular influencers or content creators on platforms like YouTube, Instagram, and TikTok – accounts with millions of followers or subscribers – has shaken up the relationship between media, brands, and audiences. Any kind of media content with a strong claim on an audience's attention will be ripe for commercialization, for being made to serve the agenda of consumer capitalism.

In this new world, some of the same tendencies from pre-social-media days remain. On these platforms, consumerism is a preeminent cultural force. Social is a type of media, like a music video and branded entertainment, where the lines between content and advertising can be so blurry as to be indiscernible. Some tendencies have been intensified: we find more selling in more ways, colonizing more of our time and attention. We use platforms like Instagram to socialize with peers, and inserting consumerism into these interactions is an invasion of brand culture into aspects of everyday life that had not previously been commercialized. We also see some sharp turns away from the mass media age: on social media, any random individual who signs up for an account can become a vector for selling, and the old ways of marketing products via professional media campaigns are being overhauled to match the audience's habits of online attention.

Of course, not all social media users are selling something. What I have in mind here are the ones who pursue opportunities afforded by these platforms to become dedicated entrepreneurs of the self, creating a brand identity out of their postings online – videos and photos of themselves – to develop substantial followings of people whose attention adds up to substantial monetary value. This kind of self-branding in user-generated online content has been described as a form of micro-celebrity, a way for ordinary people to take on some of the roles and functions of mass media celebrities like Hollywood stars (Marwick 2013). But increasingly, influencers or creators are not so micro, and what we see in social media is really an update of mass media celebrity built upon the democratizing platforms where anyone can sign up and share their content with the whole world.

The innovation of the social media influencer or content creator is that they appeal to their audiences as authentic, speaking their language, following the style of and conventions of the community. They come across as real people who happen to be big online. Their rise to fame begins with launching a YouTube Channel or Instagram or TikTok account, not with a record deal or modeling contract, or a role on television or in films. They record their content in a bedroom or a backyard, and reveal mundane details of their everyday lives. The audience comes to trust their authenticity and relates to them as quasi-friends, people you feel like you know personally. They seem like amateurs even if they are for all intents and purposes professional media and marketing workers.

Social media influencers/creators feed consumerism by monetizing their content with advertising and by selling directly to consumers whether by hawking products like their branded apparel ("merch") or by soliciting sponsorship on Patreon, which converts audiences for free content like podcasts into loyal customers. Brands have also recognized these personalities as ideal ambassadors and marketers, and some social media celebrities have created product lines in partnership with brands, for instance, in the cosmetics business.

Beauty vloggers are an exemplary type of professionalized social media celebrity. As Mingyi Hou (2019) has described in a study of these YouTubers, entrepreneurial vloggers who pursue careers in this line of work regularly upload videos focused on fashion, makeup, and lifestyle. They often combine makeup tutorials and product reviews with more personal slice-of-life content, turning their lives into ongoing narratives for audience consumption. They review new products they have acquired and show off their homes. Haul videos let audiences appreciate their newly acquired items, asking for input on which ones to review in future content. Success for a beauty vlogger will include incorporating branded content and partnering with producers of consumer goods. They display them to their subscribers who relate to the vlogger in a dynamic of intimacy and trust that comes from the connection between audience and creator. For the beauty industry, these social media influencers have become an essential conduit to the shoppers they want to reach, so the YouTubers can monetize their fame by connecting online audiences with the products that will help them follow the beauty advice of their favorite social media stars.

The TikTok/Instagram superstar Addison Rae is one of the social media celebrities who has effectively parlayed entrepreneurial beauty influencer fame into a full-blown mainstream celebrity. As a *New York Times Magazine* profile by Vanessa Grigoriadis detailed in 2021, Rae decided to start her own beauty line after realizing that her newfound TikTok fame gained from "doing slithery hip-hop dances" (at the time, she had its second-most popular account with 73 million followers) meant she needed to find a way to monetize her success. As Grigoriadis describes, the appeal of influencers for the cosmetics industry is that they "speak a fan's language and draw them close, becoming both friend and muse."

Influencers let viewers in on their secrets, and audiences feel an investment in the stars as they see them progress in their careers. They might want to duplicate their look and be inclined to trust their advice. In partnering with a cosmetics manufacturer, a social media influencer like Rae would own a share in the business of her line, Item Beauty, and the industry would own a share of her claim on a vast, desirable audience of consumers. The profile also details her branching out to promoting other brands and moving into acting in a film, and recording a pop single and accompanying video. The celebrity dynamics work in the other direction as well: celebrities from music and movies or television also launch product lines and exploit social media for their self-branding. A-list American movie stars have traditionally been reluctant to appear in US advertisements shilling for brands, a move that could seem to tarnish their image as artists, but that has been changing. As Grigoriadis (2021) notes, the two kinds of celebrities seem destined to converge. She also observes that "the relationship a celebrity can have with a fan is far more elaborate than the one between a brand and a customer, even though, at its core, those relationships are the same."

Stories like this one are exceptional, and there can only be so many megastars at one time. But the details speak to the way consumerist media have shifted as the media landscape has changed with technological developments. When we go online and create a profile, take our own photos and videos and post them, interact with other users, share links and engage in conversations, we are performing as a version of ourselves, and fashioning an identity for other users' consumption. This self-branding is a ubiquitous phenomenon, an essential activity of the internet as a communication platform. Branding of consumer products easily rides atop this behavior, and consumerist appeals have found a welcome space online by following the norms of interaction already established on social media. These are consumerist platforms through and through, from the actual advertisements slipped into the feeds to fill Facebook's coffers to the promotional content of the many brands and users whose regular streams of fresh content reward us for continually picking up our devices.

Always Be Selling

The media industries arose alongside the modern consumer society, and the two have been developing together for well over a century. Advertising-supported media are the clearest example of consumer values shaping culture and society, but there are consumerist appeals in all kinds of popular culture, and actual advertising is only part of the story. While the purpose of media to inspire consumption is a longstanding feature, it has not remained static over time, but has shifted with changes in technology and audience preferences. When we find ways to escape from advertising appeals, brands devise ways of finding us. And from radio to TikTok, when new platforms have emerged, corporations have found ways of using them to capture media audiences' attention. Anything that collects people into an audience can be harnessed to try to sell those people something. In recent years, even drivers filling up with gas or men urinating in public restrooms have had their attention captured for advertising.

We might look to blame the media industries themselves for consumerism and wonder why there aren't more spaces reserved as oases from relentless selling. And there are pockets of media that resist it or offer alternatives, like some public service broadcasting and independent outlets for journalism and the arts. Supporting more non-profit media, and more media that is not advertising-supported, could be a way of carving out spaces for culture that works in different ways and addresses different needs. But at the deepest level, media's consumerism comes out of the economic and political foundation of modern societies. Our media are the culture produced by a society in which individualism and consumption are a largely unquestioned way of life. Any critique of consumerist media will ultimately be a critique of our modern ways of living.

Discussion Questions

1. Search online for old advertisements to analyze using an image search or the Vintage Ad Browser (http://www.vintageadbrowser.com/) and analyze their appeal. Do they follow the patterns discussed here, such as speaking to our fantasies of the good life, solving novel problems, or picturing a social tableau? If not, what is their appeal?
2. Identify an example of lifestyle media and explain how it (1) fits into the agenda of consumerism and (2) appeals to its audience (or not) on the basis of gender.
3. Observe yourself using an advertising-supported social media platform like Instagram, TikTok, Facebook, or Twitter. What ads do you see, and why do you think you were served these ads in particular? Is there other consumerist content in your feed other than the advertisements? How are the ads and the other content similar and/or different from one another?

References

"Ad Age Marketing Fact Pack 2021." 2020a. *Ad Age*, December 21, 2020. https://adage.com/article/digital-edition/looking-back-biggest-newsmakers-buzzwords-and-trends-2020-ad-age-digital-edition/2302586

"Ad Age Leading National Advertisers 2020 Fact Pack." 2020b. *Ad Age*, July 13, 2020. https://s3-prod.adage.com/s3fs-public/2020-07/lnafp_aa_20200713_locked.pdf

Banet-Weiser, Sarah. 2007. *Kids Rule! Nickelodeon and Consumer Citizenship.* Durham, NC: Duke University Press.

Banet-Weiser, Sarah and Charlotte Lapsansky. 2008. "RED is the New Black: Brand Culture, Consumer Citizenship and Political Possibility." *International Journal of Communication* 2: 1248–1268.

Cohen, Lizabeth. 2003. *A Consumer's Republic: The Politics of Mass Consumption in Postwar America.* New York: Alfred A. Knopf.

Croteau, Davidand William Hoynes. 2006. *The Business of Media: Corporate Media and the Public Interest*, 2nd ed. Thousand Oaks: Pine Forge Press.

Eckert, Charles. 1978. "The Carole Lombard in Macy's Window." *Quarterly Review of Film Studies* 3.1: 1–21.

Ewen, Stuart. 2001. *Captains of Consciousness: Advertising and the Social Roots of the Consumer Culture*, 25th anniversary ed. New York: Basic Books.

Grigoriadis, Vanessa. 2021. "The Beauty of 78.5 Million Followers." *New York Times Magazine*, March 23, 2021. https://www.nytimes.com/2021/03/23/magazine/addison-rae-beauty-industry.html

Higashi, Sumiko. 1994. *Cecil B. DeMille and American Culture: The Silent Era.* Berkeley: University of California Press.

Hou, Mingyi. 2019. "Social Media Celebrity and the institutionalization of YouTube." *Convergence* 25, no. 3: 534–553.

Jones, Lindsay H. 2014. "NFL continues reach for female fans through breast cancer awareness." *USA Today*, September 30, 2014. https://www.usatoday.com/story/sports/nfl/2014/09/30/nfl-breast-cancer-awareness/16508773/

McGovern, Charles F. 2006. *Sold American: Consumption and Citizenship, 1890–1945.* Chapel Hill: University of North Carolina Press.

McGovern, Charles F. 2008. "Consumer Culture and Mass Culture." In *A Companion to American Cultural History*, edited by Karen Halttunen, 183–197. Malden: Blackwell.

Marchand, Roland. 1985. *Advertising the American Dream: Making Way for Modernity, 1920–1940.* Berkeley: University of California Press.

Marwick, Alice E. 2013. *Status Update: Celebrity, Publicity, and Branding in the Social Media Age.* New Haven: Yale University Press.

Meyers, Cynthia B. 2014. "Branded Entertainment Reshapes Media Ecosystem." *Carsey-Wolf Center Media Industries Project*, June 27, 2014. https://www.carseywolf.ucsb.edu/wp-content/uploads/2018/02/Meyers_BrandedEntertainment.pdf

Mukherjee, Rupalee and Sarah Banet-Weiser. 2012. "Introduction: Commodity Activism in Neoliberal Times." In *Commodity Activism: Cultural Resistance in Neoliberal Times*, edited by Mukherjee and Banet-Weiser, 1–17. New York: New York University Press.

Nasaw, David. 1993. *Going Out: The Rise and Fall of Public Amusements.* New York: Basic Books.

Newman, Michael Z. 2020. "Everyday Italian: Cultivating Taste." In *How to Watch Television*, 2nd ed., edited by Ethan Thompson and Jason Mittell, 329–336. New York: New York University Press.

Ohmann, Richard. 1996. *Selling Culture: Magazines, Markets, and Class at the Turn of the Century.* London: Verso.

Ryan, Maureen. 2018. *Lifestyle Media in American Culture: Gender, Class, and the Politics of Ordinariness*. New York: Routledge.

Schudson, Michael. 1986. *Advertising, The Uneasy Persuasion: Its Dubious Impact on American Society*. New York: Basic Books.

Shaw, Jenny. 2010. *Shopping: Social and Cultural Perspectives*. Cambridge: Polity.

Sperling, Nicole and Tiffany Hsu. 2021. "With Fewer Ads on Streaming, Brands Make More Movies." *New York Times*, March 23, 2021. https://www.nytimes.com/2021/03/23/business/media/branded-content-movies.html

Stole, Inger L. 2001. "Advertising." In *Culture Works: The Political Economy of Culture*, edited by Richard Maxwell, 83–106. Minneapolis: University of Minnesota Press.

Zukin, Sharon. 2004. *Point of Purchase: How Shopping Changed American Culture*. New York: Routledge.

10

TECHNOLOGY

When I teach a course called Introduction to Mass Media, I begin by defining *media* and then specifying which media are *mass* media. *Media* is the plural of *medium*, which is something in-between (Latin for "middle"). A medium cup of coffee is a size in between a large and a small, while a medium of communication is an object in-between people engaged in meaningful exchanges of ideas or symbols. In the arts, a medium is the name for the material used to create, such as bronze for sculptors and film for photographers. Mass media are also material in form, using paper and ink, or data stored on silicon chips and transmitted across cables.

In my classroom, I would say the media of communication are words and voices, neither of which we think of as technologies. Standing at the front of a large lecture hall, I switch on the wireless microphone clipped to my shirt, and call attention to the mic and the sound system in the room that allows my voice to carry effortlessly through a large space. Microphones, amplifiers, and speakers are tools created to serve human needs and extend our capabilities. I have experienced some hearing loss, and microphones help me understand people who may be far away from my ears, or who speak in soft or high voices. Microphones are a technology designed and used for improving communication.

My lecture would also be illustrated with slides, with text and illustrations. These visual aids are also media, and they combine written language, images and videos, computer hardware and software, network infrastructure for the storage of my presentation files, and a projector that throws

DOI: 10.4324/9781003007708-10

vivid, colorful pictures up on a screen. Even the electric power in the classroom can be regarded as a communication technology: we wouldn't be able to see or hear any of this without it, and it's one of the basic requirements for so many of our everyday information technologies from traffic signals to cell phone videos.

Our media are so many, and so varied, that we may forget how remarkable they are, how novel and recent these tools are in the scope of human history. Human beings have existed for hundreds of thousands of years, and our ancestors for millions before that. For most of that time, our bodies were our media of communication. Pictures and alphabets are both fairly recent inventions. As one classic text puts it: "The book is a relative newcomer in western society" (Febvre and Martin 1997, 10). Mechanical printing has existed for just a few hundred years, and writings from earlier times were usually made on animal skins rather than paper, another relatively recent invention. Snapping photographs, recording sounds, transmitting signals across wires or airwaves, making moving pictures for projection to audiences in a theater or on screens in the home: all of these are less than two centuries old as I write.

Computers as we know them are a very recent invention. They didn't exist when my grandparents were children. I remember pocket calculators being a novelty. Now we typically walk around with devices in our pockets that have more computing power than large government or corporate institutions had access to a couple of generations ago, and they are also remarkably good cameras for shooting photos and videos as well as functioning as telephones, location tracking devices, and touchscreens for playing games, writing emails, and watching shows. The fact that these have become normal, everyday objects makes it hard to see how different our technologically mediated lives must be from those of our recent ancestors who could hardly imagine such things even within the realm of science-fiction.

The existence of media as a topic for a course or for an area of study, and for a book like this one, is premised on developments in technology. All media, even those that look old to us now, are relatively recent inventions. Thinking of media this way moves us beyond analyzing media content and toward broader concerns with historical developments, with changes in society over the past several hundred years that track with changes in media technology. A key question for us here will be: what role does technology play in shaping the experience of media by its audiences and users, which is to say, the way we engage with the social world?

From Mass Media to Participatory Culture

Media, then, are technologies of information and communication that come in many varieties. Technologies, in turn, are tools and related forms of knowledge created to serve human needs. But what of *mass* media? This is a phrase we hear less and less, but much of our thinking about media technology comes from the age of mass communication. When two people have a conversation, they are engaged in one-to-one communication. But a newspaper or a radio station is capable of communicating to many readers or listeners at once. From one newsroom or TV studio, the same message can be made to transmit via printing or over the airwaves to thousands or even millions of people. This one-to-many communication is the essential feature of mass media.

Newspapers and magazines, movies, sound recordings, and radio and television are all classic cases of mass media. The invention of the printing press in 15th-century Europe is often seen as the origin point for the spread of mass media, as it led to the mass reproduction of books and of news and has been seen as a catalyst for social change (Eisenstein 1980). Before the press, the written word could be copied only by hand, which meant that texts such as history books and scripture would be rare, precious, and accessible only to a small elite of scholars and clergy with the literacy skills to read and understand them. The development of mass media was paired with an expansion of literacy and of the spread of democratic societies and a culture of print, a development that unfolded over the past few hundred years (Poe 2011).

In the middle of the 20th century, the most powerful media institutions in North American society were newspapers and magazines, radio and television networks, Madison Avenue advertising agencies, and Hollywood movie studios. This was the age of mass media, a concept suggesting a whole society shaped by the forces of one-to-many communication. A small number of channels existed for ideas, images, and stories to circulate among the public, and audiences had little opportunity to give feedback or make their own media. To many observers and critics, this gave these institutions a formidable power over the public, a power to shape opinion and behavior and mold society that was much debated in the mid-century years (Bell 1965; Mills 1956; Shils 1960). Within a few decades, however, this scenario had begun to change dramatically.

Two developments are key to this shift. The first was the proliferation of media options for consumers, epitomized by the rise of cable and satellite television in the 1970s and 1980s, new technologies that promised to open up media from the control of a small cluster of networks and studios (Streeter 1997). Rather than aiming for universal appeal, these new channels catered to smaller, narrower slices of the mass audience, often carved up by demographic characteristics like age and gender. These are often called *niche* media, hailing audiences with particular interests and backgrounds: golfers, *anime* fans, conservative news junkies, gamers, Millennial moms, etc. While media with mass appeal, such as Marvel movies and football games, continue to draw broad audiences across many segments of the public, many of us live in little worlds of *niche* rather than *mass* media. Beyond television, this can be seen in many corners of online culture from podcasts and vlogs to fan communities on Reddit or Twitch.

The second development shattering mass media's dominance was the internet. The internet has been a catalyst for changing so many things about media, and one of the biggest changes has been how it allows users to move from reading, listening, and watching to also writing, recording, creating, and participating. This has been especially important in the generation of internet services known as "Web 2.0," which emerged in the mid-2000s with the rise of blogs and photo- and video-sharing sites. Web 2.0 replaced the "read-only" format of the earlier web, where creators needed more technical knowledge and skill to post online, with a "read–write" format more typical of the age of social media. Many of the most successful online platforms since the emergence of Web 2.0 contrast with one-to-many forms of communication like TV. Often, they incorporate one-to-one (e.g., messaging) and many-to-many (e.g., social media engagement) along with one-to-many (e.g., sharing popular content).

YouTube is a good example. On YouTube, you can be a spectator and just watch the videos you find interesting. You can also make and upload videos of your own, you can respond to a video with a video, and you can like and comment on videos. The participatory aspect of YouTube makes it different from the traditional mass media, the legacy media like newspapers and TV that offer audiences much more limited opportunities for talking back and being part of a conversation. This has prompted a new configuration of the relationship between media producers and audiences/users, as these categories start blending together. As Jean Burgess and Joshua Green (2018) put it in their book about the video-sharing platform, *"participatory culture is YouTube's core business"* (vii, emphasis in original).

Any view of media technology in any particular moment will be shaped by recent experiences and the present media environment. Over a fairly short span of time, media users of the early 21st century have been through a major upheaval in communication technology that has shaken up the business of media and transformed everyday life. A handful of giant "tech" companies, including Google, Facebook, Apple, and Amazon, emerged over a brief few decades to change the way people access information and entertainment, and the way they interact with one another, rather dramatically. The legacy media companies, including the major conglomerates like Disney and Comcast and news organizations large and small, have had to adapt to this new environment not just by changing their business practices, but by transforming media platforms and formats. Tech companies and legacy companies can be seen as frenemies who need to work together while also being in fierce competition with one another.

The rise of the tech giants and the internet as a super-medium is merely the latest chapter in a long story of change upon change. We would do well to recall that previous generations also saw themselves on the cusp of a technological revolution. And some of the changes of the fairly recent past were surely as bold as those of our lifetimes, including sending messages across hundreds of miles in an instant over the telegraph wires, illuminating the night with electrical power, and wireless transmission of sounds over invisible electromagnetic waves. In their moments of emergence, these 19th-century technologies would overcome distance and speed up modern life, contributing to myriad changes in everyday affairs (Marvin 1990; Kern 2003). Whatever their actual effects on people's daily lives, they were often regarded as sources of troubling anxiety and alienation (Czitrom 1982, 20–21; Boddy 2004). The internet has surely been a catalyst for reactions like these too, but it pays to recognize that it was not the first new media technology to be so unsettling, and surely will not be the last.

New and Renewed Media

So often, it seems that just as soon as we become familiar with a particular technology, it gets replaced by something new, and we have a strong bias toward noticing novelty. This often makes the present seem like a stark break from the past. A consistent pattern across media history is that more and more of these new media keep emerging to claim our attention, while existing ones are also continuously modified as new versions are released.

Corporations with an interest in continuously selling things will bake this cycle of change into their business, releasing products intended to be used for a limited lifespan. By the time you buy a new smartphone, the companies that make them have already developed the newer version that will be better than your shiny new thing, a wasteful practice known as planned obsolescence. Whether or not this is a factor in a particular technology being cast aside for the latest model, it often seems that nothing stays the same for very long, and what we think of as one technology is, upon closer inspection, actually a series of versions and iterations that have been rolled out over a period of time.

For example, sound recording, and recorded music in particular, are not one technology, but an extensive history of formats and commercial products that have emerged one after the other for more than 100 years from tinfoil and wax cylinders to spinning disks to digital files streaming across wireless networks (McCourt 2015). Think about the way you listen to music right now, and about how this has changed over your lifetime. Even if you're not that old, you have probably experienced some change in formats or points of access. You might also use multiple different technologies for the same purpose, like having one kind of device to listen to the radio in the car (I listen to CDs and to local stations that broadcast over the air), and another kind in the kitchen (I have a smart speaker that streams online audio). YouTube might not seem like a rival to the radio, but it was found to account for almost half of the world's music consumption in 2018 (Binder 2018).

Not much more than a century ago, recorded music was scarce by today's standards. Long after recording emerged, sheet music sales still earned more than records for music composers and publishers. Sound recording devices had been invented by Thomas Edison and others in the later years of the 19th century, but a market for selling disks to be played on record players took a few decades to develop, and early record players (phonographs) could not fill a very large space with sound (Welch and Burt 1994). Alongside recorded music, radio broadcasts offered a free alternative in the home beginning in the 1920s, and live performed music continued to be a popular pastime both in the home and in public places like saloons and theaters. Early records, which spun at 78 RPM (revolutions per minute), were made of fragile shellac, contained only a few minutes of music per side, and had a somewhat noisy sound quality. Microgrooved long-playing or "LP" (12-inch, 33 1/3 RPM) vinyl records along with vinyl singles (7-inch, 45 RPM) became popular after their introduction in 1948. They were more durable than shellac, and LPs could contain an entire symphony or Broadway cast recording on a single disk (Coleman 2003, 51–70). They might be played using "high-fidelity" stereos for improved sound quality. LPs became a popular and commercially successful standard format for sale to consumers and singles filled the jukeboxes in public places like restaurants, bars, and bowling alleys.

Recording expanded as a market for consumer sales grew in the post-World War II years. After television replaced it as the most powerful broadcast medium, radio became much more music-driven, and often promoted record sales. Magnetic tape used for capturing audio (and video) was an invention of the 1920s that became widely used in the recording industry in the years after World War II (Schmidt Horning 2013). Audiotape eventually became a bona fide rival to turntable records as a consumer product. It had some advantages, including permitting home recording, and fitting into compact cassettes that could be used in portable stereos and in automobiles (Morton 2006, 164–174). Music became more mobile and ubiquitous with cassettes, which were sold alongside vinyl in record stores for several decades. Compact discs, a digital format scanned by a laser which would supposedly offer advantages of durability and noiselessness, emerged as a rival to vinyl and cassette in the 1980s, but their heyday was barely two decades long as the internet-based distribution of MP3 files assaulted their dominance in the early 2000s (Rothenbuhler 2012). CDs might offer advantages of sound quality, but MP3s were so easily shared online and thousands of them could be stored on a single small device like an iPod or smartphone.

Throughout this progression of musical formats, the place of recorded music in everyday life expanded to fill more and more different kinds of spaces, including offices, hotel lobbies, and shopping malls, and new times of day, like early in the morning and during commutes to and from work or school. Other forms of sound recording, from instructional media to answering machine greetings to podcasts, spread alongside recorded music. And moving images have also incorporated sound recordings since the rise of talking pictures in the late 1920s, and of television in the 1950s.

This thumbnail history of sound recording formats is meant to show some key principles for understanding media technology historically. First of all, technologies are constantly being updated and upgraded, or replaced with newer versions that overcome a problem or introduce a new advantage, like portability or quality of reproduction. Or, more accurately, what the business of selling recordings and recording technologies can frame as a problem/advantage in its appeals to the public. In this sense, *all media are new media*.

Second, we make sense of these technologies in relation to one another – to what they came after or improved – and to what they were used to accomplish. Recorded music was in competition with sheet music, and eventually replaced publishing as a principal way for songwriters to earn money for their work and to disseminate and popularize new songs. LPs were a rival to 78s that eventually replaced them by having advantages of sound and storage capacities, but cassette tapes and CDs and MP3s each offered something deemed lacking in their predecessors as well. Each new media technology was novel in terms of its material form – shellac, vinyl, tape, etc. – but also in the ways that it could be *used*.

Third, technologies change not from innovation for its own sake, in some kind of mythical forward march of technological progress, but to address specific needs and desires among businesses and consumers or users (Pinch and Bijker 1984). *Social and economic factors drive technological change.* In music recording, these factors included the desire to fit more music on a single disk, to make for a more robust market for selling recordings. They included making it possible for consumers to produce and copy recordings of their own, and take them out to listen to while traveling or commuting to fill more of people's lives with sound recording. A continual desire has been to produce recordings that capture the same qualities of sound as a live performance, without noises and other undesired sounds. Technologies are created and improved upon by *intention*, to serve some specific function, and do not just naturally emerge on their own (Williams 2003, 1–25), though some have been developed through serendipitous processes (e.g., x-ray, penicillin). Looking at the intentions of both businesses and consumers shows us where technologies typically come from and how different groups benefit (or not) from having them.

In some instances, corporations force change on the public from the top down, as a way of extracting more profit from their business. CDs were promoted as a great step forward in quality and durability, and while they became much cheaper than LPs or cassettes to manufacture and distribute they retailed at more than twice the price of records (Strauss 1995; Harmon 2003), and were a way for the recording industry to extract more value from existing intellectual property. The new format also promoted the sale of new hardware – CD players – often manufactured by the same firms that were responsible for the move away from LPs and cassettes, Phillips and Sony. The recording industry effectively nudged record stores and consumers to "upgrade" to a new format, which was highly profitable for the record labels, especially when consumers replaced their LPs or cassettes with CDs of the same albums.

Alternatively, in many instances, consumers drive innovation from the bottom-up, as when file-sharing for free among internet users on Napster and other platforms emerged as a popular non-commercial alternative to recordings sold as "physical media" (disks). The recording industry learned from its users that easy online distribution of songs (rather than entire albums) was a desirable way for listers to access its products, and moved within a few years of the Napster episode to serve this market, though never in a way that would be anywhere near as lucrative as CDs had been in the 1990s.

Finally, this extended example illustrates how new media hardly ever kill off their old media rivals very quickly or reliably. Some of these recording formats, like 78 records and cassettes, eventually became obsolete. But well into the 21st century, vinyl LPs persist alongside Spotify and YouTube as an economically viable format for music consumers who want to own copies of music, and for a recording industry happy to have a product to sell to them (Palm 2019). Sheet music also continues to be published and sold. Many rival formats can coexist and fill different needs for different market niches. Radio was not killed by television, and both of these mid-20th-century stalwarts remain quite popular several decades into the internet age. Books have not been killed by the internet, and television has not been killed by Netflix and other streaming platforms. But in all of these examples the older medium has had to adapt to a novel environment once its newer rival became popular and economically powerful. When old media adapt to competition from new media – such as old-school print books now routinely being released in multiple formats, including eBooks and audiobooks – we can think of them not as new media, but as *renewed* media (Peters 2009).

From Novelty to Domestication

In the example of sound recordings, I have told a story about a succession of different technologies: recording formats and playback devices, and the ways they followed one another. This is one way of looking at a medium: as a cluster or sequence of different objects that are used to accomplish a particular purpose. A medium can be more than one thing. Cinema is a medium that includes a diverse array of technologies, including cameras and projectors, but also microphones, lights, editing tools, and numerous others, not to mention movie theaters and Blu Ray players. In their early years, movie production did not include audio, but now we think of the film soundtrack as part of the medium. Even a single element like a movie camera contains many parts, such as lenses and mounts like tripods, dollies, and cranes. If you switch these up, you could end up with a different kind of movie.

But another way of thinking about this topic is to dig deeper into a more narrowly defined technology. For sound studies, this could be the Sony Walkman or the MP3 file format. When looking at a particular object like this, we observe a predictable sequence of stages in their trajectory from novelty to familiarity. Looking at this predictable pattern helps us to see new media technologies in their social and historical context, in a way that helps us appreciate not just individual inventions and their uses, but also the role of new technologies in shaping media history.

A first stage necessary to the development of a new technology will be its *invention and development*, whether by an individual tinkering in a garage or by workers in a government lab or R&D division of a company. Invention is sometimes portrayed in popular narratives as the stuff of lone, heroic geniuses inspired to dream of new possibilities in the face of great adversity, but in practice it's a form of routine work often conducted by teams of researchers pursuing specific goals within institutions, building on existing knowledge and technology.

There is no naturally occurring technological progress that is separate from human needs and desires, and from the social environment in which invention is undertaken. To take a very old example, writing is thought to have originated in ancient agricultural settlements in the form of markings on clay tokens used in counting and data-keeping and exchanged in economic activity (Schmandt-Besserat 1996). Accounting was a need felt by farmers wanting to keep track of their commodities, such as bushels of barley and jugs of oil. An agricultural society had a need for a way to make a record of production that oral communication could not satisfy, and this led to "the watershed of mathematics and communication" (125). This same basic dynamic of technologies emerging to satisfy human needs explains development of so many kinds of new media: social functions precede technical formats. In the realm of social media, for instance, new apps and new features are ways of making possible communication and socializing among people who desire connection but are separated from one another by time and distance, as people tend to be in the modern online world.

However a technology emerges, it can only be widely adopted through distribution to users. Often this requires some form of *commercialization*, especially in the case of new consumer products to be sold to the public. New technologies are often launched to great fanfare as exciting solutions to familiar problems, as in the advertising cliché of "before" and "after" shots. This revolutionary rhetoric can be the stuff of overheated marketing hype, but can also become ingrained in popular imagination. The first smartphone from Apple was hailed as the "Jesus phone" and fans of the company's products lined up for hours or days to have the opportunity to buy one. It was a fetish object. A few years later, there were millions of these commonplace black rectangles in people's pockets all over the world, and the first generation iPhone was so "old" that it would no longer work with up-to-date software. But the fact that they were commonplace means that a market for smartphones was well established, and it was a profitable business.

Distribution and commercialization can be done through already existing corporate arrangements, but many new media technologies are marketed by upstarts and outsiders with ideas for new ways of exploiting a market. This was true of the tech giants of the 21st century, which all originated as entrepreneurial startups. There was no search engine advertising establishment for Google to take on, as it was the founding company in that field. Once a market has been established for a new media technology, though, the upstarts can become the establishment, and their power can derive from holding a monopoly over a technology, as Google has over internet searching in many parts of the world. Many powerful modern media, from publishing to social networking, have succeeded in being widely distributed by being commercialized. In some societies, the state rather than private enterprise has supported this distribution, as in countries where broadcasting developed as a public service supported by state financing (e.g., the UK) rather than a private, commercial one (e.g., the US).

When a market for a new media technology has been established, it often prompts state action to set limits over its workings and uses. Some technologies may be covered in some fashion by existing government regulation. For instance, any new medium of expression may be regarded as protected by the US Constitution's First Amendment, and by other countries' free speech protections, as well as by copyright laws, laws covering libel and defamation, and many others. But new technologies also raise new problems and concerns, and new *regulation* is a predictable stage in their development.

Regulation can take many forms, such as strict policies governing who can broadcast radio and television signals over the air, which of course did not exist before radio and television were invented, but it can also be activated in a way that allows media industries much latitude in the way they operate. For most of the time they have operated, the tech giants have been rather lightly regulated, though some have advocated for new rules to constrain them in ways that would serve the public interest. If there are no state policies governing racially biased search algorithms or anti-democratic social media disinformation campaigns, the first reason is that these things have been around for a relatively short time so far. The more public concern arises, perhaps the more likely regulation of these things will become. Or perhaps the companies will decide to do something about their workings without state intervention, fearing that their business would suffer from a new regulatory environment. Regulation also can include *self-regulation*, or the regulation that companies adopt as rules for themselves, such as the content ratings systems for movies, television, and video games. Regulation and self-regulation often are institutional reactions to the adoption of new technologies to manage their social impact and ease public concern. They often serve as well to secure a predictable, profitable environment for business.

A final step in this cycle occurs once the new technology is no longer so new, when it becomes familiar to the point that it arouses much less wonder or suspicion. This stage is known as *domestication*, and we can think of that word in at least two senses. Domestication is like the taming of animals or plants to make them predictable and obedient to human control. Something domesticated has been made safe. New technologies can seem strange and unpredictable, but eventually they become trusted companions. Domestication also relates to the home as the domestic sphere, and many new technologies do become fixtures in the home, and thus elements of our everyday lives. This is certainly true of televisions and computers, but even if they are not literally found in people's homes, technologies become domesticated by their repeated presence in people's routines and in their environment (Baym 2010, 45–48; Newman 2017, 76–77).

When technologies are new, they have a tendency to provoke unsettled reactions. These can be positive or negative, *wow* or *uh oh*. Some of these reactions can prompt intense feelings and widespread worries, especially when they concern young people and young girls and women in particular.

Among modern media since the invention of the telegraph, it's hard to think of any new technology that became widely adopted that was not received with some form of *moral panic* over its supposedly harmful effects (Cohen 2002; Drotner 1999). The telephone and radio were feared for their ability to bring strangers into the home via the phone line and radio receiver, the movies were feared for their influence over vulnerable spectators who might emulate the corrupting characters onscreen, comic books were feared for provoking violence and sexual deviance and "seducing the innocent," television was feared for harming children's eyesight and making them stupid, and so on (Hadju 2009; Jowett, Jarvie, and Fuller 1996; Spigel 1992). But this is an age-old pattern: in ancient Greece, the philosopher Plato feared that the new media technology of the time, writing, would destroy memory and thus weaken the mind (Ong 1982, 79–81). In recent times, as soon as a newer technology had come along to arouse fresh public sentiment, the older one somehow ceased to be a danger. Movies receded as a cause for fear when TV became popular. These moral panics are amplified by media attention and public outrage and often lead to calls for regulation. The surest sign that a media technology has been domesticated is that it no longer supplies much fuel for panic.

Technologies as Agents, Users as Innovators

Technologies are often thought about in terms of their novel, dramatic effects on individuals and on society. Especially when they are new, technologies are framed as uniquely powerful forces with the potential to reshape the world and make deep impressions on thought and behavior. The written word, as we have just seen, was once feared for its likelihood to diminish the mental capacities of people in an oral society. New media have been represented as possessing the power to "annihilate space and time" (Galili 2020, 17–49), to diminish our ability to lead private lives (Fischer 1992, 225), and to shorten our attention spans and make us constantly anxious (Newman 2010).

In a much-discussed, panicky cover story for *The Atlantic* magazine in 2008, Nicholas Carr posited that Google was "making us stupid" by offering always-on, easily accessible information at a computer keystroke. The internet, he despaired, was "chipping away [his] capacity for concentration and contemplation." Such ideas about new technology attribute great agency to new media: the power to alter our ways of life and our very selves.

These expressions are typically overstating and misunderstanding the role of media technology in our lives, but the truth or accuracy of these ideas is not exactly what makes them popular and fascinating as discourses. They tap into our sense that the world is being transformed before our very eyes, and into our fear that novelty will upset the order of things that we have always found familiar and safe. Henry David Thoreau (1854), a naturalist who was no fan of modern inventions, wrote in the 1850s of an especially prominent new technology of his own age: "We do not ride on the railroad; it rides upon us" (100). This worry keeps coming up time and again with every new version of the railroad.

There is also a flip side to the usual doom-and-gloom rhetoric: some new media technologies are worshiped as the solution to all of our problems, as the internet was supposed to democratize politics and education and lead us all down an "information superhighway." Utopian discourses of new media, often promoted with breathless hype, tend to be future-oriented. We are ever on the cusp of an epochal change. Rather than make us stupid, Google has promised to make us smart: its stated mission on its "About" page has been "to organize the world's information and make it accessible and useful." The internet was promoted as a new "cyberspace" where we could leave our bodies behind and be whomever we want to be, overcoming many of the problems of the offline world (Barlow 1996), but earlier technologies were also presented as miracle cures to society's ills. The telegraph was seen as promising "universal communication" and "a worldwide victory for Christianity" (Czitrom 1982, 10). The advent of radio in the early decades of the 20th century led to utopian talk of the nation becoming one unified audience, which echoed similar ideas about the telegraph's power to bring far-flung people into a common community (Boddy 2004, 16–20).

Media scholars and historians of technology have a special term for this kind of talk, whether positive or negative in tone: *technological determinism*. This is a bad name that we might call certain ways of thinking that we regard as naive and unsophisticated. Deterministic thinking is a kind of logic that attributes complex phenomena to single causes, and that explains historical events in overly simple ways. Technological determinism is the philosophy that technology is what really makes everything happen, or as the historian of technology Melvin Kranzberg (1986, 545) put it, technology "is the prime factor in shaping our life-styles, values, institutions, and other elements of our society."

A famous example comes from the Canadian media theorist Marshall McLuhan (1964), whose catchphrase was "the medium is the message." This was his way of encapsulating an argument about media history, which goes like this: in any period, the most dominant medium in society will shape the environment in which people live. The world in which print is the dominant medium was a new kind of environment by comparison to the world that came before print. And the world in which TV is the dominant medium is different from the world before TV. There is much more to McLuhan's theory, but this gist of it helps us see how deterministic thinking works: we live in a world made by print, or TV, or the internet. He follows this line of argument to the nth degree, arguing that the printing press was the root cause of many developments of the modern age, including the rise of nationalism, the protestant Reformation, and the industrial revolution (McLuhan 1997, 243). The error in this logic is that any developments so broad and multi-faceted as the rise of nationalism, the Protestant Reformation, and the Industrial Revolution have many causes, and that economic, cultural, social, and political changes were important along with technological ones. It's not that technologies aren't causes, it's that they're not the only causes, and that their power is often overstated.

Even though deterministic thinking – thinking that attributes complex phenomena to single causes – is obviously flawed, it is also very appealing rhetorically and it often appears in popular discussions of media technologies and worries over their impacts. For instance, concerns about children's "screen time" often presumes that the technology of the interactive digital screen, independent of what we use screens to do, must exert a powerful force on the developing minds of young people. (This carried over from an earlier concern about the television screen being a problem needing to be managed in the lives of children.) Even if concerns about how children use these devices are often sensible and well-intentioned, thinking of the screen as a danger in itself, or as something whose use needs to be monitored carefully for safety and health, can be deterministic and reductive. "Screen time" discourse cannot account for the fact that children use screens for many different kinds of experiences, from games and videos to reading and socializing, and as a primary mode of communication for some people with disabilities (Alper 2014).

Just as print media are diverse and include news, magazines, fiction and nonfiction books, reference works, and direct mail advertising, screens offer many kinds of content. We don't think in terms of "print time" that needs to be rationed, and we hardly think of the effects of print on cognitive development and socialization except in a positive sense, as when school-children are assigned a certain amount of reading time per day. But the novelty and perceived power and addictiveness of touchscreen devices has given rise to the ubiquitous discourse of screen time as a problem to be managed. Implicit in this discourse and central to its rhetoric is an attribu-tion of agency to a technology, so that it functions as a convenient target when other issues are harder to address.

While the power of the medium should be acknowledged, the relation between technology and agency can be approached from the opposite direc-tion: from the perspective of the user, and of communities of users. Rather than asking *what technologies are doing to us*, we can explore *what users are doing with technologies*. This relocates the causal agency from media to the people who use and experience them. (The reality is surely that the agency resides in multiple locations.)

In their book about the history of Twitter (actually they call it a "biogra-phy"), Jean Burgess and Nancy Baym (2020) look at how three of the most central features of the social media platform were user-driven innovations. When it was first released, Twitter was presented to the public as a way to share your status, such as your current activity and location. Its first moment of popularity and publicity came at a large public festival, SXSW, where attendees posted on Twitter to let each other know what they were doing (Bilton 2013). Eventually, Twitter became a platform for conversation, for gathering and sharing information among communities, and for spread-ing news and amplifying certain voices. The features of Twitter that have allowed for these functions to become central to the way it is used are the @-reply (entering a user's Twitter name after the "@" to attach the tweet to them as part of a conversation thread), the hashtag (using the # symbol to contribute to the broader discussion of a topic), and the retweet (boosting what someone else tweeted by sharing it on a user's own timeline).

Burgess and Baym (2020) point out that all of these features were innova-tions that originated from communities of Twitter users, not from the com-pany that created the site and maintains it as a commercial business. Users initially typed the @-reply, #, and RT into their tweets manually without them being written into the site's code. When Twitter was new, these typo-graphical entries activated no links to other tweets and retweeting or quote tweeting was not a feature available by clicking "retweet" or "quote tweet." There were also no visible metrics of retweets. After the company saw the way users were tweeting, and recognized the value of these features, they updated the platform to incorporate their community's innovations. This makes Twitter into a media technology that was created by its software engineers and founders, but also by its users. Twitter users have exerted agency in the development of Twitter as the site we know today, one that is hard to imagine without the @-reply, hashtag, and retweet. As Burgess and Baym explain, the ways the site was being used "became code in large part through haphazard, emergent, iterative processes in which the users were crucial actors" (21).

This story of Twitter's user-driven path follows a familiar pattern. The agendas of inventors and of the people who market new media technologies are not always matched by users, who have their own ideas. Imagined uses and actual uses may often differ quite markedly. To clarify this distinction, we can think of the difference between *designer intentions* and *user affordances*. According to the accounts of their intentions (Bilton 2013), the entrepreneurs who created Twitter did not mean to invent a "second screen" experience for fans of particular television series or sports teams, who can use Twitter to join up in moment-by-moment reactions to a show or game. But a platform for offering quick reactions to an ongoing mediated event, with @-replies, hashtags, and retweets to help structure conversations, organize topics, and circulate key ideas, affords Twitter users an experience of connectivity alongside TV watching.

"Affords" in this phrasing means that the technology may be used in certain ways, whether intended or not. You instantly recognize that a wooden chair is designed to be a place to sit, but it affords other uses, too: you can step up on it to reach a high shelf, or burn it for fuel in a dire situation. "Affordances" has become a key term in studies of digital and social media used to capture the ways users shape their experiences with these platforms and networks (Nagy and Neff 2015; Bucher and Helmond 2017).

Many of the typical uses of commonplace media technologies were user innovations that exploited once unimagined affordances. The internet was not designed to be a medium for sending messages from person-to-person, but email quickly became its most popular application because a computer network affords instant communication across distance at any time of day, and helps to sustain communities (Abbate 1999, 106–110). The telephone was not designed to be a medium of sociability, and was intended by its inventors to be used for business communication, but women in particular found that a phone in the home afforded them the ability to keep in touch with friends and kin, pay "visits" without needing to go out, and overcome some of their feelings of isolation (Fischer 1992, 222–254). Radio was not invented to be a broadcast medium and was at first known as a "wireless telegraph" for point-to-point messages, but amateur radio users found that it afforded a pleasurable experience of listening in to faraway sounds, and businesses realized this affordance could be put to use for mass communication on a national scale (Douglas 1987, 292–314; Douglas 2004, 40–82).

In these and many other cases, the affordances of new media were realized by users and in turn the further development of the technology was informed by such patterns of use. Innovation followed these paths once they were established. Such examples are 180 degrees from deterministic, as they support the view of users shaping technologies to satisfy their social and personal needs and desires, and businesses adapting to serve them, rather than users being manipulated and transformed by the power of technology.

The Politics of Media Technologies

Throughout this discussion, there has been a consistent tension between two contrasting ideas about media technology, and of technology more generally. On the one hand, you can think of technology as set apart from the social world, but exerting a force over it. Deterministic thinking about technology captures this side of the tension: a new technology comes along and does something to us, like Google "making us stupid." Moral panics over new media often work this way. On the other hand, you can think of media technologies as products of the social world that are deeply embedded within it – as objects created and used by groups of people for particular purposes. These purposes may be the imperative of media companies to make money or the yearning of individuals to keep in touch with one another, stay informed, express themselves, and experience the pleasures of art and entertainment. The second of these options is the one critical media scholars tend to adopt. As products of the social world, media technologies are made and used in ways that come from and perpetuate society's unequal structures.

Kranzberg (1986), the historian of technology, argued that "technology is neither good nor bad; nor is it neutral" (547). This is to say that technologies are consequential in a way that follows from the social dynamics of their uses, often going well beyond the initial purposes of their invention. Kranzberg also observes that "the same technology can have quite different

results when introduced into different contexts or under different circum-
stances" (455–456).

Technologies are not neutral especially when it comes to their politics.
Because the social world is not neutral, nor equal or equitable, the needs
and desires that arise from the social world systematically advantage some
and disadvantage others. Technologies are often developed and used in
ways that fit into and further these dynamics of structural inequality. Those
empowered to make and market new media technologies are not representative of the whole society, and just as the dominant media industries tend
to serve the interests of the moneyed class of their owners, the dominant
media technologies also tend to serve some interests at the expense of others. These dynamics can be hard to see, especially when we naïvely accord
technologies the privilege of being neutral – of seeming like they're just
materials to be used one way or another, for whatever reasons. A critical
look at the politics of media technologies can uncover their more harmful
or oppressive functions, which exist alongside many other uses.

One key example of this is central to many kinds of cultural expression: the way that photographic reproduction (in both still and moving
images) has historically rendered white subjects differently from subjects
with darker skin tones, and assumed and constructed a norm of whiteness
in visual culture. For instance, in an old class photo of a group of children
of different racial and ethnic backgrounds, we sometimes observe that the
features of darker-skinned kids' faces are harder to discern by contrast with
those of white kids' faces, which have sharper features. You literally can't
see the Black faces as well as the white ones. (Try image-searching for 1970s
class photos to see what I mean.) Photography, and later movies and video,
developed in a context of a white-dominated society. The technology itself
was created and its uses were developed by people who assumed that the
subjects of pictures would be white people. Faces are some of the most typical subjects of photography, and there is a bias in the technology of photography toward white ones.

Photography is a technology of capturing light, and different skin tones
absorb and reflect light differently. A critical decision in taking a photo is
the *exposure*: essentially, how much light to let into the camera. The choice
of lens and aperture, the shutter speed, the film in the camera (called film
stock), and the choices made in staging and lighting the scene are all variable elements in exposure, and the photograph needs to be exposed well in
relation to its subject so that the picture will be well lit, neither overexposed

(too bright and bleached out) nor underexposed (too dark and hard to see). A subject that reflects a lot of light will need to be exposed differently from a subject that does not. A subject that combines different tones, such as racially diverse students in a class, presents a challenge to the photographer and to the tools they bring to the photoshoot. If the Black faces are underexposed and blobby, it's because the technology and technique are privileging whiteness. The technology here is not race-neutral; it discriminates.

The ability of a film stock to capture subjects that vary in how much light they absorb and reflect is called its *dynamic range*. The technology of photography could have been shaped differently if its users had demanded that dynamic range be prioritized. But because whiteness was assumed as the natural subject of photography and darker skin tones were regarded as problematic, film stock with excellent dynamic range was not the norm. As Lorna Roth (2009, 118) points out, a lack of film with extended dynamic range fits well with a society characterized by racial segregation.

Other technologies within the apparatus of photographic image-making similarly privileged whiteness. In Hollywood, the lights and makeup were key elements of this apparatus, and they were both chosen to make white faces (and white women's faces in particular) appear glamorous and glowing onscreen. The technique of backlighting, of illuminating figures from behind and above, emerged as a way to make white women's blond hair glow with a kind of halo effect. In black and white cinematography, certain colors like reds and yellows would be rendered on the film stock commonly used as dark tones, and the choice of lights and makeup were intended to avoid red and yellow hues, so that there would be no image of white faces that would render their complexion as dark, reinforcing whiteness as the image of feminine beauty (Dyer 2007, 88–102).

It's not as if the technology of photography cannot be used effectively to make images of subjects with darker skin tones. Photographers and cinematographers who work with Black, Asian, and other darker-skinned actors and models have developed excellent techniques for shooting skin tones that absorb more and reflect less light than white people's. Many African-American photographers have preferred the Japanese Fuji brand of film, as it was better with darker skin tones than many kinds of American Kodak stock (Lewis 2019). The bias within the technology and the practices of using the technology have historically treated darker skin as a problem or exception, and this is a way that the racial inequality of the social world has shaped the technology of the photographic image. As the film scholar Richard Dyer

(2007) puts it, the apparatus of photography and cinematography "came to be seen as fixed and inevitable, existing independently of the fact that it was humanly constructed" (90). If these tools of image-making systematically privilege whiteness, as he argues, "that is because they were made that way, not because they could be no other way" (90).

In this example of the racial bias of photography, we see how the inequality of the social world works through a technology that might have appeared to be a neutral means of recording images of the world. Another example of how racial oppression is perpetuated by a seemingly neutral technology can be seen in Google's search engine, which is used billions of times every day by people all over the world. As Safiya Umoja Noble (2018) writes in her book *Algorithms of Oppression*, we can see how the commercial imperatives of an advertising-driven company paired with its engineering workforce lacking in women and people of color, produces a search engine that discriminates on the basis of identities, including race and gender.

Google results have a public reputation for being "the best," and the public puts much faith in them as the most relevant and important information on the topics users type into searches. Noble argues that this trust is misplaced, and that it gives cover to the discriminatory output of the search engine. Some of the examples she offers in support of this thesis come from Google's image search: as she was researching the book, searching for "doctor" and "professor," or searching for "professional hairstyle" and "unprofessional hairstyle," returned results that expose clear gender and racial biases (82). Searching for "Black girls" returned results that sexualized the subjects in ways that carry on long-standing oppressive tropes about African-American femininity, and in a way that "white girls" were not represented (66). More generally, the results of a Google search will never simply be "the best," or the "most important" information, and will never be merely neutral and objective, but will be the results that serve the interests of the people who made the search engine and the company they work for.

The list of sites produced by Google searches are returned via an algorithm, which is basically a type of code that automates sequences of computations. It is tempting to see the automation of search as a process that takes it out of human hands so that no intention or design can be inferred from the results. But any computer program is the product of the workers – the software engineers – who wrote it, and values and intentions are expressed in whatever things human beings make. Like many online algorithms on platforms like YouTube, Facebook, and Amazon, the Google search algorithm is "black-boxed," meaning we literally can't open it up to see what it's made of. The code is Google's property and Google does not make it public. But there is a lot we can understand about how the search algorithm works without being able to peek under the hood. We can look at Google's corporate agenda and we can look at the output of its algorithm, and putting those two things together can yield a fair bit of insight into how the product works.

Google's search engine is free to the user but is a thoroughly commercial entity, and is the cornerstone of Google's advertising business. The company brings in billions of dollars annually from search advertising, and the business of making money this way orients the search algorithm in many ways. One is that advertisements appear as search results, often in a way that the user might not be able to distinguish easily from the non-ad results. Google also privileges its own products in search results, such as its own maps, images, shopping, and video services, each of which in their own way contribute to Google's commercial fortunes. And the Google algorithm can be gamed by the businesses whose success can depend on how high up the search results for key search terms they land. This is a widespread practice known as search engine optimization, or more commonly SEO. Racist and sexist results in Google searches could be the results of advertising or SEO that is premised on promoting products (like pornographic websites) that circulate sexist and racist representations.

Like photography, then, Google's search engine might not seem like an inherently biased technology. But both are imbued with the politics of the society that made these tools, and more specifically of the human agents who have developed and used them, and the big businesses that have profited from them. With the automation of algorithmic platforms and the troubling rise of artificial intelligence tools that may be used in hiring, policing, and other fields with histories of racial and gender discrimination, we must be wary of ascribing neutrality to technologies that are being employed to make critical decisions with widespread impacts, with substantial capital and political power at stake. Technologies in general, and these technologies in particular, are never neutral.

Thinking Historically

Since the rise of the Silicon Valley giants, it has become normal to refer to some technologies as "tech" and a particular cluster of businesses as the "tech industry," but there are some serious drawbacks to this way of thinking and talking. We risk losing sight of the long history of technology when only the most recent and most hyped technologies count as "tech." The media that we use all of the time include some newer and some older tools, including books and pens and pencils and touchscreens and algorithmically generated content, and looking at the technology of media over time reveals some interesting and important things. Every medium was new once, and every new medium has existed in relation to what came before. Looking historically at technology helps us observe patterns and cycles, regularities in the introduction of media technologies that tell us something useful about media and society. Thinking about technology as deeply embedded in culture shows us the significance of users and points at the thorny politics of technology as a means of engaging with others and with the broader society.

As a tool in our toolkit, technology allows us to move beyond texts and representations to the platforms and networks that we engage with every day. Looking at one particular technology or at the ensemble of technologies that constitute a medium, we can ask some basic questions to help us understand how media work, and how they have worked historically. What have been a technology's intended or authorized uses, and who has benefited from them? How have users shaped the development of a technology? How have businesses tried to capitalize on a new medium, and how have consumers responded? How have people typically talked about a technology, how have they made sense of its social functions and its effects on individuals? The answers to these questions will often help us recognize how fundamental media technologies have been to people's everyday lives for as long as these tools have existed, whether we are talking about paper and books or apps and algorithms. The answers are likely to go to the heart of how media and society shape one another.

Discussion Questions

1. Choose a media technology that is no longer new and research how people talked about when it first emerged by looking at newspaper and magazine stories that introduced it to the public. What similarities and differences do you find to the way people talk about new media today?

2. What are some similarities and differences between mass media and new media? Choose one example of each to illustrate the comparison.

3. What are the affordances of media? Choose an example of a media technology and describe its affordances, and what they tell us about the value of the technology to users.

4. What does to it mean to say that a technology is "not neutral"? Choose an example of a media technology and explore how the technology itself might have a bias or a politics.

References

Abbate, Janet. 1999. *Inventing the Internet*. Cambridge, MA: MIT Press.

Alper, Meryl. 2014. *Digital Youth With Disabilities*. Cambridge, MA: MIT Press.

Barlow, John Perry. 1996. "A Declaration of the Independence of Cyberspace." Electronic Frontier Foundation, February 8, 1996. https://www.eff.org/cyberspace-independence

Baym, Nancy K. 2010. *Personal Connections in the Digital Age*. Malden: Polity.

Bell, Daniel. 1956. "The Theory of Mass Society: A Critique." In *Mass Communication and American Social Thought: Key Texts 1919–1968*, edited by John Durham Peters and Peter Simonson, 364–373. Lanham: Rowman & Littlefield.

Burgess, Jean and Nancy K. Baym. 2020. *Twitter: A Biography*. New York: New York University Press.

Bilton, Nick. 2013. *Hatching Twitter: A True Story of Money, Power, Friendship, and Betrayal*. New York: Portfolio/Penguin.

Binder, Matt. 2018. "YouTube accounts for 47 percent of music streaming, study claims." *Mashable*, October 10, 2018. https://mashable.com/article/youtube-47-percent-of-on-demand-music-streaming/

Boddy, William. 2004. "Wireless Nation: Defining Radio as a Domestic Technology." In his *New Media and Popular Imagination: Launching Radio, Television, and Digital Media in the United States*, 16–43. Oxford: Oxford University Press.

Bucher, Taina, and Anne Helmond. 2017. "The affordances of social media platforms." *The SAGE Handbook of Social Media*, edited by Jean Burgess, Alice Marwick, and Thomas Poell, 233–253. Thousand Oaks: SAGE.

Burgess, Jean and Joshua Green. 2018. *YouTube: Online Video and Participatory Culture*. 2nd ed. Cambridge: Polity.

Carr, Nicholas. 2008. "Is Google Making Us Stupid?" *The Atlantic* (July/August). https://www.theatlantic.com/magazine/archive/2008/07/is-google-making-us-stupid/306868/

Cohen, Stanley. 2002. *Folk Devils and Moral Panics: The Creation of the Mods and Rockers*, 3rd ed. London: Routledge.

Coleman, Mark. 2003. *Playback: From the Victrola to MP3, 100 Years of Music, Machines, and Money*. Boston: Da Capo Press.

Czitrom, Daniel J. 1982. *Media and the American Mind: From Morse to McLuhan*. Chapel Hill: University of North Carolina Press.

Douglas, Susan. 1987. *Inventing American Broadcasting, 1899–1922*. Baltimore: Johns Hopkins University Press.

Douglas, Susan. 2004. *Listening In: Radio and the American Imagination*. Minneapolis: University of Minnesota Press.

Drotner, Kristin. 1999. "Dangerous Media? Panic Discourses and Dilemmas of Modernity." *Paedagogica Historica* 35.3: 593–619.

Dyer, Richard. 2007. *White*. London: Routledge.

Eisenstein, Elizabeth. 1980. *The Printing Press as an Agent of Change: Communications and Cultural Transformations in Early-Modern Europe*. Cambridge: Cambridge University Press.

Febvre, Lucien and Henri-Jean Martin. 1997. *The Coming of the Book: The Impact of Printing 1450–1800*, translated by David Gerard. London: Verso.

Fischer, Claude S. 1992. *America Calling: A Social History of the Telephone to 1940*. Berkeley: University of California Press.

Galili, Doron. 2020. *Seeing by Electricity: The Emergence of Television, 1878–1939*. Durham, NC: Duke University Press.

Hadju, David. 2009. *The Ten Cent Plague: The Great Comic Book Scare and How It Changed America*. New York: Picador.

Harmon, Amy. 2003. "What Price Music?" *New York Times*, October 12, 2003. https://www.nytimes.com/2003/10/12/arts/music-what-price-music.html

Jowett, Garth S, Ian C. Jarvie, and Kathryn H. Fuller. 1996. *Children and the Movies: Media Influence and the Payne Fund Controversy*. Cambridge: Cambridge University Press.

Kern, Stephen. 2003. *The Culture of Time and Space, 1880–1918*. Cambridge, MA: Harvard University Press.

Kranzberg, Melvin. 1986. "Technology and History: 'Kranzberg's Laws.'" *Technology and Culture* 27.3: 544–560.

Lewis, Sarah. 2019. "The Racial Bias Built Into Photography." *New York Times*, April 25, 2019. https://www.nytimes.com/2019/04/25/lens/sarah-lewis-racial-bias-photography.html

McCourt, Tom. 2015. "Recorded Music." *Communication and Technology*, edited by Lorenzo Cantoni and James A. Danowski, 79–10. Berlin: De Gruyter Mouton.

McLuhan, Marshall. 1964. *Understanding Media: The Extensions of Man.* New York: McGraw-Hill.

McLuhan, Marshall. 1997. "Playboy Interview: A Candid Conversation with the High Priest of Popcult and Metaphysician of Media." In *The Essential McLuhan*, edited by Eric McLuhan and Frank Zingrone, 233–269. London: Routledge.

Marvin, Carolyn. 1990. *When Old Technologies Were New: Thinking About Electric Communication in the Late Nineteenth Century.* Oxford: Oxford University Press.

Mills, C. Wright. 2004. "The Mass Society." In *Mass Communication and American Social Thought: Key Texts, 1919–1968*, edited by John Durham Peters and Peter Simonson, 387–400. Lanham: Rowman & Littlefield.

Morton, Jr., David L. 2006. *Sound Recording: The Life Story of a Technology.* Baltimore: Johns Hopkins University Press.

Nagy, Peter and Gina Neff. 2015. "Imagined Affordance: Reconstructing a Keyword for Communication Theory." *Social Media + Society* 1.2. doi: 10.1177/2056305115603385

Newman, Michael Z. 2010. "New Media, Young Audiences, and Discourses of Attention: From *Sesame Street* to 'Snack Culture.'" *Media, Culture & Society* 32.4: 581–596.

Newman, Michael Z. 2017. *Atari Age: The Emergence of Video Games in America.* Cambridge, MA: MIT Press.

Noble, Safia Umoja. 2018. *Algorithms of Oppression: How Search Engines Reinforce Racism.* New York: New York University Press.

Ong, Walter J. 1982. "Writing Restructures Consciousness." *Orality and Literacy: The Technologizing of the Word*, 78–116. London: Methuen.

Palm, Michael. 2019. "Keeping it Real? Vinyl Records and the Future of Independent Culture." *Convergence: The International Journal of Research into New Media Technologies* 25.4. https://doi.org/10.1177/1354856519835485

Peters, Benjamin. 2009. "And Lead Us Not Into Thinking The New Is New: A Bibliographic Case for New Media History." *New Media & Society* 11.1–2. https://doi.org/10.1177/1461444808099572

Pinch, Trevor J. and Wiebe E. Bijker. 1984. "The Social Construction of Facts and Artefacts: Or How the Sociology of Science and the Sociology of Technology Might Benefit Each other." *Social Studies of Science* 14: 399–441.

Poe, Marshall T. 2011. *A History of Communications: Media and Society from the Evolution of Speech to the Internet.* New York: Cambridge University Press.

Roth, Lorna. 2009. "Looking at Shirley, the Ultimate Norm: Colour Balance, Image Technologies, and Cognitive Equity." *Canadian Journal of Communication* 34: 111–136.

Rothenbuhler, Eric W. 2012. "The Compact Disc and Its Culture: Notes on Melancholia." In *Cultural Technologies: The Shaping of Culture in Media and Society*, edited by Göran Bolin,
36–50. London: Routledge.
Schmandt-Besserat, Denise. 1996. *How Writing Came About*. Austin: University of Texas Press.
Schmidt Horning, Susan. 2013. *Chasing Sound: Technology, Culture, and the Art of Studio Recording from Edison to the LP*. Baltimore: The Johns Hopkins University Press.
Shils, Edward. 1960. "Mass Society and Its Culture." *Daedalus* 89.2: 288–314.
Spigel, Lynn. 1992. *Make Room for TV: Television and the Family Ideal in Postwar America*. Chicago: University of Chicago Press.
Strauss, Neil. 1995. "Pennies That Add Up to $16.98: Why CD's Cost So Much." *New York Times*, July 5, 1995. https://www.nytimes.com/1995/07/05/arts/pennies-that-add-up-to-16.98-why-cd-s-cost-so-much.html
Streeter, Thomas. 1997. "Blue Skies and Strange Bedfellows: The Discourse of Cable Television." In *The Revolution Wasn't Televised: Sixties Television And Social Conflict*, edited by Lynn Spigel and Michael Curtin, 221–242. New York: Routledge.
Thoreau, Henry D. 1854. *Walden; Or, Life in the Woods*. Boston: Ticknor and Fields.
Welch, Walter L. and Leah Brodbeck Stenzel Burt. 1994. *From Tinfoil to Stereo: The Acoustic Years of the Recording Industry 1877–1929*. Gainesville: University of Florida Press.
Williams, Raymond. 2003. *Television: Technology and Cultural Form*, 3rd ed. London: Routledge.

11

GLOBAL AND LOCAL

As a child growing up in Canada during the 1970s and 1980s, I was an avid consumer of many kinds of popular culture: television, movies, music, video games, newspapers and magazines, and mass-market paperbacks. The media of my childhood were often Canadian in origin. I watched Toronto Maple Leafs games on the Canadian Broadcasting Corporation's weekly *Hockey Night in Canada*, and numerous episodes of the children's television series *The Polka-Dot Door*, *Mr. Dressup*, and *The Friendly Giant*, all produced in Toronto a few kilometers from my living room. On the radio, I heard music by Canadian artists like Rush and Neil Young. Canadian news, both print and broadcast, contained local and national stories, as well as plenty of coverage of international affairs. On Sundays I would go out with my dad to find a copy of the *New York Times*, but the rest of the week the newspaper in my home was the Toronto *Globe and Mail*. The local sports section, with its heavy coverage of home teams, was my gateway to reading the news. I collected and traded Canadian O-Pee-Chee hockey cards, packaged with sticks of bubble gum.

Canada is a relatively small country that shares a long border with a much larger neighbor (by population), the United States. Radio and television signals easily reach Toronto from Buffalo, New York, so I also watched *Sesame Street* and other educational programming on PBS, as well as American network sitcoms and dramas like *Happy Days*, *Dukes of Hazzard*, and *Hill Street Blues*, and a ton of American sports. Much of the music on the radio was American or British: Led Zeppelin, Michael Jackson, Madonna, David Bowie. The movies I saw in theaters or on home video came mainly from Hollywood. Even

DOI: 10.4324/9781003007708-11

movies shot on location in Canada, a common practice that saves production costs, were often American. I read Judy Blume and Stephen King novels (US authors) and subscribed to *Sports Illustrated* and *Rolling Stone* (US magazines). On the whole, I probably was exposed to more American than Canadian media, though this kind of thing is hard to quantify.

I also consumed media from other parts of the world. Two of the cartoons I especially liked when I was little were Japanese, *Fables of the Green Forest*, and French, *Barbapapa*. *Pac-Man* and *Space Invaders*, both Japanese, were among my first favorite video games, and a few years later a Soviet game, *Tetris*, became an obsession. Both the television set in the living room and my portable music player ("Walkman") were Sony products from Japan. Occasionally the radio would play a hit song from Germany ("99 Luftballons") or Norway ("Take On Me"), and there were plenty of reggae songs on the radio, a genre from Jamaica, often via Britain. A surprisingly popular movie that I saw in the mid-1980s was *The Gods Must Be Crazy*, a comedy shot in Namibia by South African and Botswanan producers. It ran at a theater near my home for more than a year in the mid-1980s.

The experience of any media consumer in the later 20th and early 21st centuries will probably be similar to mine from childhood in at least one way: most of us consume a mix of local media products and imports from elsewhere. The imported media is likely to be from another country that is nearby or that shares a common language or both, as in the case of Canada and the US. It's also true for many media consumers that the imports tend to come from richer countries with more robust cultural industries, like the American film studios, broadcast networks, and record labels. In other parts of the world, there are similar patterns: bigger or richer countries like Japan, South Korea, India, France, the UK, Brazil, and Nigeria are often more prolific media exporters than smaller neighbors with less powerful economies. Around the world, many people are likely to have some exposure to American mass media exports: popular music, film and television, and social media have a strong American presence across the globe, as do some kinds of American video games and sports. America is a large, rich country with a long history of success in the media industries. But it has a lot of competition from local and national industries around the world, and from major regional and global exporters like Japan.

For media consumers in the United States, the situation is a bit different than in many other countries, though it's hard to generalize about a diverse nation of 330 million souls. Living in a dominant global media producer means less exposure to the cultural exports of other nations, and American audiences tend to be, at least according to conventional wisdom, monolingual and hostile to subtitles. Yet millions of Americans in the 21st century often have experiences of passionate engagement with South Korean pop music, English football, Japanese pop culture (e.g., manga, anime, and games), and online video content from all over the planet. As a Canadian in the US, I am often conscious of the presence here of Canadian talent – numerous writers, actors, recording artists, journalists, etc. – but also of my consumption of global media in the form of European TV shows and Asian movies.

The tens of millions of US residents who are recent immigrants from other places, or children or grandchildren of immigrants from Mexico, China, India, and dozens of other countries, are often deeply connected to diasporic communities that maintain cultural ties and practices through media consumption. The movie theaters near me in Wisconsin regularly screen films in Tamil and Mandarin, and there are radio stations in every US city that play Spanish music (whether domestic or imported). Via television or internet feeds, it's possible for North Americans to keep cheering for the home team (e.g., the cricket sides in the Indian Premier League) from a distance of many time zones. And major international media events, such as the Olympics and FIFA World Cup, and the weddings and funerals of princesses and other celebrities, assemble massive audiences from every corner of the earth.

The name we give this phenomenon of importing and exporting culture from place to place, is *media globalization*. It is part of a wider globalization that has been going on for hundreds of years, at least since the age of discovery and colonization, and which has intensified with economic and technological developments. These include the introduction of media infrastructure like undersea cables that allow for instantaneous transmission of messages from one continent to another, satellite communication that makes it possible to broadcast live television to the whole world at once, and the internet, a global medium that stitches computer users together in a vast network of instant gratification. Globalization in general and media globalization in particular have undoubtedly transformed our societies and our everyday lives, sometimes quite radically. Our ancestors might have encountered a few hundred other human beings during an entire lifetime. We are connected to billions of others all the time.

But we are not actually in touch one-on-one with billions of people, or even with thousands. And we don't ordinarily encounter large amounts of media from dozens of different countries and cultures. We often prefer to consume content from our own region, in our own language. And this can be true of some kinds of media more than others. News does not travel as well as music and movies. News doesn't even travel that well within a particular country: I consume local news about restaurants, road construction, and the weather. These topics would be of little interest to someone even a couple of hours' drive away. I also consume national news about American politics. But even if the topic of media isn't specifically national, as politics often is, there are still reasons why media would appeal mainly to audiences that share a national identity with its creators. Some forms and genres call on shared frames of reference and common backgrounds and are hard to translate. Comedy often calls upon particular kinds of knowledge and can be rooted in particulars of experiences, including language. Some kinds of media are better at transcending these barriers: action movies, athletic competitions, and catchy dance beats have more of a universal appeal and depend little on translation.

There is a well-known saying that all politics is local, and the same can be said of media. No matter where it comes from, you experience it where you are, in the context of your life situation and your location in a particular place. So there is a tension when it comes to media globalization between media that often comes from "elsewhere," like Afrobeat music for me, and experiences of media that occur right here and now, like listening to Afrobeat while I make dinner in my kitchen in the US, thousands of miles away from where it was recorded, in a very different environment from West Africa. This is the tension between the global and the local. It is between the meanings and values encoded in media by its creators and the meanings and values derived from it by its audiences and users.

Global and local are two poles of this tension, but national media sits right in between them making trouble. Media are shaped in myriad ways by their nations of origin. State media policy and regulation occurs on the national level. Media like newspapers have been essential to the very formation of nations, of the "imagined communities" that collect dispersed, diverse populations into one body politic that shares a common identity (Anderson 2006). Media industries segment their audiences by nation; each country has its own release dates, its own charts for bestselling books or recordings or video games, its own version of Google. Intellectual property laws maintain these boundaries, sometimes making it hard to access online video from one nation in another. Advertising campaigns can be global but are often more specifically rooted in place, with different commercial appeals for different national audiences. The rise of global media is often seen as marking a shift of power away from the nation toward a larger, higher-level category that transcends national identity. This is happening to some degree, but the centrality of the nation in media production, distribution, and consumption is still considerable.

Globalization has played out in ways that serve some people's interests more than other people's. Media globalization's winners have succeeded at gaining larger audiences and market shares for their products, spreading their images, sounds, and stories across the world. Local and national media often struggle in the face of competition from global media. But as it travels, global media has to be made appealing to local audiences, framed and formatted to suit their tastes. Texts are routinely adapted or translated or in some other way transformed in the process. The dynamics among these levels of scale, from macro to micro or vice versa, shape the passage of media from place to place (Couldry and McCarthy 2004). Globalization has not been a smooth or uniform process, and has not produced one techno-utopian world society. The local and the national still matter, but they have been thrown into ever more complicated arrangements with the spread of transnational media content.

Media and Empire

Less than one century ago, on the eve of World War II, many parts of the globe were under the colonial rule of a cluster of Western powers: Great Britain, France, Italy, The Netherlands, Belgium, Portugal, and the United States. Japan was also an imperial power occupying the Korean peninsula, parts of what is now the People's Republic of China, and other territories in East Asia. The lands claimed by the imperial Western nations were in Latin America, Africa, Asia, and Oceania. When I was in high school, several decades later, these places were usually known collectively as "The Third World," but more up-to-date usage favors "the developing world" (though many consider this term to imply Western superiority) or increasingly, "the Global South." The most extensive empire was the British: it once claimed much of North America, and in 1940 still included territory in every region of the globe. India, Burma (Myanmar), Singapore, Hong Kong, many parts of Africa and the Middle East, and several Caribbean islands were British colonies at the beginning of the 1940s. The French colonies included much of

Africa and French Indochina, territories that today include Laos, Cambodia, and Vietnam.

An era of decolonization and independence followed the end of the war. India and Pakistan were decolonized in the late 1940s, and many African nations gained independence in the 1950s and 1960s. Western empires are now the stuff of history lessons. But the power and influence exerted by richer, mostly Western, nations over other territories have hardly gone away. In the postcolonial period, the inequalities of earlier eras have been maintained in ways other than literal imperialism of conquering foreign lands and forcing their people to become subjects of a distant king. Economic or cultural domination has often served a function similar to political subjection and rule by force. The most powerful of the Western world's nations in this period, the United States, has also been the one whose media and communication systems have had the greatest international presence and influence. The popularity of Western popular culture in the Global South has been an ongoing concern for scholars of media globalization (Tomlinson 1991; Miller et al. 2005; Tunstall 2008; Mirrlees 2013), not to mention for many citizens of the Global South. Does such popularity signal a continuation of the same unequal dynamics from the colonial era?

In addition to movies, television, music, and other forms of media, American soft drinks, fast food, apparel, and lifestyles have also spread to many parts of the world, making the globe into a vast market for American-style mass consumption, and filling the pockets of American (and multinational) corporations. This has been described in some glib terms like Coca-Colonization, implying that the global spread of American consumer culture makes the rest of the world subservient to American power. In media studies, the most common phrase for capturing this dynamic is *cultural imperialism*, or sometimes *media imperialism* (Tomlinson 1991). According to the logic of cultural or media imperialism, what empires once achieved by military might and outright plunder, now they achieve by effective marketing.

The cultural imperialism thesis has been much debated over the years. The strongest version of it has been articulated by Marxist critics who regard the global exchange of media and communication as a form of capitalist domination by the economic world powers, principally the United States and its corporations. The political economist Herbert Schiller (1976, 1992), who formulated some of the key arguments about cultural imperialism in the 1970s, described it as a process that converts the old system of colonialism into a "modern mode of organization and control" (Schiller 1976, 9).

In this global media landscape, cultural imperialism meant that the societies that only recently had become independent of colonial rule were still made to follow "the values and structures of the dominating center of the system" (9). According to Schiller, it was the media, and especially commercial television, that influenced media audiences to favor capitalism and the Western way of life. The presence of Western media in the regions of the Global South, such as Latin America, was not necessarily unwelcome to the inhabitants of those places, including elites in business who benefited financially from the commercial broadcasting of American programs. But in the mind of critics like Schiller, the effects of the spread of media from a core of Western powers to the periphery of other regions was nevertheless a vehicle for the spread of Western ideology all over the world and for maintaining Western power.

And the presence of Western media in these regions was hardly a new thing in the postwar years. Hollywood was so successful at exporting films that within a few decades of the invention of cinema, even Western countries had instituted regulations to protect them from the dominance of foreign (American) films on their theater screens. For instance, in the late 1920s, Britain instituted a quota system that required that a percentage of the films screened in UK cinemas be British, a law passed to help develop a more successful national film industry in the face of American dominance, which did succeed at increasing the presence of British films in the UK (Street 2009).

Popular cinemas across the world are often regarded as adopting a Hollywood style of production, technique, and storytelling, as industry nicknames like Bollywood (B for Bombay) and Nollywood (N for Nigeria) reveal. The influence of Hollywood's global exports on social life, fashion, beauty culture, and music is hard to overestimate. American movie stars were international celebrities, and American film genres – westerns, gangster films, musicals – were familiar to audiences on every continent. Beginning around World War I, when European film production was disrupted by the war more than American production, America became the West's premier cinema exporter and a dominant force in the world's market for films (Thompson 1985). Classical Hollywood had a big advantage in a large domestic audience, the world's most popular stars, and an efficient vertically integrated studio system. The export of American films was aided by the US government, who regarded motion pictures as a form of trade that would benefit American corporations, but also as a means of exerting what is now often called "soft power" in international politics, spreading American values along with American images and stories (Fraser 2005). Hollywood's international influence has become an essential part of the mythology of American global cultural dominance. As a character in the 1976 West German film *Kings of the Road* puts it, "The Yanks have colonized our subconscious."

In more recent years, Hollywood has been the epitome of a globalized media industry. Disney has its theme parks in Europe and Asia. Mainstream American films are made for foreign as much as domestic theaters, and the expansion of emerging markets like China has been appealing to American media's thirst for ever more audiences to reach. The franchise blockbuster is a product engineered to travel well, to be beyond translation, to appeal to the eye and the ear and to the appetite for celebrity bodies and storytelling experienced as a roller-coaster ride. American cinema has an incredible track record over 100 years of being popular practically all over the world, and foreign markets have often earned substantial revenue for the American movie studios, rivaling their domestic earnings.[1] In the age of streaming media, the movie theater box office is often less significant than the revenue from media viewed in the home or on mobile devices, and one index of the power of American content is the presence of Netflix as a global alternative to conventional television. Netflix is available in dozens of nations, and is stocked with large amounts of American film and TV, in addition to productions in many languages from many nations of origin (Lobato 2019). Like German cars and French wines, American movies – and popular culture more generally – are surrounded by an aura, a mystique, and a reputation for quality.

Cultural imperialism has been debated over many decades. Defenders of the cultural imperialism thesis believe that the popularity of Western media in the Global South is a form of domination, typically of an American hegemony that makes the whole world a welcome space for a consumer society and free-market corporate capitalism. In other words, the Americanization of an emerging global society. To them, media globalization enriches the already wealthy industries of the West at the expense of local and national media in less powerful regions. This dominance is maintained by polluting the airwaves and cinema screens with American propaganda, at least according to the strongest versions of this school of thought.

While it is undoubtedly true that global exports of Western media are a form of influence and that they benefit the West in general and America in particular, there is another side to this debate, which holds that the cultural imperialism thesis has been overstated and that its argument misses much of what is actually going on in local and national media environments. Most critical media scholars are probably not happy to accept the imperialism thesis without reservations. A crude version of the thesis gives the impression that the Global South and even smaller Western countries like Canada are nothing more than victims of a constant onslaught of American media warfare, but the reality is more nuanced – and more interesting – than that.

There are several ways of looking at the globalization of media that undercut the imperialism thesis. First, while imperialism suggests a single direction of influence and exploitation, from the dominant West to the subordinate Global South, we can instead consider multi-directional flows of media and culture, which are often shaped by *cultural proximity* and other kinds of affinity. These flows are not just from the West to the Global South but also from the Global South to the West, as well as from neighbor to neighbor within particular regions.

Second, there is *hybridity* in media produced for global circulation. Media cannot always be identified exclusively with a single place or culture of origin. Global media markets incentivize the production of hybrid forms of media, such as localized versions of television series for different countries, using personnel who speak the language and incorporating elements of local culture. Hybrid media have qualities of both the local and the global, or they have been customized to appeal to certain markets while still retaining qualities that bridge across differences.

And third, there are practices of local audience reception that give meaning to global media. Rather than media from elsewhere imposing its agenda and ideology on local audiences, local audiences can use their intellectual resources and culturally specific knowledge to make sense of global media and appropriate it for their own purposes, merging the macro and micro levels of global and local. In the process, neither local nor global is the right concept all by itself, because media can be both at once. Sometimes this is called *glocalization*, a term that can also be used similarly to *hybridization*, expressing a combination of the universal (global) and the particular (local).

In each of these ways of looking at media globalization, we see an interplay between different nations and regions of the globe and also between production and consumption. Each of them is a way of looking at the relationship between the global and the local as more dynamic than is implied by "cultural imperialism," while still keeping in mind the inequalities and injustices that structure the global marketplace and mediascape.

Global Media Flows

In global studies, *flow* describes movements of many kinds from place to place, often across distances separated by oceans and continents. Media texts like news stories, videos, and sound recordings flow alongside people, capital, technology, and ideology, all of which are key elements of globalization (Appadurai 1990). The task for critical studies of global media is to capture the dynamics and implications of media flows in relation to these other flows.

It has often been asserted or assumed that media originating from centers of power, such as Hollywood, have an effect of *homogenization* on the populations that receive them, of producing a sameness across the globe as everyone watches the same shows and listens to the same songs, just as they eat the same fast food and wear the same athletic apparel. Critical scholarship has pushed back against this notion, arguing that diversity coexists with global media flows, and that the planet has hardly become home to a single corporate monoculture through the export of American or Western popular culture. Difference and divergence remain and even thrive despite globalization.

The imperialism thesis identifies flows from the West to the rest of the world as a driver of inequality. There are several ways that close attention to media flows can complicate this account. First of all, there are limits to how much media travels, and different kinds of media are more or less likely to circulate globally. One significant barrier to global flow remains the nation-state. Some forms of media, particularly radio and television, are regulated by national governments in a way that protects local markets from international competition. Audiences in Canada cannot receive American TV content via cable subscriptions except using Canadian services that retransmit American channels, which substitute Canadian ads and promos for some American commercials and are required to offer certain percentages of Canadian content. This is a matter of national regulation that protects Canadian media industries and contributes to their economic success while promoting a national culture.

National policies can include state censorship, like the "Great Firewall of China," which prevents Chinese internet users from accessing Google, Facebook, and Wikipedia, among other sites. This functions as a means of stifling opposition to state policy, such as the oppression of minority groups. Less ideological cases of national restrictive policies would be the "geoblocking" of online content, such as videos, that are not available in some territories because they have not been licensed for those markets. International copyright only "succeeds" insofar as national governments participate in a global system that enforces restrictions of some content in some territories. Much of the media we consume continues to be national and local because of the power of governments to support their national and local industries and cultural sectors, and to inhibit global media flow when it advances national interests, whether political or economic or both.

Another barrier is language, and more generally cultural specificity. Print media like books, newspapers, and magazines tend not to circulate as much globally as TV, movies, and music, and one reason is that their primary medium is language. Another is that much news is addressed to local, regional, or national audiences and covers topics primarily of interest to them. Some kinds of movies and TV flow more easily than others. American sitcoms have succeeded on the global TV market in syndicated reruns (e.g., The Big Bang Theory has been popular around the world). English-language news circulates well in places where people speak English (which is many places), but news in other languages such as Arabic or Spanish faces obstacles in being accessible to monolingual American or British English speakers. Local or national news and talk shows are often preferable to imports.

The kinds of media that flow most effectively are often those designed for just this purpose. There are many varieties of media whose ability to transcend place is a design feature. Popular music might be the most promiscuous of global media, as rhythm, melody, and harmony work no matter what language you speak, and having lyrics in English seems to be a minor obstacle (if any) to worldwide success. Many video games offer pleasures and challenges that might not be universally compelling, but appeal to players around the world. Hollywood makes franchise films for a global audience, and many kinds of television, including children's programs and prestige dramas travel well across borders and succeed in translated versions. Netflix is a powerful presence in dozens of countries, and its original series and movies, such as The Crown and Roma, are often made to have international appeal. Some kinds of films are made not for multiplexes and mainstream streaming platforms, but for the international film festival circuit, where critical acclaim and prizes are their own kind of currency, and cosmopolitan audiences pride themselves on their appreciation of "world cinema." Some kinds of popular online videos have a similar basic appeal that works on practically anyone who looks at their images of impossible skateboard tricks or meteors landing by the side of the road.

There is no denying that American media flow more outwards from the US than foreign media flow into America. But the notion that American media have colonized the rest of the world's unconscious overstates the case for rhetorical effect. The presence of popularity of American media in many other places has also shifted over time. In 1977, a widely-cited book on this subject by Jeremy Tunstall appeared with the title *The Media Are American*, and its editorializing cover portrays Mickey Mouse nibbling on hunks broken off from a globe made of cheese. The sequel that he published in 2008 is called *The Media Were American*. It makes the case that the flow of Western content to the rest of the world significantly diminished over the three decades between publications, and that American's global media supremacy was in the past, especially considering that in many parts of the globe (e.g., in Asia, with its population in the billions), national media commands much more attention than Western imports.

Tunstall acknowledges the success of American cinema in newer markets like China, but also points out that most people around the world spend only a few hours a year at the movies, and asserts that "hundreds of millions of people in Asia and Africa have never seen even one Hollywood film" (xii). The point here isn't to question whether or not Hollywood in particular and the American media industries more broadly have been successful as exporters, but to consider in the most general terms what kinds of media are consumed by audiences on a global scale, how much of their media comes from elsewhere, and where that elsewhere might be. Tunstall generalizes about this in *The Media Were American* in a way that pushes back against the notion of imperialism and global hegemony:

> Most people around the world prefer to be entertained by people who look the same, talk the same, joke the same, behave the same, play the same games, and have the same beliefs (and worldview) as themselves. They also overwhelmingly prefer their own national news, politics, weather, and football and other sports.
>
> (xiv)

Global media flows are successful to the extent that they can either overcome this set of preferences – as transmedia franchises, internationally popular TV series, and global pop stars evidently accomplish – but also by satisfying them.

They can satisfy them by producing versions of media for local or national markets that appeal to particular rather than universal audiences, but also by following the flows of people (e.g., migration, displacement, exile) who form global *diasporas*, communities separated from a common homeland. When videotapes and DVDs were dominant formats for movies and TV content, diasporic supermarkets would sell or rent them to their customers. An Indian or Korean or multi-ethnic grocery store in North America would thus offer several kinds of connection to home for their communities, with both food and media satisfying similar needs for familiar kinds of nourishment. Diasporic media takes numerous forms: newspapers, podcasts, television shows, music, social media. It can be media from home accessed in new locations, or media made in new locations for diasporic communities in many places. The Hindi films or Brazilian music that travels from Asia or South America to Europe or North America help us see that flows of media often run from the Global South to the West and not the other way around.

Probably the most effective way that media flows satisfy audiences' desires for images and stories that reflect themselves is by moving most effectively between places that are alike and nearby. In Latin America, television dramas circulate among countries within the region, with Mexico as the biggest exporter. American shows also flow to Latin America, but there is no question that audiences have a preference for regional or local content in Spanish or Portuguese. In many regions of the globe, regional flows are just as important as global flows. This is true of movies, television, and popular music in Africa, South Asia, East Asia, and Latin America. As Joseph Straubhaar (1991) has observed in his study of Latin American television flows, audiences seek out "cultural relevance or proximity" when it is available among their media options (39). Some nations, such as Brazil, have successfully satisfied their own national audiences as well as successfully created export products. Smaller Latin American nations like the Dominican Republic import more of their media from elsewhere, but audiences in the Dominican still have preferred local or regional media, when available, to imports from outside of Latin America. Trade in media is not so different from other kinds of trade in this regard: most of it happens between neighbors and within regions. The United States trades more with Canada and Mexico than with China or any other more distant nation.

Cultural proximity is a key factor in global media flows, explaining how national and regional media continue to compete with global media exports from the West or from regional economic powers in Africa, Asia, and Latin

America. There are some ways that global media flows both overcome and satisfy these preferences at the same time, by adapting global products for local markets, and by speaking to audiences in a way that allows them to appropriate global products on their own terms.

Global Media Hybridity

Perhaps you've had a Vietnamese banh mi, a sandwich that's not too hard to find in cosmopolitan cities of the West. The banh mi typically is made of one or more kinds of meat such as roast pork, thin strips of crunchy vegetables, cilantro (aka coriander), and sliced green chiles all stuffed into a split baguette spread with mayonnaise. This is the epitome of a postcolonial food: crusty French bread and mayonnaise are combined with Asian ingredients like cilantro, hot peppers, and vegetable pickles. The legacy of European empire in what was once called French Indochina is contained in this sandwich, as are the fresh, bright flavors of Southeast Asia. The banh mi is neither purely Asian nor purely Western, and rather than being purely anything, it is a hybrid of different cultures. The fact that I can find one to have for lunch in the Midwestern US is a product of modern globalization.

Hybridity is crucial to pushing back against the assumption that global flows of media simply spread Western culture around the world. Media producers have many ways of combining forms, styles, values, and meanings from multiple contexts, especially mixing elements from one place with elements from another. Hybridity, according to the subtitle of Marwan Kraidy's 2006 book, is "the cultural logic of globalization." This logic is the polar opposite of homogenization: rather than making everything uniformly the same, globalization has produced hybrids combining features of different cultures, of the global and the local. This hybridity comes in diverse forms. It is both a feature of media industry strategies, and of media consumption and appropriation of global content for local purposes.

An epitome of hybridization would be the global media franchise adapted differently for different markets and territories. MTV and CNN have versions created for different regions, such as MTV Latin America and CNN International Asia Pacific. The localized identity of the cable channel extends an American brand internationally, while the content on the channel is customized to address audiences in a particular place, whether a region in these examples or a specific country or language in the case of some international versions of MTV (e.g., MTV channels in German, Spanish, or Danish).

You might think of this as the media version of American global restaurant chains having menus adapted to local diets by offering many vegetarian items in India and serving halal food in Muslim places, while still maintaining their iconic brand identities like McDonald's arches and red/yellow color scheme.

Sometimes, hybrids from "elsewhere" flow back into the place of origin in a way that complicates assumptions of American dominance. The US cable channel HGTV has many international versions, including the Canadian HGTV, which is partly owned by an American parent company, Discovery Inc., and partly by a Canadian media conglomerate, Corus. To satisfy Canadian regulations, some of the Canadian HGTV content has been produced in Canada, but some of these home renovation and redecorating shows became popular and successful on the American version of HGTV, including *Property Brothers* and *Love It or List It*. This led to the production of some seasons of these Canadian television shows in the US. It can be hard to tell sometimes where episodes of these programs take place as they seem to avoid giving us too much specific information about locations, and in particular avoid seeming to be set in Canada (McNutt 2017). Astute viewers might recognize Canadian or American accents or landscapes, but the hybridity of *Property Brothers* makes it both Canadian and American at the same time, a North American text that could be interpreted as representing either nation depending on how you look at it.

A similar aesthetic is at work in another successful Canadian export, the teen TV franchise *Degrassi* about generations of students and staff at a multicultural Toronto school where everyone seems to be grappling with serious social issues and relationship drama. Originally a domestic public television series, the various iterations of *Degrassi* became popular in the US after being run on American television networks (first public broadcasters, then cable channels). In order to cater to the global TV market, and in particular the American market, the producers have shaped the show's representations in a way that helps it appeal internationally without sacrificing its distinctive Canadian-ness. Audiences must often know the program originates in Canada, and the accents and references to Toronto sports teams can be a giveaway, but like many Canadian exports, the specificity of place often seems dialed down. In some of its versions, *Degrassi* has been produced with the expectation of distribution on one of Viacom's cable channels for young viewers, and the demands of the American channel (as a proxy for the American audience) make this a show that can be read as both Canadian and not-too-Canadian, or as a hybrid of specific/Canadian and global/universal (Levine 2009).

One genre especially well suited to hybridization is the reality TV competition. Unlike scripted shows, which are more expensive and have characters played by actors who can become stars through their identification with a particular role, reality series use cheaper labor and change casts for each season, with only hosts or judges recurring from year to year. This makes them easily adapted for different regions and nations. A reality TV format is a template that travels from one country to another, including a show "bible" of instructions covering elements such as "characters" like hosts and judges, set design, graphics, and direction (Moran 2014, 76). The creator of this intellectual property (IP) licenses the format to production companies in different territories, earning revenue each time they sell the same IP. The producers localize the variable elements of the format, while the structure remains more or less the same from place to place.

Reality formats come from various points of origin, mainly in the West. A number of successful global reality franchises, including *Big Brother*, have been the work of one Dutch media company, Endemol. Many have been British (e.g., *Pop Idol*, which spawned *American Idol* and many others, and *Strictly Come Dancing*, adapted as *Dancing with the Stars* in the US). One especially successful TV format has been *Who Wants to Be a Millionaire?*, which began in the late 1990s in the UK, and eventually was made into local versions in most of the world's countries, in dozens of languages, inspiring the Oscar-winning UK film *Slumdog Millionaire* (2008), set in Mumbai where a version of the show is being produced in Hindi. Wikipedia counts 104 instances of the show, with dozens of versions of the catchphrase "Is that your final answer?" in different languages. Each *Millionaire* is localized with a popular celebrity as host and questions and answers that draw on the cultural competencies of the home population.

While it has been a prolific exporter of television content, many of the biggest hits among American reality competitions have used formats from other places. Shows based on imported formats include *Who Wants to Be a Millionaire?*, *Survivor*, *American Idol*, *America's Got Talent*, *Dancing with the Stars*, and *The Voice*, while American formats (e.g., *The Bachelor*) are not as popular globally as some of the European and British franchises. And what we see in American reality competitions is similar to what we see in other countries: the American production gives the text a flavor of the local, Americanizing the format, while maintaining the basic premise of the show.

The examples so far have been unscripted and non-fictional television series, but formats come in other varieties, and have been a mainstay of the global television marketplace since the 1990s (Moran 2014). A key example of a highly successful fictional, scripted global television franchise has been the Colombian primetime serial, Yo soy Betty, la fea (originally produced 1999–2001, adapted in the US as Ugly Betty, 2006–2010). This show centers on an assistant at a fashion design firm who finds herself in love with the company president. They are a romantic mismatch: she is unattractive but brilliant, and he is rich and handsome but not very smart. Unlike the reality formats above, Betty is from Latin America, a region sometimes portrayed as a victim of Western media imperialism. The series and its many versions is a key example of the multi-directional flows of hybrid global media. Not only was Yo soy Betty, la fea a popular export from Colombia to Spanish-speaking territories in Europe and the Americas, following lines of cultural proximity, but the program was sold as a format on the global television market, and versions were produced not only in the US, but in Mexico, Brazil, India, Russia, China, Germany, and more than two dozen countries in all.

In some ways, the Betty format taps into an archetypal story, the Cinderella or ugly duckling fairy tale of a humble character's rise in fortune. If not truly universal, this kind of storytelling spans many cultures and eras. In a study of four adaptations of the Colombian telenovela, Lothar Mikos and Marta Perrotta (2013) found that many changes were made to localize each version, from changing names to fit a Russian or German character to incorporating locations in each production site. Some adaptations stayed more true to the form of the telenovela (a primetime Latin American version of the US daytime soap opera), while some blended drama with comedy or went deeper into character psychology. "Each of the five adaptations," the authors argue, "shows differences that are strongly related to national production cultures" (13).

Telenovelas are not like American serials with their indefinitely expanding timeframes covering potentially dozens of years. Rather, they tell a story with a beginning, middle, and end, and come to a conclusion at the end of between 100 and 300 nightly episodes. The American Ugly Betty was neither a soap opera nor a telenovela, but a weekly dramedy mixing together tones of sitcom and melodrama. This is a form of primetime series typical of American network TV. The Russian version showed more of the telenovela influence than Ugly Betty, which Mikos and Perrotta attribute to telenovelas having been popular in Russia since the 1990s (18). In all, the varied styles from country to country show how hybrid media texts function by localizing formats that are popular on the global market for culture, customizing storytelling conventions to suit both audience and industry expectations. *Ugly Betty* and many shows like it, scripted and unscripted, are not either local or global, Western or non-Western, homogenized or culturally specific. They exist in a realm of yes-and, not either-or.

Audiences and Users as Localizers

When media texts become popular in places distant from their place of origin, how do audiences or users make sense of them? The imperialism thesis implies that the ideologies conveyed by media are expressions of their producer's culture, so that exporting media to other places transforms the receiving culture by imposing Western ideology. This is a crucial element of the rhetoric of global media homogenization. It's not just that everyone watches the same movies and TV and listens to the same music (which of course they do not), but that the globally dominant images and sounds make a global society in the image of the West.

Critical cultural scholars of global media have rejected this account in favor of an alternative way of thinking that ascribes far more agency to local audiences or users to shape the meanings and values that they take from global media. As Ien Ang (1996) puts it, globalized mass media is "differentially responded to and negotiated with in concrete local contexts and conditions" (153), which is to say that the same media does not necessarily produce the same understanding from place to place.

Ang gives as an example the reception of the long-running American soap opera, *The Young and the Restless* (Y&R), on the Caribbean island of Trinidad, where it was incredibly popular in the 1980s and a constant topic of everyday conversations. Citing research by the anthropologist Daniel Miller (1992), Ang describes how Trinidadian audiences interpreted the storytelling through their local concept of *bacchanal*, a nationally-specific term with connotations of scandal, confusion or disorder, and revealing what has been hidden (Ang 1996, 160). Miller relates the interest in Y&R to a Trinidadian culture of gossip and confrontation associated with bacchanal, especially concerning matters of sexual desire, giving audiences opportunities for debate and discussion about characters on Y&R in a specifically local way, transforming an example of thoroughly American media into a national obsession regarded locally as "True True Trini" (Miller 1992, 179).

The American and Trinidadian viewer of Y&R would see the same pictures and stories, but would not have the same experience. In appropriating the show in their specific way, Trinidadian audiences transformed its meanings according to the specificities of their culture. In this and virtually infinite other examples, we observe that local audiences *inflect* global media, making sense of imported texts through their interpretive activity within communities that share common perspectives.

In the work audiences do to inflect and appropriate media in their own ways, hybridity from the production side overlaps with *localizing* from the reception side – of media made to flow globally by adapting to specific markets, but also taken up by active audiences using their cultural resources. A good example is popular music, including rock and roll and hip-hop, two American genres that became global formats of popular culture.

In the first place, American popular music is thoroughly hybrid and globalized as a product of the patterns of migration that made the US population what it has been for centuries. American music is unimaginable without African-American influences, including folk spirituals, work songs, blues, ragtime, jazz, gospel, soul, and rhythm and blues. It also draws on European-American traditions of song structure, and the formats of 19th- and 20th-century entertainment from traveling minstrel shows and vaudeville to Broadway and Hollywood. This mix of influences and styles produced a globally popular culture in the form of rock music, which would then be localized by creative artists and industries around the world, writing and recording songs in many different languages, with the influence of local musical traditions of song and instrumentation. And unlike some other media, popular music has often been a culture of protest and resistance, especially rock music in the era of the 1960s counterculture, and hip-hop in its more politicized, critical forms calling out for racial justice.

In creating music following American styles outside of the West, artists use basic materials of Western culture but also speak to their own experiences and inflect Western global media with local meaning. Hip-hop has traveled from African-American communities and American pop charts to become a form of local pop culture in countries around the world. In Japan, for instance, hip-hop music (which is also closely related to hip-hop dance and graffiti), takes a Western cultural form and localizes it with elements of Japanese culture. Just as hip-hop has been at odds with mainstream ideals in the US, Japanese hip-hop has functioned as a form of social criticism questioning the popular consensus on matters such as Japan's World War

II history, the place of work in Japanese culture, and support for American foreign policy during the 9/11 era.

As Ian Condry (2006) puts it in his book *Hip-Hop Japan*, the way hip-hop has been developed in Japanese culture shows the limitations of assuming American media imports spell Americanization of other societies. In Japan, hip-hop has sometimes been a platform for criticism of America. And hip-hop in Japan also incorporates specifically Japanese elements, such as the *katana* (Samurai sword), imagery of the ninja and geisha, and the vocal styles of kabuki and bunraku theater, layering Japanese elements over a global form of popular media, while also glorifying some of the same things as American hip-hop, like the figure of the "gangsta" or "thug." This example is not one of hybridization of something American like a television channel or theme park to appeal to a foreign market. Rather, we have creators and artists of another culture inflecting an originally American media style with their own meanings and values, which are not at all the ideology of American global dominance.

Japanese popular culture is also omnipresent in the US, so the flow here moves in both directions. Pokémon is one particularly popular example. The media franchise began in the 1990s to become a global phenomenon that includes television series, trading cards, and branded merchandise, with Nintendo games at the heart of the brand. Pokémon has been called the highest-grossing media franchise to date. It is thoroughly hybridized, with translations in several widely spoken languages localizing the content, e.g., by creating names for the Pokémon that make sense in the language of translation rather than carrying over Japanese names. Many characters in Pokémon follow the Japanese practice of *mukokuseki* (representation lacking distinctive ethnic features, typical of anime and manga), making the content less likely to be perceived as culturally different by varied audiences (Tobin 2004). Pokémon television series intended for American audiences have been modified in many ways, including changes in musical score, representations of sex and violence, and on-screen Japanese text (Katsuno and Maret 2004).

The 2016 mobile augmented reality (AR) game *Pokémon Go* takes localization a step further in the way it layers the Japanese/hybridized content of Pokémon over local maps and locations, inviting users or players to explore physical spaces where they play to create geographically specific experiences. The objective in *Pokémon Go* is to catch Pokémon and take over Gyms by battling others, but this only works by navigating to locations such as PokéStops to obtain necessary items, collecting Pokémon along the way.

The PokéStops and Gyms are virtual sites matched to landmarks such as businesses, parks, and places of worship. The Pokémon themselves are scattered around the map to be acquired by a player as they walk. When *Pokémon Go* was released and when it became a popular sensation, primarily in the summer of 2016, there were many controversies and criticisms around its presence in different kinds of spaces, but it was also celebrated as a digital game that would encourage physical activity and outdoor exploration. These discourses around the game are revealing of the ways that local concerns can be expressed in relation to global media.

Near the university where I teach is a historic park on a bluff looking over Lake Michigan. Lake Park was designed by Frederick Law Olmstead (of Central Park fame) in the 1890s. Its 138 acres contain meadows and trees, winding paths, bridges, tennis courts, lawn bowling greens, a golf course, a lighthouse, a playground, wooded trails, and a French bistro, all nestled into a neighborhood of historic mansions. This genteel urban oasis was a popular destination for *Pokémon Go* players in the summer of 2016 as it was filled with PokéStops, but many of the park's neighbors were unhappy with evening crowds descending on them. They cited a shortage of restrooms and parking spots, trash accumulation, and damage to the landscape. It was undeniable that the demographics of the *Pokémon Go* players were a contrast to those of the nearby residents, who were by and large older and more affluent than the new visitors, and unused to large nighttime gatherings. Local officials attempted to regulate the game to curtail its presence in the park, while fans and players expressed their outrage that their new pastime was threatened by powerful interests (Wild 2016).

These concerns among different groups were as much about visitors to a neighborhood as they were global media flows, but this kind of episode shows how the experience and meaning of global media products like the Pokémon franchise can be overlaid with local issues of identity, politics, and culture. The popular pleasure of the game transformed the serene park into a buzzing hub of activity for many evenings one summer. This clash of interests and many others during the first months of *Pokémon Go* were opportunities to think about who has the freedom and privilege to circulate in certain spaces and whose mobility is more regulated and circumscribed, whether because of disability, race and ethnicity, class, gender and sexuality, or age. Playing *Pokémon Go* involved negotiating these power-laden dynamics in public while also trying to "catch 'em all" (Feldman 2018; Tekinbaş 2017).

In my own family life, *Pokémon Go* had a different kind of importance. A couple of years after the Lake Park summer, my 9-year-old son and I would explore our neighborhood while playing *Pokémon Go*, and the app turned familiar spots in our environment into places with significance for playing the game. The Lutheran church, the public library, the post office, and the veterinary hospital were now PokéStops or Gyms and our outings were newly purposeful as catching Pokémon was a whole reason to get out and explore the streets. Noah was at a good age for being able to start exploring more on his own, without adult supervision, and *Pokémon Go* gave him a sense of mastery of the neighborhood and familiarity with its streets and landmarks. He didn't know that the building on the corner of the next block was a church until it became a place with a purpose in the game. Every *Pokémon Go* player surely has their own version of this spatial transformation, as the natural and built environments become invested in new meanings for play. If you think about this as a moment where local and global meet, we have a Japanese media franchise with monsters or creatures designed by Japanese artists but given English names to export to English-speaking territories appropriated via the mapping of an American augmented reality company, Niantic Inc., as a game you play by localizing the experience of catching the creatures and battling with them. You succeed in this virtual game by mastering your "real" local environment, which in turn gives new significance to everyday spaces.

A term used in the study of globalization can help us capture the significance of these intersections of the global and local: *glocalization* (Robertson 2018). Glocalization is a kind of adaptation, present in the examples above from *Ugly Betty* and *The Young and the Restless* to Japanese hip-hop and *Pokémon Go*. When ideas and texts and media forms and styles flow, they change. Whether by the work of media producers and industries or of audiences and users, localizing global media causes transformations in meaning, but does not drain away global characteristics. As with hybridity, glocal means both/ and. Top-down and bottom-up meanings coexist in a glocalized culture that blends the universal and particular.

Asymmetry and Interconnection

As is true within national boundaries, media on a global scale are shaped by the power structures that undergird international relations. Richer countries and world regions are in an asymmetrical relationship with weaker ones when it comes to media (and to trade more generally). The West exports more media to the Global South than it imports, and larger nations export more than smaller ones. Even a Western nation like Canada is subject to these dynamics, being neighbors with such a powerful media producer.

The key question about global media is not whether the West exerts influence over the Global South, but how we understand this asymmetry – among others – in global flows. Cultural imperialism sees the relationship in terms of exploitation and domination, while other approaches can reveal more complexity, including approaches that consider the multiple directions of media flows, the salience of cultural proximity, the abiding power of national media, the hybridity of global media, and the localization (or glocalization) of media as it moves from place to place. These approaches are unlikely to reveal a utopian global village of equal relations among nations and regions. Global media flows are asymmetrical and unequal because of stark inequality on a global scale, the product of a legacy of imperialism and colonialism.

Thinking about media on a global scale gives us an opportunity to appreciate the way media bridges divides and speaks to many different people in a diversity of contexts. We can think of the global mediascape as a vast network of interconnection. The availability of so much media from elsewhere is unprecedented in human history, though we generally tap into only a tiny fraction of the options available to us. The primacy of the local endures as audiences and users need to make sense of media, wherever it comes from, in relation to their own everyday lives and communities. This is why global media is always inflected in the process of reception: everything comes from a particular place, and is experienced in a particular place, and both of these places matter.

Discussion Questions

1. In your own everyday experience, how much of the media you encounter is local, how much is national, and how much is global? Do you see differences in which examples of media are more likely to be each of these kinds?

2. Choose examples of media you know well that are (a) from your own place, (b) from someplace culturally proximate, e.g., a neighboring country or a place where you would understand the language, and (c) from a place distant from you, e.g., another continent or a place where you don't understand the language. How does your understanding of

these different media change depending on whether they are more "global" or "local" in relation to you?

3. What is hybridity in global media? Choose an example of hybrid media that you know well and consider how it combines elements of two or more cultures.

4. Do you find the cultural imperialism thesis to be persuasive? Why or why not? Formulate arguments both for and against it.

Note

1   The economic and cultural importance of global markets to Hollywood filmmaking is explored in much detail in Miller (2005).

References

Anderson, Benedict. 2006. *Imagined Communities: Reflections on the Origins and Spread of Nationalism*, rev. ed. London: Verso.

Ang, Ien. 1996. *Living Room Wars: Rethinking Media Audiences for a Postmodern World* London: Routledge.

Appadurai, Arjun. 1990. "Disjuncture and Difference in the Global Cultural Economy." *Theory Culture Society* 7: 295–310.

Condry, Ian. 2006. *Hip-Hop Japan: Rap and the Paths of Cultural Globalization.* Durham, NC: Duke University Press.

Couldry, Nick and Anna McCarthy. 2004. "Orientations: Mapping Media Space." In *MediaSpace: Place, Scale, and Culture in a Media Age*, edited by Couldry and McCarthy, 1–18. New York: Routledge.

Feldman, Benjamin. 2018. "Agency and Governance: Pokémon-Go and Contested Fun in Public Space." *Geoforum* 98 (November): 289–297.

Fraser, Matthew. 2005. *Weapons of Mass Distraction: Soft Power and American Empire.* New York: Thomas Dunne Books.

Katsuno, Hirofumi and Jeffrey Maret. 2004. "Localizing the Pokémon TV Series for the American Market." In *Pikachu's Global Adventure: The Rise and Fall of Pokémon*, edited by Joseph Tobin, 80–107. Durham: Duke University Press.

Kraidy, Marwan. 2006. *Hybridity, or the Cultural Logic of Globalization.* Philadelphia: Temple University Press.

Levine, Elana. 2009. "National Television, Global Market: Canada's *Degrassi: The Next Generation*." *Media Culture & Society* 31.4: 515–531.

Lobato, Ramon. 2019. *Netflix Nations: The Geography of Digital Distribution.* New York: New York University Press.

McNutt, Myles. 2017. "Some Locations Matter: HGTV's Uneven Relationship with Spatial Capital." *Flow*, April 24, 2017. https://www.flowjournal.org/2017/04/some-locations-matter/

Mikos, Lothar and Marta Perrrotta. 2013. "Global *Ugly Betty*: International Format Trade and the Production of National Adaptations." *The International Encyclopedia of Media Studies*, 1st ed., edited by Angrahad N. Valdivia; Volume II: Media Production, edited by Vicki Maye, 1–22. Malden: Blackwell, 2013.

Miller, Daniel. 1992. *"The Young and the Restless* in Trinidad: A Case of the Local and the Global in Mass Consumption." In *Consuming Technologies: Media and Information in Domestic Spaces*, edited by Roger Silverstone and Eric Hirsch, 163–182. London: Routledge.

Miller, Toby, Nitin Govil, John McMurria, Richard Maxwell, and Ting Wang. 2005. *Global Hollywood 2*. London: British Film Institute.

Mirrlees, Tanner. 2013. *Global Entertainment Media: Between Cultural Imperialism and Cultural Globalization*. New York: Routledge.

Moran, Albert. 2014. "Program Format Franchising in the Age of Reality Television." *In A Companion to Reality Television*. 1st ed., edited by Laurie Ouellettte, 74–93. Hoboken: John Wiley & Sons.

Robertson, Roland. 2018. "Glocalization." *The International Encyclopedia of Anthropology*, edited by Hilary Callan, 1–8. Malden: John Wiley & Sons. doi:10.1002/9781118924396.wbiea2275

Schiller, Herbert. 1976. *Communication and Cultural Domination*. White Plains: International Arts and Sciences Press, Inc.

Schiller, Herbert. 1992. *Mass Communications and American Empire*, 2nd ed. Boulder: Westview Press.

Straubhaar, Joseph D. 1991. "Beyond Media Imperialism: Asymmetrical Interdependence and Cultural Proximity." *Critical Studies in Mass Communication* 8: 39–59.

Street, Sarah. 2009. "British Film and the National Interest, 1927–39." In *The British Cinema Book*, 3rd. ed., edited by Robert Murphy, 185–191.

Tekinbaş, Katie Salen. 2018. "Afraid to Roam: The Unlevel Playing Field of *Pokémon Go*." *Mobile Media & Communication* 5.1. https://journals.sagepub.com/doi/10.1177/2050157916677865

Thompson, Kristin. 1985. *Exporting Entertainment: America in the World Film Market 1907–34*. London: BFI.

Tobin, Joseph. 2004. "Conclusion: The Rise and Fall of the Pokémon Empire." In *Pikachu's Global Adventure: The Rise and Fall of Pokémon*, edited by Tobin, 257–292. Durham: Duke University Press.

Tomlinson, John. 1991. *Cultural Imperialism: A Critical Introduction*. Baltimore: Johns Hopkins University Press.

Tunstall, Jeremy. 1977. *The Media Are American: Anglo-American Media in the World*. New York: Columbia University Press.

Tunstall, Jeremy. 2008. *The Media Were American: U.S. Mass Media in Decline*. New York: Oxford University Press.

Wild, Matt. 2016. "Lake Park's Pokemon Go Meeting Was Boring, Livid, And Gloriously Absurd." *Milwaukee Record*, September 8, 2016. https://milwaukeerecord.com/city-life/lake-parks-pokemon-go-meeting-was-boring-occasionally-livid-gloriously-absurd/

INDEX

Note: Page numbers followed by "n" denote endnotes.